ARMED FORCES IN THE MIDDLE EAST

The Begin–Sadat (BESA) Center for Strategic Studies at Bar-Ilan University is dedicated to the study of Middle East peace and security, in particular the national security and foreign policy of Israel. A non-partisan and independent institute, the BESA Center is named in memory of Menachem Begin and Anwar Sadat, whose efforts in pursuing peace laid the cornerstone for future conflict resolution in the Middle East.

Since its founding in 1991 by Dr Thomas O. Hecht of Montreal, the BESA Center has become one of the most dynamic Israeli research institutions. It has developed cooperative relationships with strategic study centres throughout the world, from Ankara to Washington and from London to Seoul. Among its research staff are some of Israel's best and brightest academic and military minds. BESA Center publications and policy recommendations are read by senior Israeli decision-makers, in military and civilian life, by academicians, the press and the broader public.

The BESA Center makes its research available to the international community through three publication series: *BESA Security and Policy Studies*, *BESA Colloquia on Strategy and Diplomacy* and *BESA Studies in International Security*. The Center also sponsors conferences, symposia, workshops, lectures and briefings for international and local audience.

ARMED FORCES
IN THE
MIDDLE EAST

Politics and Strategy

Edited by

BARRY RUBIN

Begin–Sadat Center for Strategic Studies,
Bar-Ilan University

and

THOMAS A. KEANEY

School of Advanced International Studies,
Johns Hopkins University

FRANK CASS
LONDON • PORTLAND, OR

First published in 2002 in Great Britain by
FRANK CASS PUBLISHERS
Crown House, 47 Chase Side, Southgate
London N14 5BP

and in the United States of America by
FRANK CASS PUBLISHERS
c/o ISBS, 5824 N.E. Hassalo Street
Portland, Oregon, 97213-3644

Website: www.frankcass.com

British Library Cataloguing in Publication Data

Armed forces in the Middle East: politics and strategy. –
(BESA studies in international security)
1. Middle East – Armed forces 2. Middle East – History,
Military – 20th century 3. Middle East – Politics and
government – 1945–
I. Rubin, Barry II. Keaney, Thomas A. III. Begin-Sadat Center
for Strategic Studies
355' .00956

ISBN 0-7146-5255-5 (cloth)
ISBN 0-7146-8245-4 (paper)
ISSN 1368-9541

Library of Congress Cataloging-in-Publication Data

Armed forces in the Middle East: politics and strategy / edited by
Barry Rubin and Thomas A. Keaney.
    p. cm. – (BESA studies in international security)
  ISBN 0-7146-5255-5 (cloth). – ISBN 0-7146-8245-4 (paper)
  1. Middle East–Military policy. 2. Middle East–Defenses. 3.
Middle East–Strategic aspects. I. Rubin, Barry M. II. Keaney, Thomas
A. III. Series.
 UA832 .A755 2001
 355'.03356–dc21

                                                              2001047217

Typeset in 11/13pt Goudy Old Style by Vitaset, Paddock Wood, Kent
Printed in Great Britain by
MPG Books Ltd, Bodmin, Cornwall

Contents

Notes on Contributors

Oksana Antonenko is program director for Russia and Eurasia at the International Institute for Strategic Studies (IISS). Her recent publications include 'Russia, NATO and European Security after Kosovo', *Survival* (Winter 1999–2000) and *Russia's Armed Forces* (IISS Strategic Comments No. 10, 2000).

Amatzia Baram is head of the Jewish-Arab Center and the Gustav Von Heinemann Middle East Institute, Haifa University. His books include *Culture, 'History and Ideology in the Formation of Ba'thist Iraq, 1968–89* (1991) and *Building Toward Crisis: Saddam Husayn's Strategy for Survival* (1998). He was co-editor (with Barry Rubin) of *Iraq's Road to War* (1994).

Alexander Bligh is a senior lecturer at Bar-Ilan University, as well as head of the Department of Middle Eastern Studies and director of the Israel National Strategic Assessment Center (INSAC) at the College of Judea and Samaria. His publications include *The Political Legacy of King Hussein* (2001); *From Prince to King: Succession to the Throne in Modern Saudi Arabia* (1984); 'The Intifada and the New Political Role of the Israeli Arab Leadership', *Middle Eastern Studies*, Vol. 35, No. 1 (January 1999).

Stuart A. Cohen is a professor of political science at Bar-Ilan University. His publications include *The Formation of British Policy towards Mesopotamia – 1903–1914* (1975); *The Jewish Polity* (with D. J. Elazar) (1988); *The Scroll or the Sword: Dilemmas of Religion and Military Service in Israel* (1998). He edited *Democratic Societies and their Armed Forces: Israel in Comparative Context* (2000), which was also published in this series.

Norvell De Atkine is a retired US Army colonel and director of Middle East Studies at the John F. Kennedy US Army Special Warfare Center and School at Fort Bragg NC. As a former US Army Foreign Area Specialist he traveled extensively in the Middle East and graduated from the master of arts Arab Studies Program at the American University in Beirut. In addition to eight years of assignments in the Middle East, he served other overseas tours of duty as an artillery officer in Korea, Vietnam and Germany.

Michael Eisenstadt is a senior fellow at the Washington Institute for Near East Policy specializing in Arab–Israeli and Persian Gulf security affairs. He is co-author, with Eliot Cohen and Andrew Bacevich, of *Knives, Tanks, and Missiles: Israel's Security Revolution* (1998). His articles include 'Living with a Nuclear Iran', *Survival* (London), Vol. 41, No. 3 (Autumn 1999), pp. 124–48 and 'US Military Capabilities in the Post-Cold War Era: Implications for Middle East Allies', *MERIA Journal*, Vol. 2, No. 4 (December 1998).

Marvin C. Feuer is a professorial lecturer in strategic studies at the Paul H. Nitze School of Advanced International Studies (SAIS), Johns Hopkins University, Washington, DC, and Director for Defense and Strategic Issues at the American Israel Public Affairs Committee. He received his PhD from Harvard University. He has served in positions on Capitol Hill, in the White House, the US State Department and the Office of the Secretary of Defense.

Hillel Frisch is senior lecturer in the Department of Political Studies, Bar-Ilan University and Senior Researcher at the BESA Center for Strategic Studies. He is the author of *Countdown to Statehood: Palestinian State-Building in the West Bank and Gaza* (1998) and many articles on Arab and Palestinian politics.

Thomas A. Keaney is the executive director of the Foreign Policy Institute and senior adjunct professor of strategic studies at the Paul H. Nitze School of Advanced International Studies (SAIS), Johns Hopkins University, Washington, DC. A retired officer with 30 years service in the US Air Force, his recent publications include *Revolution in Warfare? Air Power in the Persian Gulf* (1995) and (as joint editor with Barry Rubin) *US Allies in a Changing World* (2000), which was the previous book in this series.

Gal Luft is a former battalion commander in the Israel Defense Forces (IDF) and currently a doctoral candidate in the Department of Strategic Studies of the Johns Hopkins University's Paul H. Nitze School of Advanced International Studies (SAIS). Luft is a research associate of the Washington Institute for Near East Policy. He is the author of *The Palestinian Security Services: Between Police and Army* (1998).

Umit Sakallioglu is an associate professor at Bilkent University. She has been a Fulbright Research Scholar and a Jean Monnet Research Fellow. Her writings include *Politics and Military in Turkey in the 21st Century* (EUI, Robert Schuman Center for Advanced Studies Working Papers, No. 2000/24, June 2000) and 'Turkey's Kurdish Problem: A Critical Analysis of Boundaries, Identity and Hegemony', in Ian Lustick, Brendan O'Leary and Thomas Callaghy (eds), *Rightsizing the State* (2001).

Barry Rubin is director of the Global Research in the International Affairs Center and editor of the *Middle East Review of International Affairs* (MERIA) journal. He is deputy director of the Begin–Sadat Center for Strategic Studies. His books include *The Transformation of Palestinian Politics: From Revolution to State-Building* (1999); *Cauldron of Turmoil: America in the Middle East* (1992); *Modern Dictators: Third World Coupmakers, Strongmen, and Populist Tyrants* (1987); *The Arab States and the Palestine Conflict*; *Paved with Good Intentions: The American Experience and Iran*; and *The Great Powers in the Middle East 1941–1947: The Road to Cold War*. His co-edited books include *Turkey in World Politics: An Emerging Multi-Regional Power* (2001); *America and Its Allies* (2000); and *Iraq's Road to War: Politics, Economics, and Foreign Relations* (1994).

Eyal Zisser is a senior research fellow at the Moshe Dayan Center for Middle East and African Studies, and a senior lecturer in the department of Middle Eastern and African History, Tel Aviv

University. He is author of *Asad's Syria at a Crossroads* (in Hebrew, 1999); *Lebanon: The Challenge of Independence* (2000); *Asad's Legacy – Syria in Transition* (2000). He is also author of 'Decision-making in Asad's Syria', *MERIA Journal*, Vol. 2, No. 2 (May 1998) and 'Hizballah: New Course or Continued Warfare?', *MERIA Journal*, Vol. 4, No. 3 (September 2000).

Preface

Unquestionably, the armed forces are one of the most important institutions of every Middle East country and have played a key role in the overwhelming majority of vital events in the region. This has been true not only because of the frequency of war and crisis in the area but also because of the role in domestic politics played by armies and officers. Clearly, the region's armed forces remain, and will continue to be, central considerations in maintaining peace or fighting wars in the region.

In past decades, the armed forces were a focal point for research on the Middle East. More recently, though, in part because their role has changed somewhat, there has been far less study of military institutions. Yet precisely because of new features in doctrine, technology, armaments, and composition – as well as in their political function – Middle East armed forces require careful consideration and a fresh examination.

To achieve this goal, the Begin–Sadat (BESA) Center for Strategic Studies of Bar-Ilan University and the Foreign Policy Institute of Johns Hopkins University's Paul H. Nitze School of Advanced International Studies (SAIS) jointly launched a research project on this topic. These efforts culminated in an international conference held at the BESA Center on 14–16 November 2000. This book is the product of that project and meeting.

Our goal was to look at the region's armed forces both as military establishments and as key sociopolitical institutions. On the professional side, participants were asked to look at the armed forces' doctrine, priorities and missions, as well as their ability to meet these objectives in terms of armaments, training and personnel. In addition, they would examine the interaction between politics and the military. Of special interest are the impact of social changes, new technologies, and the advent of Weapons of Mass Destruction (WMD) as a factor in the region's arsenals.

We especially wish to thank the Lynde and Harry Bradley Foundation for its generous grant, which made this project possible. We also wish to thank the staffs of our two institutions for their help in this project. From the BESA Center for Strategic Studies, those who helped include Professor Efraim Inbar, the Center's director, Cameron Brown, Elisheva Brown and Elisheva Rosman. From the Foreign Policy Institute, Ms Courtney Mata managed all administrative and financial details.

1

The Military in Contemporary Middle East Politics

BARRY RUBIN

Our views of the military's role in Middle East politics have largely been formed by the history of the 1950s, 1960s and 1970s in the region. Those years were the golden age of coups in the Arab world, a time when every Arab military officer could hope to become his country's ruler some day. The armed forces were highly politicized and rulers generally failed to control them. During this period, too, the armed forces were the most effective national institutions and, at times, the only effective one.

Officers argued that politics was too important to be left to the politicians, whom they saw – by no means inaccurately – as incompetent and corrupt. The 1948 defeat, failure to gain Arab unity, a perceived subservience to Western states, and the slow pace of the development process were among the grievances that motivated officers to seek political power.

At the same time, coups by military officers often in fact represented revolts by various ethnic, religious, class and regional groups that were well represented in the officer corps while largely excluded from the political and economic elites. Thus, these coups were actually social revolutions in the form of military takeovers. At the time, many Western scholars saw Arab militaries as the necessary instruments for creating governments capable of nation-building and mass mobilization.

The current era, beginning in the 1970s, was shaped by these military regimes and by the remaining civilian rulers who had learned how to survive this threat. They were determined to prevent military officers from staging any fresh coups. Indeed, governments did have a great deal of success in preventing their armies from intervening in politics.[1] They have also built militaries that can successfully maintain internal order. But the price of that accomplishment is severe damage to their ability to function as armed forces actually fighting wars.[2]

Perhaps the biggest asset of Middle East militaries is that they often have more influence than their Western counterparts in obtaining the level of financial support they seek. They need not worry about public criticism. At the same time, though, few Middle Eastern armed forces can equal the professional qualities and operational advantages enjoyed by their counterparts in democratic states.

The limits placed on the regular militaries as a tool for fighting external wars have made it more necessary for states to develop other means of projecting power, ranging from sponsorship of terrorism to obtaining Weapons of Mass Destruction (WMD). Certainly, the high level of conflict in the Middle East has led to periodic wars. Yet this history has clearly shown the risks involved in normal warfare and the frequency of defeat for Arab and Iranian armies. The possession of strong deterrence, especially by Israel, has also discouraged direct assault.

After the 1980s, the decline of one superpower sponsor in the region, the Soviet Union, and the relative strength and willingness to intervene of the sole remaining superpower, the United States, accelerated this trend. Consequently, such tools as the use of proxies, subversion, terrorism and an attempt to obtain WMD have become important means of power projection, compared with the use of regular armed forces.

THE ARMED FORCES AND STATE POWER

The first requirement for any government is to ensure its own survival. In the Arab world, this has meant finding a way to prevent the armed forces from seizing power in a coup. Simultaneously, governments have given the armed forces privileges, while also trying to weaken them in order to redirect their interests away from politics. Ironically, though, the armed forces have been kept out of politics only by measures that subordinate them to the government's policy decisions, making governments dependent on keeping the officers happy, and making the actual use of the armed forces a dangerous strategy that is likely to produce defeats.

Today, only two of the 14 main Arab countries – Egypt and Libya – have rulers who are in power because they were career military officers.[3] And even in these two cases, the chief executives (Husni Mubarak and Muammar Qadhafi, respectively) left active duty more than a quarter century ago.

Two more peripheral and less developed Arab states, Yemen and Sudan, have military dictatorships more typical of the Middle East in the 1950s–70s period. Sudan, which in many ways is different from other members of the Arab League, had military coups in 1958, 1969, 1985 and 1989. The current leader is Lieutenant General Omar Hasan Ahmad al-Bashir, and the government portrays itself as Islamist. Yemen had its latest coup in 1979 and is led by Ali Abdallah Salah, who promoted himself to field marshal. He is a Ba'thist with strong pro-Iraq sympathies. Both of these countries have turbulent histories and a lack of alternative civilian political institutions relative to other Arab states.

In order to ensure that the military did not try to seize power, Arab governments followed several policies. There were two general ways by which politicians sought to win the armed forces' backing: through material incentives for individuals and for the collective military institution.

First, officers are kept happy by high pay and special privileges. These benefits have been many and varied. In Syria, they can be said to include the right to smuggling and other illicit profits deriving from Damascus's control over Lebanon. Special housing is another common perquisite.

Of course, while such privileges inflate budgets, the wage rates (especially for enlisted men) are relatively low. If economies were booming and a large middle class was being created, professionals and high-tech employees would be earning more than soldiers, creating problems of morale and retention. These problems exist especially in Israel.[4]

Arab military systems are still largely geared to recruiting and retaining less-educated, poorer people from the sectors most loyal to the regime. In many Arab states, military careers are still relatively lucrative, compared to the other options open to rural and disadvantaged people who can qualify for such jobs. Yet already urban, college-educated young people are reluctant to enter the armed forces. As time goes on, Arab militaries will have a harder time keeping up with the growing importance of high technology, advanced communications and other new features of warfare requiring highly trained elite personnel, as well as innovation and flexibility.

This problem already exists in the Gulf Arab monarchies, where easier high-paying jobs are available, but is solved by employing foreign mercenary soldiers. These countries have also tried to manage their manpower shortages by cooperating through the Gulf Cooperation Council (GCC), although efforts to develop a joint military force have had only limited success.[5]

Second, the armed services have been given high proportions of national budgets, thus detracting from development and social spending in order to ensure the military's loyalty.

That point, while obvious, may be often missed by Western observers, who expect that the prospect of obtaining an economic 'peace dividend' is an incentive for ending regional conflicts. Given their importance for maintaining domestic stability, as well as the threats from neighbors faced by every state, military budgets are unlikely to decline. A purely 'rational' argument based on economics will not appeal to leaders who know they need a strong and happy military to survive.

Expensive weapons purchases are often undertaken based on military commanders' preferences, rather than on the nation's need for these specific arms or the armed forces' ability to maintain them. Again, the demand for top-of-the-range weapons is important for rulers' egos, national prestige and the deterrence of regional threats, yet these rationales, too, are often responses to the desires or decisions of military commanders.[6] Turkey has a similar situation, since generals there can intervene constitutionally in the budget process to ensure their demands are met.[7]

Nevertheless, as military budgets and the costs of specific weapons systems climb higher, governments are forced to apply the brakes on spending. This has already been seen in such countries as Syria and Turkey. The need to obtain financing for weapons purchases can also affect foreign policy. For example, Syria portrays itself as a front-line state battling Israel in order to seek money from Gulf Arab monarchies. Iraq used a similar approach in defining itself as the Arab world's defender against Iran.

In the case of the Gulf Arab monarchies, another motive for huge arms purchases from the United States is to create additional links to make certain that the superpower will play the role of protector for the regimes. As a result of seeking prestige and protection, however, civilian and military leaders often waste huge amounts of money without creating a more effective military establishment. For example, the United Arab Emirates buys advanced planes for which it does not have pilots, or even, perhaps, suitable runways.

Governments employ six other successful methods designed to weaken and divide the armed forces' ability to threaten the government. These policies also, however, damage the military's ability to fight external adversaries.

1. Multiple military branches and intelligence services are maintained to cancel each other out in terms of power and influence. This leads to wasted resources and poor coordination among forces. It also corrupts the intelligence-gathering process, since a premium is put on information that pleases rulers and discredits rivals, rather than on accurate data. Much of the intelligence effort goes to gather information on the military itself, including officers' attitudes and any dissent that might exist in the ranks.

Asked why he needed so many security forces for the Palestinian Authority (PA), Yasir Arafat replied, 'The Syrians have 14, the Egyptians have 12. I only have 6 to protect me'.[8] Actually, he had as many as 12 different military agencies. These forces sometimes feuded and even fought among themselves.

For example, in 1998, Military Intelligence, led by Musa Arafat, a relative of Yasir Arafat, raided an office of the Tanzim, Fatah's armed militia headed by Marwan Barghuti, Fatah's leader in the West Bank. Barghuti then led a march on the Military Intelligence's headquarters in Ramallah in which Musa Arafat's men opened fire and killed one youth, nephew of a Palestinian Authority cabinet minister. Barghuti's men then issued a leaflet stating, 'Musa Arafat and his dogs suck Palestinian blood by dealing with stolen cars, whorehouses, and selling weapons. They prefer to be Israeli prostitutes, working here as the Israeli intelligence arm to separate the Palestinian leadership and the Palestinian people.'[9]

During the fighting against Israel in the intifada that began in 2000, different forces refused to share ammunition and supplies.[10] In doing so, they were not flouting Arafat's instructions but fulfilling the divide-and-rule structure that he had deliberately created to forestall future coup possibilities even before a state was established. Of course, fully independent states created more order and discipline among their various forces, but the basic principle of using multiple forces to enhance control remained the same.

In Arab countries, these units have overlapping responsibilities, spy on each other, and have no ability to coordinate among themselves. They are, then, deliberately put into competition with each other. While Arafat plays off different forces as more or less equal, in Arab states and Iran they form a hierarchy ranging from more apolitical and multi-ethnic regular units to increasingly elite forces tied closely to the regime through communal and ethnic interests. To ensure this support, the elite groups are subjected to more ideology, as well as favored with greater privileges. The concept is to make sure the special units and their officers feel their fate is closely linked to the regime's survival.

In Iran, aside from the regular military, there is the Islamic Revolutionary Guard Corps and the Basij militia, both ideologically reliable and loyal to the regime, or at least the hardline faction. Given internal Iranian conflicts, these latter two forces are also, in a sense, a party militia that could be used in a factional civil war.[11]

Saudi Arabia has both its regular forces and the tribal-based 'White Army'. A special feature of the elite units is that they are more likely to be used in quelling internal unrest, since they can be considered reliable against anti-regime rebels who may come from a different religious, ethnic and geographical background.

Within Iraq, this multi-force system is developed to its peak of complexity and specialization.[12] Kurds are not drafted into the regular army – though there are pro-regime Kurdish militias. In the regular armed forces, there is a large proportion of Shi'a Muslims, who can even attain the rank of general. Beyond this, however, is a complex hierarchy. As Amatzia Baram has written:

> In the army, as opposed to the Republican Guard (RG), support for the president is far less staunch. Thus, the RG is placed between all army units and the capital city, and the Special Republican Guard (SRG) is stationed inside of Baghdad, and thus between the RG and the inner rings guarding the president. As long as the regime looks stable, the RG, the SRG, Special Security (SS), and the Palace Guard (or Presidential Guard, *Himayat al-Ra'is*) will remain essentially loyal to [President] Saddam Husayn. If he is removed they have too much to lose: power and prestige, higher salaries than those of their army counterparts, and other privileges that increase in relation to a soldier's proximity to the president.[13]

2. Promotions and assignments are based more on political loyalty than ability. This approach can make a distinction between professionally able and politically correct officers. Those who devote more time to proving their pro-regime credentials can advance more quickly, and this priority can mean sacrificing military effectiveness for meeting the regime's preferences and expectations. Such organizational politics exists in all the world's armies, of course, but the question is how important such considerations are in the overall mix of decision-making.

At the top, key positions may also be given to those with special connections to the regime through family – as happens with many Saudi princes and several Iraqi commanders – or ethnic, geographical or tribal connections.

To put a premium on political loyalty makes eminent political sense, of course, since the regime's first priority is to stay in power, but it also lowers the military's quality. In the real world, less competent officers are often more eager to portray, or assume, ideological zeal precisely in order to ensure their successful careers, since they lack other assets for doing so. The point is whether apolitical officers – as opposed to those antagonistic to the regime – suffer.

3. Higher-ranking officers are frequently rotated to avoid their establishing strong ties of loyalty with their troops or subordinate officers. Periodic transfers are also common in armies throughout the world, but other armed forces want to build good links within the officer corps and between officers and enlisted personnel. The issue here is to what extent such relationships might be deliberately curtailed as a matter of policy.

4. Initiative among individual officers is discouraged, a doctrine that has high costs during battles and military campaigns. Indeed, mistrust can be encouraged, making officers reluctant to share information. Coordination among units can be inhibited and combined operations can be made very difficult, even impossible. These problems are increased by cultural tendencies, but may be worsened by deliberate regime policies.

5. Special formations based on ethnic and sectarian religious membership are used as elite forces and deployed in sensitive places, especially close to the rulers and the capital.

As already noted above, Iraq's elite units are overwhelmingly Sunni in composition and are recruited from tribes and areas close to President Saddam Husayn's home area. In Syria, the same practice is followed but with Alawites from the community of the ruling Asad family.

Jordan, in apparent contrast to other countries, has always relied on a highly professional military without competing alternative units. But since the regular armed forces are overwhelmingly comprised of 'East Bank Jordanians', with only very limited numbers of Palestinians permitted, it does constitute an ethnic-communal force in its own right. Israel drafts only Jewish citizens, as well as traditionally loyal Druze and Circassian minorities, into its army. Although Muslim and Christian Arabs are accepted as volunteers, it is perceived that the level of loyalty and reliability that can be expected is unsatisfactory.

Certainly, there are exceptions to such practices, notably in Egypt, where religion does not seem to be a major criterion in assignments and promotions. Especially interesting are two other cases. Lebanon, where the country's communal-democratic system makes a nominally multi-ethnic army a necessity, has the least effective armed forces in the entire region. Since it is so representative, the military is hard to use reliably against any given group.

As a result of this problem, as well as many other factors, of course, the central government has remained weak. Ethnic militias sprang up, controlled most of the country's territory and fought a long civil war. Even after the fighting ended, Hizballah, a Shi'a Islamist militia, continues to operate independently and even to wage its own war against neighboring Israel.

The other interesting exception is Turkey, a country based on a strong unitary nationalism with a very large army based on a universal draft. Denying the existence of a separate Kurdish national group, Turkey never made any distinction among citizens even during the height of fighting against Kurdish separatists.

6. Officers suspected of harboring other political loyalties, or even excessive ambitions, are periodically purged. All the region's armies, excepting Iran, try to keep Islamists out of the officer corps. A failure to do so can be costly, as shown by the 1981 assassination of Egyptian President Anwar al-Sadat by a small group of soldiers at a military parade. Turkey's armed forces are so powerful and adamant on this point that they even forced Prime Minister Erbakan, leader of the Islamist party, to endorse the expulsion of his own supporters from the military.

Essentially, all of the above policies have worked in preventing successful coups and even serious attempts at takeovers. There has not been a coup or serious attempt to seize power by soldiers in Egypt since 1952, Syria since 1970, or in Iraq since 1968. Syria had about eight coups during 22 years (1949–71), while Iraq had three within ten years (1958–68). As of the year 2000, neither had had such an event for 30 years. It is easy to forget that the last coup during which soldiers seized power for themselves in a major Arab state (outside of Yemen and Sudan) were those of Asad in 1970 and Muammar Qadhafi in Libya in 1969.

The reasons for this dramatic transformation are not hard to find. In the earlier period, the state system had not yet stabilized and institutionalized itself. The military was the one institution that had the cohesiveness and tools to take power. Thereafter, the officers who took power finally learned how to keep it, or civilians discovered the same lesson. The new system made officers less eager and able to try to seize power, while also defeating any plots more effectively before they are well organized.

As a result, the armed forces found a new role as the incumbent regime's guardian rather than as its principal challenger. Of course, this is the proper role of the military, though in this function its political behavior may exceed that considered appropriate in the West. In Turkey, the armed forces have staged several coups to implement their interpretation of preserving the country's unity and democratic system. Preserving the secular republic against Islamist rule motivated the generals to force Prime Minister Erbakan's resignation.

A parallel situation took place in Algeria. When it appeared certain that Islamists would come to power through elections, the military seized power and canceled the balloting. This action set off a bloody civil war, though the armed forces preferred to hand control back to civilian politicians.

Of course, a key element in successful coup avoidance is an Arab leader's personal connection to the armed forces. Egyptian President Husni Mubarak and Syrian President Hafiz al-Asad were commanders of their countries' air forces. King Husayn of Jordan was a graduate of Sandhurst, the British military academy, and devoted great personal attention to the army. Even some civilian leaders, like Saddam Husayn and Yasir Arafat, frequently appear in uniform.

As for the next generation, King Abdallah was an officer who was given command of Jordan's important special forces' units. If he had not become king at such a young age he would have continued in his military career. An interesting contrast that illustrates the same point is Syrian ruler Bashar al-Asad. An eye doctor with no military background, he was quickly made an officer and rapidly promoted after it became clear that he would succeed his father.[14]

Gulf Arab monarchies have developed a number of control mechanisms to ensure that the armed forces remain servants of the state. One effective measure is to have members of the ruling family hold high military ranks and control key units.[15]

Of course, many Arab leaders are civilian politicians. In the Gulf Arab monarchies, except for Saudi Arabia, the governments depoliticize the militaries by hiring foreign mercenaries. While this raises a theoretical problem of their loyalty and willingness to fight, in practice the officers stay out of local politics. An excellent example is the preference of Gulf Arab monarchies for non-Arab and even non-Muslim cadres over Egyptian and Syrian units, even when encouraged to turn to the latter after the 1991 Kuwait War. Having even Arab Muslim forces who were political allies on their soil was considered far more dangerous in political terms than any advantage that might be gained in external security.

Finally, there are some important negative social and cultural factors that damage the capability of Arab armies. These are hard to measure and controversial to enumerate, as well as being intensified by some of the political factors identified above. They might include excessively rigid hierarchies and reluctance to take initiative.

An American army officer with extensive experience as an adviser to Arab armies, Norvell De Atkine, has concluded:

> Until Arab politics begin to change at fundamental levels, Arab armies, whatever the courage or proficiency of individual officers and men, are unlikely to acquire the range of qualities which modern fighting forces require for success on the battlefield. For these qualities depend on inculcating respect, trust and openness among the members of the armed forces at all levels, and this is the marching music of modern warfare that Arab armies, no matter how much they emulate the corresponding steps, do not want to hear.[16]

THE ARMED FORCES AND INTERNAL CONTROL

For Middle East governments, the armed forces play an important role in maintaining internal security. The requirements of this political objective have taken many forms and varied strategies.

11

On the political level, it should be noted that the armed forces' loyalties lie with the regime rather than with the general population, a democratic system or the nation as an abstraction. The main exceptions are Turkey, where the military sees itself as the guardian of the republic, and Israel. Of course, it should be emphasized that the program of most Arab governments over decades was designed precisely to break any such linkages. The only time that military formations are wedded to ideology is when they have been formed by regimes for precisely that purpose: for example, the Iranian Islamic Revolutionary Guard Corps to support radical Islamic rule and the Iraqi Republican Guard to support Ba'thist rule.

In general, outside of Iran (and perhaps even in Iran's own regular army), professional military formations do not seem sympathetic to radical Islamist views. Does this indicate some inevitable orientation? To some extent, it may be due to tradition. In the 1950s, of course, the revolutionary officers in various countries were always tied to secularist views. Moreover, the armed forces had more contact with foreign ideas and personnel than virtually any other institution in Middle East countries. Perhaps the pragmatic and patriotic ethos of the professional militaries discouraged traditional piety. Unquestionably, too, Islamists and strong religious believers were attracted to other professions, while frequent purges in many armies kept their numbers limited.

Even Israel's army was traditionally dominated by secularists. Observant Jews are now becoming a more important factor than ever before, but are still quite limited in number in the higher ranks. Turkey's armed forces are explicitly secular, viewing that as one of the Turkish republic's most important values. Israel and Turkey are also relatively unique in stressing the military's role in national integration, in bringing people from different areas, backgrounds and social levels together to forge them into a single nation. These two countries have a very broad draft policy to put a relatively large proportion of their citizens through some experience of military service.

Armed forces may also play an important socioeconomic role. They absorb excess labor, which might otherwise be unemployed and thus politically disruptive. Egypt seems to fit this situation. As noted above, though, as economies develop, the armed forces can be a drain on the workforce, removing people from potentially productive jobs. The armed forces can also be used for development projects, and Egypt also furnishes a good example in this respect.[17]

To some extent, the military can be said to have lost its internal control function to various security forces. At the same time, however, regular militaries often prefer such a division of labor, preferring not to be involved in conflicts which, they argue, detract from their prime function of protecting against external enemies. Such internal security problems, officers argue, require operations for which they are neither equipped nor trained. Among other reasons that military forces don't like to engage in such activities, is the danger of creating friction between the armed forces and the citizenry, opening up divisions in their own ranks, and detracting from training.

While each situation is quite different, the highest-level internal conflicts in which Middle Eastern militaries have participated include the following:

Algeria A bloody, full-scale civil war against Islamists has been fought since 1992, after the army intervened to cancel the second round of elections that would have been won by the opposition group. The armed forces were easily able to prevent the rebels from taking power and apparently made some progress in battle against them. But the military also seemed to lack any strategy for achieving victory. During this period, the army had strong influence over the civilian leaders, though it did not always determine their policies.

Egypt A low-level military force, used mostly for guard duty, revolted in 1986 over pay and conditions, but was put down by the armed forces within a few days.

Iran The regular army crumbled during the 1978–79 revolution due to soldiers' refusal to fire on civilian revolutionaries, as well as some dissension in its lower ranks, demoralization at the Shah's uncertain strategy, and key officers' conclusions that the Islamist opposition was going to win. This outcome – while by no means attributable only to the military's behavior – was the greatest failure of any Middle Eastern military to maintain internal security in the last quarter of the twentieth century.

Iraq The army fought wars against Kurdish separatists in their mountain strongholds during the 1960s and 1970s, which resulted in enough of a stalemate to provide the government with a victory. Following the 1991 defeat in Kuwait, the armed forces put down Shi'a and Kurdish rebellions with great bloodshed, but international intervention prevented them from occupying the Kurdish-populated areas of northern Iraq.[18]

Israel Most of the 'internal' activities of Israel's army were conducted not within the country's own borders (where police units have jurisdiction), but in the areas captured during the 1967 war – the West Bank and Gaza Strip. The army has been used to counter specific terrorist operations within Israel, for example hostage-taking incidents, from the late 1960s onward and especially during the 1970s. It was used extensively during the first (1987–90) and second (2000–) Palestinian intifadas. These activities involved tactics and restraints quite different from conventional war. The army also governed the West Bank and Gaza Strip from 1967 to 1994 and the areas retained by Israel, which were gradually reduced during the post-Oslo Agreement peace process.[19]

Jordan In 1970–71, the Jordanian army fought and defeated PLO (Palestine Liberation Organization) forces after some elements in the Palestinian organization became increasingly involved in a bid to overthrow King Husayn. The armed forces performed very effectively and won a total victory.

Lebanon The most notable point about Lebanon's army is its lack of involvement in internal security matters. It was not involved in the civil war of the 1970s and 1980s, fought by ethnic-communal militias, and the government even refused to deploy it up to the border after Israel withdrew from southern Lebanon in the year 2000. The army did play a role, however, in policing the post-civil war situation, though its ability to act was always minimized by the more powerful Syrian military presence and the remaining militias.

Sudan Since the 1970s, and especially since 1983, the army has been periodically involved in fighting secessionist rebels in the south led by a former officer, John Garang, a member of the Dinka tribe and leader of the Sudanese People's Liberation Army (SPLA). The army has never been able to defeat the rebellion and there has been a complex mix of fighting and truces during this period.

Syria After the army ceased seeking direct state power, follow-ing Hafiz al-Asad's coup of 1970–71, its place in maintaining internal security was largely taken by Ba'th party and Alawi ethnic forces especially loyal to the regime. The most significant internal security operations included the war against Islamist rebels in the 1970s, which culminated in the massive killings in the city of Hama in 1982 that crushed any armed opposition.

Turkey The longest continuous and largest-scale internal security operation by regular armed forces was the Turkish struggle with Kurdish separatists of the Kurdish Workers' Party (PKK) during the 1980s and 1990s. The fighting involved the country's southeast provinces, terrorist operations in Turkish cities, and Turkish military incursions into northern Iraq. While fought originally by the gendarmerie, the army became increasingly involved over time in using counter-guerrilla warfare techniques. Aided by the capture of the PKK's leader and his own call – under threat of a death sentence – to end the rebellion, Turkish forces had achieved victory by 2000.

Yemen The country has a relatively 'traditional' military regime ruled by a career officer, Field Marshal Ali Abdallah Salah, since 1979. Other members of the government are also officers and one of them, the minister of interior, controls a 50,000-man security force. The Yemeni army seized control of south Yemen in the 1990s – which could be viewed abroad as power projection or as the reunification of the country – and has fought border skirmishes with Saudi Arabia and Eritrea. Aside from the regular army, there are also tribal levies.[20]

Several basic conclusions can be drawn from this inventory of diverse events and operations:

1. Internal security forces are increasingly important. In part, this is due to the effort to depoliticize the army. But officers generally support their exclusion from having to deal with such

15

problems, preferring to focus on external threats and more conventional military operations.

2. Regular armies can fight with a large degree of success in situations of ethnic-national (as in Iraq, Turkey and Israel) and Islamist (Algeria) rebellions, though only political solutions can end these conflicts.

3. In contrast to other regional states, the armed forces continue to play a full political role in Sudan and Yemen. In Algeria and Turkey, situations have developed in which the military feels free to intervene temporarily as guardian of the state (and especially of secularism), but returns power to civilians as quickly as possible.

4. The two great internal security failures of regular militaries were in Iran and Lebanon, where political constraints played an important factor in each case.

In general, then, armed forces remain reliable instruments for maintaining internal regime authority, though they do not necessarily prefer this role. They also lack the training and equipment to perform such tasks.

NATIONAL DEFENSE AND POWER PROJECTION

While the armed forces have important duties regarding the preservation of regime stability and internal control, their main job is supposed to be the care of national defense and power projection. Regarding this task, the failure of Arab and Iranian armies is an important factor in the modern Middle East's history.

Most obviously, Arab armies were unable to destroy Israel or even to inflict defeats on that country during the wars of 1948, 1956, 1967, 1969–70 (war of attrition), 1973 or 1982 (Lebanon). While the Egyptian army can be said to have contributed to its state's regaining of the Sinai peninsula, through its successes in the early part of the 1973 war, this is about the sole gain that can be cited during the five decades of Arab–Israeli conflict. In power-projection terms, the Arab states failed to eliminate, dominate, defeat or force significant concessions from Israel.

A second area of general failure in Arab power projection was the efforts to use military force to promote pan-Arab nationalist objectives or, to put it another way, to ensure one Arab state's regional hegemony and absorption of neighbors. Among these cases can be listed Egypt's failed intervention in the Yemen civil war, and its unsuccessful effort to stop Syria from seceding from the United Arab Republic (1961); Syria's move (canceled due to Israeli threats) toward intervening in Jordan during the Jordan–PLO war of 1970; and Iraq's wars against Iran (1980–88) and Kuwait (1990–91). The story of the Iraqi army shows an especially impressive contrast between a military that was highly successful in preserving the regime and remarkably unsuccessful in expanding its power through warfare.[21]

There are three cases, however, where such efforts can be said to have succeeded: Syria's domination of Lebanon from the mid-1970s onwards through a 30,000-soldier expeditionary force, Morocco's successful expansion into the former Spanish Sahara after defeating a local insurgency, and Yemen's virtual annexation of south Yemen.

In Iran's case, the armed forces were able to repel an Iraqi invasion, but not to defeat and destroy the Baghdad regime. Otherwise, the Iranian leaders have preferred to rely on more indirect efforts – including propaganda, terrorism and development of surrogate client groups – to spread the influence of their state and ideology. Such groups have included Hizballah, Hamas, Islamic Jihad, various organizations in the Persian Gulf and also the direct covert operations of Iranian intelligence.

Israel can certainly be considered the most successful country at using power projection, with two important reservations. First, Israeli objectives were always limited – far more so than most Arabs perceived them – and defense-oriented. These goals included preserving the state's existence, trying to prevent neighboring countries from letting their territory be used to launch third-party attacks on Israel, damaging the infrastructure of terrorist/guerrilla groups operating from other countries against Israel, and pressuring neighboring states to make peace or at least deter them from engaging in war. Another goal was to stop or slow down the development of nuclear weapons by Iraq, which was achieved in the 1981 raid on the Osiraq reactor.

Within this context, Israel's failures must be seen as more modest. Perhaps the most prominent would be the inability to defeat Hizballah through Israeli operations and support for surrogate forces in south Lebanon. From the standpoint of deterring and reducing attacks on Israeli territory during the 1982–2000 period, however, Israel's military was able to achieve a far better result than achieved during the 1971–82 period.

One possible lesson from all of these events is that, if conventional war and direct engagement by national militaries seems too costly or unproductive, governments could turn to other means for projecting power. These instruments can include subversion, support for surrogate forces, terrorism, diplomatic solutions, civil insurrections (notably the two Palestinian inti-fadas), the development of WMD, and seeking the help of external great powers to deter or fight wars. These last two factors will be discussed separately below.

WEAPONS OF MASS DESTRUCTION (WMD)

At first glance, the efforts of various countries to obtain WMD equipment (missiles, nuclear, chemical and biological arms) seem to enhance the strength of Middle East regular armed forces. But it should be remembered that governments control such weapons very closely and give them only to special military formations deemed especially reliable, and may view them as an alternative to using their regular armed forces.

In part, too, obtaining these weapons are attempts to overcome a perceived deadlock in the balance of power that reduces the power projection and deterrence of Arab and Iranian militaries. Clearly, WMD armaments add a new dimension to the doctrine and strategy of Middle East armed forces. These weapons have already been used in the Iran–Iraq War – with both sides firing missiles at the other's cities and, especially in Iraq's case, using chemical weapons with great effectiveness on the battlefield. Iraq also fired missiles at Saudi Arabia and Israel during the 1991 Kuwait War. Iran is developing missiles and nuclear warheads under the control of the Islamic Revolutionary Guard Corps forces. Israel has long had missile and nuclear capability, but these weapons have had little effect on its doctrine and military structure.

It should be emphasized, of course, that even the presence of WMD in the Middle East would not supplant or render irrelevant the existing regular armies. On the contrary, if such armaments break the existing deterrence deadlock they could make the armed forces an even more important tool for power projection.[22]

EXTRA-REGIONAL SOURCES OF TRAINING AND SUPPLY

Since no Middle Eastern military can supply all the arms and equipment it needs, finding a source for weapons and *matériel* is an important defining factor which has major political implications. In 1955, when Nasser's Egypt turned to Soviet supplies, this was a major turning point in the region's history, as was Egypt's break with the USSR in the early 1970s and its move to the American camp later in the same decade. The same can be said for Israel's loss of French supplies in 1967 and its switch to US equipment in the 1970s, or for Iran's break with US weapons necessitated by the 1979 Iranian revolution and the hostage crisis.

In addition to the weaponry used by the armed forces, the outside supplier has influence regarding training, doctrine and the actual use of military force. Europe tried to pressure Turkey regarding Kurdish issues by denying it certain types of equipment imports. The US boycott of Iran and, even more significantly, the international sanctions against Iraq following the 1991 Kuwait War, have had profound effects on the relevant armed forces' competence and style.

By the 1970s, the United States and the USSR were the only two powers able to supply all of a Middle Eastern military's import needs. By 1990, the Soviet Union had largely dropped out of the picture, though Russia, its successor state, has returned to some extent. The end of the Cold War, with the United States emerging victorious, penalized countries like Iran, Iraq, Libya and Syria, which depended on Soviet weaponry.[23] The technological gap between the two main suppliers could also be expected to grow over time, with US equipment becoming increasingly superior to Russian armaments. There are important implications for an armed force's political stand in this situation, since the officer corps is likely to favor maintaining good relations with the country that is its chief arms supplier.

To cite some examples of this, a US-supplied Middle Eastern military today is less likely to stage a coup against a pro-US government. Moreover, such an army would be less likely to attack Israel, since this would lead to the loss of US spare parts. The loss of Soviet equipment and Russia's unwillingness to provide arms on credit has crippled the capacity of the Syrian military. More broadly, the loss of Soviet aid, low prices and reliable supplies greatly weakened the armed forces – and hence the power projection capabilities – of Syria, Libya and Iraq.

The exception to the US monopoly is most glaring in the area of WMD supply. Countries like Iran, Iraq, Libya and Syria can turn to alternative sources of arms and technology, notably China, North Korea and Russia. This situation also creates new policy dynamics for the armed forces of those Middle Eastern states. Since this WMD equipment is obtained without any political restraints, such arms might be more likely used, if not as weapons at least as strategic leverage for power projection.[24]

CONCLUSIONS

The decline in the Middle East armed forces' tendency to seize power is not irreversible, but is likely to remain the predominant trend. No ruler can ignore, however, the views of his generals and the institutional interests of the armed forces. The militaries of various countries have a major role in terms of advising the government, setting budget priorities and maintaining internal order.

Another strong, but not inevitable, tendency is the current deadlock among states in terms of deterrence and the lack of an extra-regional sponsor encouraging the use of force in international disputes. Given the ineffectiveness of conventional armed forces for power projection, alternative military means (surrogates, terrorism, WMD, subversion etc.) remain attractive.

Certain structural flaws in regional – especially Arab – military establishments are also important factors in limiting their political role and utility. The growing importance of high technology, rapid communications and flexibility in military strategy tend to play up the weaknesses of Arab and Iranian armed forces.

Politicization usually undermines professionalism. But government efforts to depoliticize the armed forces, often by bringing politicization into their ranks, can have the same effect. This is the paradox of Middle East states historically, and its legacy today. At the same time, governments can choose to accept the military's internal autonomy – so long as it does not impinge on political matters – as a solution to this problem.

This chapter's analysis is not meant to imply that the Middle East armed forces are unimportant factors in the region's politics. On the contrary, in that part of the world where war and conflict is most likely – and most often evidenced – military power is relatively more important than anywhere else. But in a place where, to cite the Chinese revolutionary leader Mao Zedong, political power once directly grew out of the barrel of a gun, today the region's countries embody a situation in which politics is definitely in command.

NOTES

1. For an analysis of the social and institutional management techniques of such regimes, see Barry Rubin, *Modern Dictators: Third World Coupmakers, Strongmen, and Populist Tyrants* (New York: Harcourt, 1987).
2. For a discussion of the region's overall issues, conflicts, and balance of forces, see Barry Rubin, 'The Geopolitics of Middle East Conflict and Crisis', *Middle East Review of International Affairs (MERIA) Journal*, Vol. 2, No. 3 (September 1998). To view this and other *MERIA Journal* articles listed below, see http://meria.biu.ac.il.
3. Morocco, Tunisia, Algeria, Libya, Egypt, Lebanon, Jordan, Saudi Arabia, Kuwait, UAE, Bahrain, Oman, Qatar and Jordan. King Abdallah of Jordan was a career military officer, but rules, of course, as heir to his father.
4. See Stuart Cohen, 'Portrait of the New Israeli Soldier', *MERIA Journal*, Vol. 1, No. 4 (December 1997). See also Stuart Cohen, 'The Israel Defense Force: Continuity and Change', in Barry Rubin and Thomas Keaney (eds), *Armed Forces in the Middle East* (London: Frank Cass, 2001), Chapter 9.
5. Turki al-Hamad, 'Will Gulf Monarchies Work Together?' *MERIA Journal*, Vol. 1, No. 2 (May 1997).
6. These were factors, for example, in the military overspending of the Shah's regime which contributed to its fall. See Barry Rubin, *Paved with Good Intentions* (New York: Viking Penguin, 1980).

7. Gencer Özcan, 'The Turkish Foreign Policymaking Process and the Influence of the Military', in Barry Rubin and Kemal Kirisci (eds), *Turkey in World Politics: An Emerging Multi-Regional Power* (Boulder, CO: Lynne Rienner, 2001).

8. Shiham Bahatia, 'Arafat's Torturers Shock Palestinians', *Guardian Weekly*, 24 September 1995.

9. *Palestine Report*, 30 October 1998; *Ha'aretz*, 22 December 1998.

10. Gal Luft, 'The Palestinian Armed Forces', *MERIA Journal*, Vol. 3, No. 2 (June 1999); 'Palestinian Military Performance and the 2000 Intifada', *MERIA Journal*, Vol. 4, No. 4 (December 2000) and Chapter 7 in Rubin and Keaney (eds), *Armed Forces*.

11. Darius Bazargan, 'Iran: Politics, the Military and Gulf Security', *MERIA Journal*, Vol. 1, No. 3 (September 1997).

12. Mark A. Heller, 'Iraq's Army: Military Weakness, Political Unity', in Amatzia Baram and Barry Rubin (eds), *Iraq's Road to War* (New York: St Martin's Press, 1993).

13. Amatzia Baram, 'Saddam Husayn between his Power Base and the Community', *MERIA Journal*, Vol. 4, No. 4 (December 2000).

14. Eyal Zisser, 'Decisionmaking in Asad's Syria', *MERIA Journal*, Vol. 2, No. 2 (May 1998).

15. Daniel L. Byman and Jerrold D. Green, 'The Enigma of Political Stability in the Persian Gulf Monarchies', *MERIA Journal*, Vol. 3, No. 3 (September 1999), and Sean Foley, 'The UAE: Political Issues and Security Dilemmas', *MERIA Journal*, Vol. 3, No 1 (February 1999).

16. Norvell De Atkine, 'Why Arab Armies Lose Wars', in Rubin and Keaney (eds), *Armed Forces*, Chapter 2.

17. See Hillel Frisch, 'Guns and Butter in the Egyptian Army', in Rubin and Keaney (eds), *Armed Forces*, Chapter 5.

18. The best account of the Iraqi military's role in putting down the 1991 revolts is in Kanan Makiya, *Cruelty and Silence: War, Tyranny, and Uprising in the Arab World* (New York: W. W. Norton, 1994).

19. It could be easily argued that the Israeli military's involvement in the West Bank and Gaza fits better under the power projection category. The discussion of these issues under the section on internal security is not meant to make any political point, but seems more logical since the armed forces had already captured these territories and they were under Israeli administration for a protracted period of time.

20. Thanks to Eric Watkins for help on these points.

21. For an evaluation of the contemporary Iraqi armed forces, see Kenneth M. Pollack, 'Current Iraqi Military Capabilities', *MERIA News*, No. 4 (February 1998).

22. George Tenet, 'Weapons of Mass Destruction: A New Dimension in US Middle East Policy', *MERIA Journal*, Vol. 4, No. 2 (June 2000).

23. For a discussion of US military capabilities in the region, see Michael Eisenstadt, 'US Military Capabilities in the Post-Cold War Era: Implications for Middle East Allies', *MERIA Journal*, Vol. 2, No. 4 (December 1998).

24. See, for example, Bates Gill, 'Chinese Arms Exports to Iran', *MERIA Journal*, Vol. 2, No. 2 (May 1998); Barry Rubin, *North Korea's Threat to the Middle East and the Middle East's Threat to Asia* (Tel Aviv: BESA Center for Strategic Studies monographs, 1997); Barry Rubin, 'China's Middle East Strategy', *MERIA Journal*, Vol. 3, No. 1 (February 1999); Robert O. Freedman, 'Russia and the Middle East: The Primakov Era', *MERIA Journal*, Vol. 2, No. 2 (May 1998); Robert O. Freedman, 'Russian–Iranian Relations in the 1990s', *MERIA Journal*, Vol. 4, No. 2 (June 2000).

2

Why Arab Armies Lose Wars

NORVELL DE ATKINE[1]

Arabic-speaking armies have been generally ineffective in the modern era. Egyptian regular forces did poorly against Yemeni irregulars in the 1960s.[2] Syrians could only impose their will in Lebanon during the mid-1970s by the use of overwhelming weaponry and numbers.[3] Iraqis showed ineptness against an Iranian military ripped apart by revolutionary turmoil in the 1980s and could not win a three-decades-long war against the Kurds.[4] The Arab military performance on both sides of the 1990–91 Kuwait War was mediocre[5] and the Arabs have done poorly in nearly all the military confrontations with Israel. Why this unimpressive record? There are many factors – economic, ideological, technical – but perhaps the most important has to do with culture and certain societal attributes which inhibit Arabs from producing an effective military force.

It is a truism of military life that an army fights as it trains, and so, following my many years of first-hand observation of Arabs in training, I draw conclusions about the ways in which they go into combat. The following impressions derive from personal experience with Arab military establishments in the capacity of US military attaché and security assistance officer, observer officer with the British-officer Trucial Oman Scouts (the security force in the emirates prior to the establishment of the United Arab Emirates), as well as some 30 years' study of the Middle East.

FALSE STARTS

Including culture in strategic assessments has a poor legacy, for it has often been spun from an ugly brew of ignorance, wishful thinking and mythology. Thus, the US army in the 1930s evaluated the Japanese national character as lacking originality, and drew the unwarranted conclusion that the country would be permanently disadvantaged in technology.[6] Hitler dismissed the United States as a mongrel society[7] and consequently underestimated the impact of America's entry into the war. As these examples suggest, when culture is considered in calculating the relative strengths and weaknesses of opposing forces, it tends to lead to wild distortions, especially when it is a matter of understanding why states unprepared for war enter into combat flushed with confidence. The temptation is to impute cultural attributes to the enemy state that negate its superior numbers or weaponry. Or the opposite: to view the potential enemy through the prism of one's own cultural norms. US strategists assumed that the pain threshold of the North Vietnamese approximated to their own and that the air bombardment of the North would bring it to its knees.[8] Three days of aerial attacks were thought to be all the Serbs could withstand; in fact, 78 days were needed.

It is particularly dangerous to make facile assumptions about abilities in warfare based on past performance, for societies evolve, as does the military subculture with it. The dismal French performance in the 1870 Franco-Prussian war led the German High Command to an overly optimistic assessment prior to the First World War.[9] The tenacity and courage of French soldiers in the First World War led everyone from Winston Churchill to the German High Command vastly to overestimate the French army's fighting abilities in the Second World War.[10] Israeli generals underestimated the Egyptian army of 1973, based on Egypt's hapless performance in the 1967 war.[11]

Culture is difficult to pin down. It is not synonymous with an individual's race or ethnic identity. The history of warfare makes a mockery of attempts to assign rigid cultural attributes to individuals – as the military histories of the Ottoman and Roman Empires illustrate. In both cases it was training, discipline, *esprit* de corps and élan which made the difference, not the individual soldiers' origins.[12] The highly disciplined, effective, Roman legions, for example, were recruited from throughout the Roman Empire, and the elite Ottoman Janissaries (slave soldiers) were Christians forcibly recruited as boys from the Balkans.

THE ROLE OF CULTURE

These problems notwithstanding, culture does need to be taken into account. Indeed, awareness of prior mistakes should make it possible to assess the role of cultural factors in warfare. John Keegan, the eminent historian of warfare, argues that culture is a prime determinant of the nature of warfare. In contrast to the usual manner of European warfare, which he terms 'face to face', Keegan depicts the early Arab armies in the Islamic era as masters of evasion, delay and indirection.[13] Examining Arab warfare in this century leads to the conclusion that Arabs remain more successful in insurgent, or political, warfare[14] – what T. E. Lawrence termed 'winning wars without battles'.[15] Even the much-lauded Egyptian crossing of the Suez in 1973 entailed at its core a masterful deception plan. It may well be that these seemingly permanent attributes result from a culture that engenders subtlety, indirection, and dissimulation in personal relationships.[16]

Along these lines, Kenneth Pollack concludes his exhaustive study of Arab military effectiveness by noting that 'certain patterns of behavior fostered by the dominant Arab culture were the most important factors contributing to the limited military effectiveness of Arab armies and air forces from 1945 to 1991'.[17] These attributes included over-centralization, discouraging initiative, lack of flexibility, manipulation of information and the discouragement of leadership at the junior officer level.

The barrage of criticism leveled at Samuel Huntington's notion of a 'clash of civilizations'[18] in no way lessens the vital point he made – that however much the grouping of peoples by religion and culture rather than political or economic divisions offends academics who propound a world defined by class, race and gender, it is a reality, one not diminished by modern communications.

But how does one integrate the study of culture into military training? At present, it has hardly any role. Paul M. Belbutowski, a scholar and former member of the US Delta Force, succinctly stated a deficiency in our own military education system: 'Culture, comprised of all that is vague and intangible, is not generally integrated into strategic planning except at the most superficial level.'[19] And yet it is precisely 'all that is vague and intangible' which defines low-intensity conflicts. The Vietnamese Communists did not fight the war the United States had trained for, nor did the Chechens and Afghans fight the war for which the Russians had prepared. This entails far more than simply retooling weaponry and retraining soldiers. It requires an understanding of the enemy's cultural mythology, history, attitude toward time, etc. – demanding a more substantial investment in time and money than a bureaucratic organization is likely to authorize.

Mindful of walking through a minefield of past errors and present cultural sensibilities, I offer some assessments of the role of culture in the military training of Arabic-speaking officers. I confine myself principally to training for two reasons. First, I observed much training but only one combat campaign (the Jordanian Army against the Palestine Liberation Organization in 1970). Secondly, armies fight as they train. Troops are conditioned by peacetime habits, policies and procedures; they do not undergo a sudden metamorphosis that transforms civilians in uniform into warriors. General George Patton was fond of relating the story about Julius Caesar, who, 'In the winter time ... so trained his legions in all that became soldiers and so habituated them to the proper performance of their duties, that when in the spring he committed them to battle against the Gauls, it was not necessary to give them orders, for they knew what to do and how to do it.'[20]

INFORMATION AS POWER

In every society, information is a means of making a living or wielding power, but Arabs husband information and hold it especially tightly. US trainers have often been surprised over the years by the fact that information provided to key personnel does not get much further than them. Having learned to perform some complicated procedure, an Arab technician knows that he is invaluable so long as he is the only one in a unit to have that knowledge; once he dispenses it to others, he no longer is the only font of knowledge and his power dissipates. This explains the commonplace hoarding of manuals, books, training pamphlets and other training or logistics literature. On one occasion, an American mobile training team working with armor in Egypt at long last received the operators' manuals that had laboriously been translated into Arabic. The American trainers took the newly minted manuals straight to the tank park and distributed them to the tank crews. Right behind them, the company commander, a graduate of the armor school at Fort Knox and specialized courses at the Aberdeen Proving Grounds ordnance school, collected the manuals from the crews. Questioned why he did this, the commander said that there was no point in giving them to the drivers because enlisted men could not read. In point of fact, he did not want enlisted men to have an independent source of knowledge. Being the only person who can explain the fire control instrumentation of boresight artillery weapons brings prestige and attention. In military terms, this means that very little cross-training is accomplished and that, for instance in a tank crew, the gunners, loaders and drivers might be proficient in their jobs but are not prepared to fill in for a casualty. Not understanding one another's jobs also inhibits a smoothly functioning crew. At a higher level, it means there is no depth in technical proficiency.

EDUCATION PROBLEMS

Training tends to be unimaginative, cut and dried, and not chal-lenging. Because the Arab educational system is predicated on rote memorization, officers have a phenomenal ability to commit vast amounts of knowledge to memory. The learning system tends to consist of on-high lectures, with students taking voluminous notes and being examined on what they were told. (It also has interesting implications for foreign instructors; for example, their credibility is diminished if they must resort to a book.) The emphasis on memorization has a price, and that is in diminished ability to reason, or engage in analysis based upon general principles. Thinking outside the box is not encouraged; doing so in public can damage a career. Instructors are not challenged and neither, in the end, are students.

Head-to-head competition among individuals is generally avoided, at least openly, for it means that someone wins and someone else loses, with the loser humiliated. This taboo has particular import when a class contains mixed ranks. Education is in good part sought as a matter of personal prestige, so Arabs in US military schools take pains to ensure that the ranking member, according to military position or social class, scores the highest marks in the class. Often this leads to 'sharing answers' in class – often in a rather overt manner – or junior officers concealing scores higher than their superior's.

American military instructors dealing with Middle Eastern students learn to ensure that, before directing any question to a student in a classroom situation, particularly if he is an officer, the student does possess the correct answer. If this is not assured, the officer will feel he has been set up for public humiliation. Furthermore, in the often paranoid environment of Arab political culture, he will believe this set-up to have been purposeful. This student will then become an enemy of the instructor and his classmates will become apprehensive about their also being singled out for humiliation – and learning becomes impossible.

OFFICER VS. SOLDIERS

Arab junior officers are well trained on the technical aspects of their weapons and tactical know-how, but not in leadership, a subject given little attention. For example, as General Sa'd ash-Shazli, the Egyptian chief of staff, noted in his assessment of the army he inherited prior to the 1973 war, they were not trained to seize the initiative or volunteer original concepts or new ideas.[21] Indeed, leadership may be the greatest weakness of Arab training systems. This problem results from two main factors: a highly accentuated class system bordering on a caste system, and lack of a non-commissioned officer (NCO) development program.

Most Arab officers treat enlisted soldiers with a total lack of respect. When the winds in Egypt one day carried biting sand particles from the desert during a demonstration for visiting US dignitaries, I watched as a contingent of soldiers marched in and formed a single rank to shield the Americans; Egyptian soldiers, in other words, are used on occasion as nothing more than a wind-break. The idea of taking care of one's men is found only among the most elite units in the Egyptian military. On a typical weekend, officers in units stationed outside Cairo will get in their cars and drive off to their homes, leaving the enlisted men to fend for themselves by trekking across the desert to a highway and flagging down buses or trucks to get to the Cairo rail system. Garrison cantonments have no amenities for soldiers. The same situation, in various degrees, exists elsewhere in the Arabic-speaking countries – less so in Jordan, even more so in Iraq and Syria.

The young draftees who make up the bulk of the Egyptian army hate military service for good reason and will do almost anything, including self-mutilation, to avoid it. In Syria, the wealthy buy exemptions or, failing that, are assigned to non-combatant organizations. As a young Syrian told me, his musical skills came from his assignment to a Syrian army band, where he learned to play an instrument. In general, the militaries of the Fertile Crescent enforce discipline by fear; in countries where a tribal system is still in force, such as Saudi Arabia, the innate egalitarianism of the society mitigates against fear as the prime motivator, so a general lack of discipline pervades.[22]

The social and professional gap between officers and enlisted men is present in all armies, but in the United States and other Western forces, the non-commissioned officer (NCO) corps bridges it. Indeed, a professional NCO corps has been critical for the American military to work at its best; as the primary trainers in a professional army, NCOs are essential to training programs and to the enlisted men's sense of unit *esprit*. Most of the Arab world either has no NCO corps or it is non-functional, severely handicapping the military's effectiveness. With some exceptions, NCOs are considered in the same low category as enlisted men, and so do not serve as a bridge between enlisted men and officers. Officers instruct, but the wide social gap between enlisted man and officer tends to make the learning process perfunctory, formalized and ineffective. The show-and-tell aspects of training are frequently missing, because officers refuse to get their hands dirty and prefer to ignore the more practical aspects of their subject matter, believing this below their social station. A dramatic example of this occurred during the Gulf War, when a severe wind-storm blew down the tents of Iraqi officer prisoners of war. For three days they stayed in the wind and rain rather than be observed by enlisted prisoners in a nearby camp working with their hands.

The military price for this is very high. Without the cohesion supplied by NCOs, units tend to disintegrate in the stress of combat. This is primarily a function of the fact that the enlisted soldiers simply do not trust their officers. Once officers depart the training areas, training begins to fall apart as soldiers start drifting off. An Egyptian officer once explained to me that the Egyptian army's catastrophic defeat in 1967 resulted from a lack of cohesion within units. The situation, he said, had only marginally improved in 1973. Iraqi prisoners in 1991 showed a remarkable fear and enmity toward their officers.

DECISION-MAKING AND RESPONSIBILITY

Decisions are made and delivered from on high, with very little lateral communication. This leads to a highly centralized system, with authority hardly ever delegated. Rarely does an officer make a critical decision on his own; instead, he prefers the safe course of being identified as industrious, intelligent, loyal – and compli-ant. Bringing attention to oneself as an innovator or someone prone to make unilateral decisions is a recipe for trouble. As in civilian life, conformism is the overwhelming societal norm; the nail that stands up gets hammered down. Orders and information flow from top to bottom; they are not to be reinterpreted, amended or modified in any way.

US trainers often experience frustration obtaining a decision from a counterpart, not realizing that the Arab officer lacks the authority to make the decision – a frustration amplified by the Arab's understandable reluctance to admit that he lacks that authority. This author has several times seen decisions that could have been made at the battalion level, concerning such matters as class meeting times and locations, requiring approval from the ministry of defense. All of which has led American trainers to develop a rule of thumb: a sergeant first class in the US army has as much authority as a colonel in an Arab army. Methods of instruction and subject matter are dictated from higher authorities. Unit commanders have very little to say about these affairs. The politicized nature of the Arab militaries means that political factors weigh heavily and frequently override military considerations. Officers with initiative and a predilection for unilateral action pose a threat to the regime. This can be seen not just at the level of national strategy, but in every aspect of military operations and training. If Arab militaries became less politicized and more professional in preparation for the 1973 war with Israel,[23] once the fighting ended, old habits returned. Now, an increasingly bureaucratized military establishment weighs in as well. A veteran of the Pentagon turf wars will feel like a kindergartener when he encounters the rivalries that exist in Arab military headquarters.

Taking responsibility for a policy, operation, status, or training program rarely occurs. American trainers can find it very frustrating when they repeatedly encounter Arab officers placing blame for unsuccessful operations or programs on the US equipment or some other outside source. A high rate of non-operational US equipment is blamed on a 'lack of spare parts' – pointing a finger at an unresponsive US supply system, despite the fact that American trainers can document ample supplies arriving in country and disappearing in a malfunctioning supply system. (Such criticism was never caustic or personal, and often so indirect and politely delivered that it wasn't until after a meeting that oblique references were understood.) This imperative works even at the most exalted levels. During the Kuwait War, Iraqi forces took over the town of Khafji in north-east Saudi Arabia, after the Saudis had evacuated the place. General Khalid bin Sultan, the Saudi ground forces commander, requested a letter from General

Norman Schwarzkopf, stating it was the US general who ordered an evacuation from the Saudi town.[24] And in his account of the Khafji battle, General bin Sultan predictably blames the Americans for the Iraqi occupation of the town.[25] In reality, the problem was that the light Saudi forces in the area left the battlefield.[26] The Saudis were in fact outgunned and outnumbered by the Iraqi unit approaching Khafji, but Saudi pride required that foreigners be blamed.

As for equipment, a vast cultural gap exists between the US and Arab maintenance and logistics systems. The Arab difficulties with US equipment are not, as sometimes simplistically believed, a matter of 'Arabs don't do maintenance', but something much deeper. The American concept of a weapons system does not convey easily. A weapons system brings with it specific maintenance and logistics procedures, policies and even a philosophy, all of them based on American culture, with its expectations of a certain educational level, sense of small unit responsibility, tool allocation and doctrine. Tools that would be allocated to a US battalion (a unit of some 600–800 personnel) would most likely be found at a much higher level – probably two or three echelons higher – in an Arab army. The expertise, initiative and, most importantly, the trust indicated by delegation of responsibility to a lower level are rare. The US equipment and its maintenance are predicated on a concept of repair at the lowest level, and therefore require delegation of authority. Without the needed tools, spare parts or expertise available to keep equipment running, and loath to report bad news to his superiors, the unit commander looks for scapegoats. All this explains why I many times heard in Egypt that US weaponry is 'too delicate'.

I have observed many in-country US survey teams: invariably, hosts make the case for acquiring the most modern of military hardware and do everything to avoid issues of maintenance, logistics and training. They obfuscate and mislead to such an extent that American teams, no matter how earnest their sense of mission, find it nearly impossible to help. More generally, Arab reluctance to be candid about training deficiencies makes it extremely difficult for foreign advisers properly to support instruction or assess training needs.

COMBINED ARMS OPERATIONS

A lack of cooperation is most apparent in the failure of all Arab armies to succeed at combined arms operations. A regular Jordanian army infantry company, for example, is man-for-man as good as a comparable Israeli company; at battalion level, however, the coordination required for combined arms operations, with artillery, air and logistics support, is simply absent. Indeed, the higher the echelon, the greater the disparity. This results from infrequent combined arms training; when it does take place, it is intended to impress visitors (which it does – the dog-and-pony show is usually done with uncommon gusto and theatrical talent) rather than provide real training.

This problem results from three main factors. First, the renowned lack of trust among Arabs for anyone outside their own kin group adversely affects offensive operations.[27] Exceptions to this pattern are limited to elite units (which throughout the Arab world have the same duty – to protect the regime, rather than the country). In a culture in which almost every sphere of human endeavor, including business and social relationships, is based on a family structure, this orientation is also present in the military, particularly in the stress of battle. Offensive action, basically, consists of fire and maneuver. The maneuver element must be confident that supporting units or arms are providing covering fire. If there is a lack of trust in that support, getting troops moving forward against dug-in defenders is possible only by officers getting out front and leading, something that has not been characteristic of Arab leadership.

Second, the complex mosaic system of peoples creates additional problems for training, as rulers in the Middle East make use of the sectarian and tribal loyalties to maintain power. The 'Alawi minority controls Syria, East Bankers control Jordan, Sunnis control Iraq and Nejdis control Saudi Arabia. This has direct implications for the military, where sectarian considerations affect assignments and promotions. Some minorities (such as the Circassians in Jordan or the Druze in Syria) tie their well-being to the ruling elite and perform critical protection roles; others (such as the Shi'a of Iraq) are excluded from the officer corps. In any case, the assignment of officers based on sectarian considerations works against assignments based on merit.

The same lack of trust operates at the interstate level, where Arab armies exhibit very little trust of one another, and with good reason. The blatant lie Gamal Abdel Nasser told King Husayn in June 1967 to get him into the war against Israel – that the Egyptian air force was over Tel Aviv (when most of its planes had in fact been destroyed) – was a classic example of deceit.[28] Sadat's disingenuous approach to the Syrians to entice them to enter the war in October 1973 was another (he told them that the Egyptians were planning total war, a deception which included using a second set of operational plans intended only for Syrian eyes).[29] With this sort of history, it is no wonder that there is very little cross- or joint training among Arab armies and very few command exercises. During the 1967 war, for example, not a single Jordanian liaison officer was stationed in Egypt, nor were the Jordanians forthcoming with the Egyptian command.[30]

Third, Middle Eastern rulers routinely rely on balance-of-power techniques to maintain their authority.[31] They use competing organizations, duplicate agencies and coercive structures dependent upon the ruler's whim. This makes building any form of personal power base difficult, if not impossible, and keeps the leadership apprehensive and off-balance, never secure in its careers or social position. The same applies within the military; a powerful chairman of the joint chiefs is inconceivable.

Joint commands are paper constructs that have little actual function. Leaders look at joint commands, joint exercises, combined arms and integrated staffs very cautiously, for all Arab armies are a double-edged sword. One edge points toward the external enemy and the other toward the capital. The land forces are a regime-maintenance force and threat at the same time. No Arab ruler will allow combined operations or training to become routine; the usual excuse is financial expense, but that is unconvincing, given their frequent purchase of hardware whose maintenance costs they cannot afford. In fact, combined arms exercises and joint staffs create familiarity, soften rivalries, erase suspicions and eliminate the fragmented, competing organizations that enable rulers to play off rivals against one another. This situation is most clearly seen in Saudi Arabia, where the land forces and aviation are under the Minister of Defense, Prince Sultan, while the National Guard is under Prince Abdullah, the Deputy Prime Minister and Crown Prince. In Egypt, the Central Security Forces balance the army. In Iraq and Syria, the Republican Guard does the balancing.

Politicians actually create obstacles to maintain fragmentation. For example, obtaining aircraft from the air force for army airborne training, whether it is a joint exercise or a simple administrative request for support of training, must generally be coordinated by the heads of services at the ministry of defense; if a large number of aircraft is involved, this probably requires presidential approval. Military coups may be out of style, but the fear of them remains strong. Any large-scale exercise of land forces is a matter of concern to the government and is closely observed, particularly if live ammunition is being used. In Saudi Arabia, a complex system of clearances required from area military commanders and provincial governors – all of whom have differing command channels to secure road convoy permission, obtain ammunition and conduct exercises – means that, in order for a coup to work, it would require a massive amount of loyal conspirators. Arab regimes have learned how to be coup-proof.

SECURITY AND PARANOIA

Arab regimes classify virtually everything as vaguely military. Information the US military routinely publishes (about promotions, transfers, names of unit commanders and unit designations) is top secret in Arabic-speaking countries. To be sure, this does make it more difficult for the enemy to construct an accurate order of battle, but it also feeds the divisive and compartmentalized nature of the military forces. The obsession with security can reach ludicrous lengths. Prior to the 1973 war, Sadat was surprised to find that within two weeks of the date he had ordered the armed forces be ready for war, his Minister of War, General Muhammad Sadiq, had failed to inform his immediate staff of the order. Should a war, Sadat wondered, be kept secret from the very people expected to fight it?[32] One can expect to have an Arab counterpart or key contact changed without warning and with no explanation as to his sudden absence. This might well be simply a transfer a few doors down the way, but the vagueness of it all leaves foreigners with dire scenarios – scenarios that might be true. And it is best not to inquire too much; advisers or trainers who seem overly inquisitive may find their access to host military information or facilities limited.

The presumed close US–Israel relationship, thought to be operative at all levels, aggravates and complicates this penchant for secrecy. Arabs believe that the most mundane details about them are somehow transmitted to the Mossad via a secret hotline. This explains why a US adviser with Arab forces is likely to be asked early and often about his opinion of the 'Palestine problem', then subjected to monologues on the presumed Jewish domination of the United States.

INDIFFERENCE TO SAFETY

In terms of safety measures, there is a general laxness, a seeming carelessness and indifference to training accidents, many of which could have been prevented by minimal efforts. To the (perhaps overly) safety-conscious Americans, Arab societies appear indifferent to casualties and show a seemingly lackadaisical approach to training safety. There are a number of explanations for this. Some would point to the inherent fatalism within Islam,[33] but perhaps the reason is less religiously based and more a result of political culture. As any military veteran knows, the ethos of a unit is set at the top, or, as the old saying has it, units do well those things that the boss cares about. When the top political leadership displays a complete lack of concern for the welfare of its soldiers, such attitudes percolate down through the ranks. The prime example was the betrayal of Syrian troops fighting Israel in the Golan in 1967: having withdrawn its elite units, the Syrian government knowingly broadcast the falsehood that Israeli troops had captured the town of Kuneitra, which would have put them behind the largely conscript Syrian army still in position. The leadership took this step to pressure the great powers to impose a truce, though it led to a panic by the Syrian troops and the loss of the Golan Heights.[34]

CONCLUSION

It would be difficult to exaggerate the cultural gulf separating American and Arab military cultures. In every significant area, American military advisers find students who enthusiastically take in their lessons and then resolutely fail to apply them. The culture they return to – the culture of their own armies in their own countries – defeats the intentions with which they took leave of their American instructors.

When they had an influence on certain Arab military establishments, the Soviets reinforced their clients' cultural traits far more than, in more recent years, Americans were able to do. Like the Arabs, the Soviet military culture was driven by political fears bordering on paranoia. The steps taken to control the sources (real or imagined) of these fears, such as a rigidly centralized command structure, were readily understood by Arab political and military elites. The Arabs, too, felt an affinity for the Soviet officer class's contempt for ordinary soldiers and the Soviet military hierarchy's distrust of a well-developed, well-appreciated, well-rewarded NCO corps.

Arab political culture is based on a high degree of social stratification, very much like that of the defunct Soviet Union, and very much unlike the upwardly mobile, meritocratic, democratic United States. Arab officers do not see any value in sharing information among themselves, let alone with their men. In this, they follow the example of their political leaders, who not only withhold information from their own allies, but routinely deceive them. Training in Arab armies reflects this: rather than prepare as much as possible for the multitude of improvised responsibilities that are thrown up in the chaos of battle, Arab soldiers, and their officers, are bound in the narrow functions assigned them by their hierarchy. That this renders them less effective on the battlefield, let alone places their lives at greater risk, is scarcely of concern, whereas, of course, these two issues are dominant in the American military culture and reflected in American military training.

Change is unlikely to come until it occurs in the larger Arab political culture, although the experience of other societies (including our own) suggests that the military can have a democratizing influence on the wider political culture, as officers bring the lessons of their training first into their professional environment, then into the larger society. It obviously makes a big difference, however, when the surrounding political culture is not only avowedly democratic (as are many Middle Eastern states), but functionally so. Until Arab politics begin to change at fundamental levels, Arab armies, whatever the courage or proficiency of individual officers and men, are unlikely to acquire the range of qualities which modern fighting forces require for success on the battlefield. For these qualities depend on inculcating respect, trust and openness among the members of the armed forces at all levels, and this is the marching music of modern warfare that Arab armies, no matter how much they emulate the corresponding steps, do not want to hear.

NOTES

1. This chapter first appeared as an article in *Middle East Quarterly*, December 1999. The opinions expressed in the article are strictly the author's and do not represent the views of the US government.
2. Saeed M. Badeeb, *The Saudi–Egyptian Conflict over North Yemen 1962–1970* (Boulder, CO: Westview Press, 1986), pp. 33–42.
3. R. D. McLaurin, *The Battle of Zahle* (Aberdeen Proving Grounds, MD: Human Engineering Laboratory, September 1986), pp. 26–7.
4. Anthony Cordesman and Abraham Wagner, *The Lessons of Modern War, Volume II: The Iran–Iraq War* (Boulder, CO: Westview Press, 1990), pp. 89–98; Phebe Marr, *The Modern History of Iraq* (Boulder CO: Westview Press, 1985), pp. 222–3, 233–4.
5. Kenneth M. Pollack, 'The Influence of Arab Culture on Arab Military Effectiveness' (PhD, Massachusetts Institute of Technology, 1996), pp. 259–61 (Egypt); pp. 533–6 (Saudi Arabia); pp. 350–5 (Iraq). Syrians did not see significant combat in the 1991 Gulf War but conversations with US personnel in liaison with them indicated a high degree of paranoia and distrust toward Americans and other Arabs.
6. David Kahn, 'United States Views of Germany and Japan', in Ernest R. May (ed.), *Knowing One's Enemies: Intelligence Before the Two World Wars* (Princeton, NJ: Princeton University Press, 1984), pp. 476–503.
7. Gerhard L. Weinberg, *The Foreign Policy of Hitler's Germany: Diplomatic Revolution in Europe, 1933–1936* (Chicago, IL: University of Chicago, 1970), p. 21.

8. Stanley Karnow, *Vietnam: A History* (New York: Penguin Books, 1984), p. 18.
9. Paul Kennedy, *The Rise and Fall of Great Powers* (New York: Random House, 1987), pp. 186–7. The German assessment from T. Dodson Stamps and Vincent J. Esposito (eds), *A Short History of World War I* (West Point, NY: United States Military Academy, 1955), p. 8.
10. William Manchester, *Winston Spencer Churchill: The Last Lion Alone, 1932–1940* (New York: Dell Publishing, 1988), p. 613; May, 'Conclusions', in *Knowing One's Enemies*, pp. 513–14. Hitler thought otherwise, however.
11. Avraham (Bren) Adan, *On the Banks of the Suez* (San Francisco, CA: Presidio Press, 1980), pp. 73–86. 'Thus the prevailing feeling of security, based on the assumption that the Arabs were incapable of mounting an overall war against us, distorted our view of the situation', Moshe Dayan stated. 'As for the fighting standard of the Arab soldiers, I can sum it up in one sentence: they did not run away.' *Moshe Dayan: Story of My Life* (New York: William Morrow, 1976), p. 510.
12. John Keegan, *A History of Warfare* (New York: Alfred A. Knopf, 1993), p. 18.
13. Ibid., p. 387.
14. John Walter Jandora, *Militarism in Arab Society: A Historiographical and Bibliographical Sourcebook* (Westport, CT: Greenwood Press, 1997), p. 128.
15. T. E. Lawrence, *The Evolution of a Revolt* (Ft Leavenworth, KS: CSI, 1990), p. 21. (Reprint of article originally published in *British Army Quarterly and Defence Journal*, October 1920.)
16. Author's observations buttressed by such scholarly works as Eli Shouby, 'The Influence of the Arabic Language on the Psychology of the Arabs', in Abdullah M. Lutfiyya and Charles Churchill (eds), *Readings in Arab Middle Eastern Societies and Culture* (The Hague: Mouton Co., 1970), pp. 688–703; Hisham Shirabi and Muktar Ani, 'Impact of Class and Culture on Social Behavior: The Feudal-Bourgeois Family in Arab Society', in L. Carl Brown and Norman Itzkowitz (eds), *Psychological Dimensions of Near Eastern Studies* (Princeton, NJ: Darwin Press, 1977), pp. 240–56; Sania Hamady, *Temperament and Character of the Arabs* (New York: Twayne Publishers, 1960), pp. 28–85; Raphael Patai, *The Arab Mind* (New York: Charles Scribner's Sons, 1973), pp. 20–85.
17. Pollack, 'Influence of Arab Culture', p. 759.
18. Samuel P. Huntington, 'The Clash of Civilizations', *Foreign Affairs* (Summer 1993), pp. 21–49.
19. Paul M. Belbutowski, 'Strategic Implications of Cultures in Conflict', *Parameters* (Spring 1996), pp. 32–42.
20. Carlo D'Este, *Patton: A Genius for War* (New York: HarperCollins, 1996), p. 383.
21. Saad el-Shazly, *The Crossing of the Suez* (San Francisco: American Mideast Research, 1980), p. 47.
22. Jordan may be an exception here; however, most observers agree that its effectiveness has declined in the past 20 years.
23. Pollack, 'Influence of Arab Culture', pp. 256–7.
24. H. Norman Schwarzkopf, *It Doesn't Take A Hero* (New York: Bantam Books, 1992), p. 494.
25. Khaled bin Sultan, *Desert Warrior: A Personal View of the War by the Joint Forces Commander* (New York: HarperCollins, 1995), pp. 368–9.
26. Based on discussions with US personnel in the area and familiar with the battle.
27. Yehoshafat Harkabi, 'Basic Factors in the Arab Collapse during the Six Day War', *Orbis* (Fall 1967), pp. 678–9.
28. James Lunt, *Hussein of Jordan, Searching for a Just and Lasting Peace: A Political Biography* (New York: William Morrow, 1989), p. 99.
29. Patrick Seale, *Asad of Syria: The Struggle for the Middle East* (Berkeley: University of California Press, 1988), pp. 197–9; Shazly, *The Crossing of the Suez*, pp. 21, 37.
30. Samir A. Mutawi, *Jordan in the 1967 War* (Cambridge: Cambridge University Press,

1987), p. 161.
31. James A. Bill and Robert Springborg, *Politics in the Middle East* (New York: HarperCollins, 1990, 3rd edn), p. 262.
32. Anwar el-Sadat, *In Search of Identity* (New York: Harper & Row, 1978), p. 235.
33. Hamady, *Temperament and Character*, pp. 184–93; Patai, *The Arab Mind*, pp.147–50.
34. Joseph Malone, 'Syria and the Six-Day War', *Current Affairs Bulletin* (26 January 1968), p. 80.

3

US Policy and Middle East Armed Forces

MARVIN C. FEUER[1]

US military policy in the Middle East and south-west Asia is based upon American interests in this region. Perhaps the most succinct statement of those interests is found in the White House's annual National Security Strategy statement, and elaborations thereof by other senior officials. In the year 2000, the Clinton administration indicated that American interests in the region were:

1. Pursuing a just, lasting and comprehensive Middle East peace.

2. Ensuring the security and well-being of Israel.

3. Helping Arab friends provide for their security and promotion of regional stability.

4. Maintaining the free flow of oil from the region, particularly since world dependence is expected to rise dramatically. This in turn requires freedom of navigation, access to commercial markets, protection of US citizens and property abroad.

5. Promotion of political and economic reform.[2]

Former Secretary of Defense William Perry characterized American interests in the Middle East in the mid-1990s in a similar way. According to Perry's list, these interests included:

1. Assured access to Gulf oil.

2. A durable Arab–Israeli peace.

3. The security of key regional partners, including Israel, Egypt and Saudi Arabia.
4. The protection of US citizens and property.
5. Freedom of navigation.
6. Successful reform in the former Soviet Union.
7. Human rights and democratic development.
8. Access to regional markets.[3]

American military activity is based on the pursuit of these interests in the face of threats posed to them both from within the region and without.

US THREAT PERCEPTIONS

The United States looks at Middle East threats from a variety of perspectives, including threats to its own military and civilians, and aggression against American allies and friends. The Middle East region poses challenges to the United States across a wide spectrum, ranging from Weapons of Mass Destruction (WMD) and missiles to conventional forces, terrorism, narcotics, crime and information warfare. American analysts believe that many Middle East threats are becoming increasingly transnational. For example, countries like Iran, Iraq and Syria may no longer be mere recipients of WMD technology from more advanced countries like Russia and China, but are developing the capability to produce and export such technologies within the Middle East. Terrorist organizations are cooperating across borders and using advances in missile technology. At the same time, traditional threats of war and subversion also continue in the region, led largely by Iran and Iraq. The following are the main elements of the threat, as outlined by US officials:[4]

Proliferation of WMD
From the US perspective, this is a dangerous and worsening situation in the Middle East. Potential adversaries believe they can preclude US force options and offset US conventional military capability by developing WMD and missiles. More generally, many Middle East states are motivated by their own regional threat

perceptions. For example, the use of missiles against its cities during the 1980–88 Iran–Iraq War galvanized Iran's WMD efforts. States like Iran, Iraq, Libya and Syria have clearly indicated that their development of WMD is meant in part as a means of challenging Israel and deterring its assumed military superiority.

Most US intelligence analysts believe that Iran could test an ICBM (intercontinental ballistic missile) capable of delivering a light payload to the United States in the next few years, and that Iraq could develop such an ICBM in the next decade. These two countries already possess short- and medium-range missiles that pose a more immediate threat to US forces, interests and allies in the Middle East. Iraq has retained some WMD and missile capabilities despite the sanctions. The lack of intrusive inspection and disarmament mechanisms permits it to enhance these capabilities. The United States is increasingly concerned about deployment of biological and nuclear programs in the Middle East. In the assessment of the Director of the Defense Intelligence Agency, 'all told, the prospects for limiting proliferation are slim'.[5]

Iraq
Apart from its WMD capabilities, Iraq continues to pose a conventional threat to its Gulf neighbors. Despite the decline of Iraqi military capabilities since the 1991 Gulf War, the country's ground forces continue to be formidable in regional terms.[6] In 2000 the Iraqis paraded 1,000 tanks in an impressive show of force in Baghdad. Iraq could threaten its neighbors, if not restrained by external forces, and could participate if there were a conventional war between Israel and the Arab states. Iraq deployed troops near its western border during the crisis between Israel and the Palestinians, which began in fall 2000. Its terrorist and WMD capabilities might also cause the United States to scale back its presence and harm US military effectiveness in the region.

Iran
American officials believe that Iran seeks to dominate the Gulf area. To be sure, Iran's armed forces remain significantly limited with regard to modern weapons systems, mobility and logistics infrastructure. Nonetheless, Iran has embarked on a military build-up designed to ensure regime security, increase its influence

in the Middle East and Central Asia, deter Iraq and limit US regional influence. Iran is doing this by developing capabilities including subversion, terrorism, and capabilities to interdict maritime access around the Strait of Hormuz. At the same time, Iran is acquiring WMD and longer-range missiles to deter the United States and to intimidate its neighbors. Iran remains the world's largest sponsor of terrorism, and its foreign policy remains hostile to US interests – most clearly demonstrated by its rejection of the Middle East peace process and efforts to energize rejectionist Palestinian and Hizballah movements.

Terrorism and Extremism

US officials perceive terrorism as a very significant threat to American interests at home and abroad. They believe this threat will grow as disgruntled groups focus on America as the source of their troubles. The US military is vulnerable, due to its overseas presence and status as a symbol of US power, interests and influence. The attack on the USS *Cole* on 12 October 2000 clearly demonstrated this vulnerability. American officials believe that state sponsors of terrorism (primarily Iran) and individuals with the financial means (such as Usama bin Laden) will continue to provide much of the economic and technological support needed by terrorists.

In addition, American officials believe that extremist forces in the Middle East may challenge traditional rulers. This premise has been reinforced in the wake of local disturbances accompanying the violent clashes between Palestinians and Israelis in October 2000, which led to the placing of US forces in the Persian Gulf and Turkey on alert.[7] Perhaps more disturbing was a public opinion poll showing that three-quarters of Palestinians supported military attacks against the American presence in the Middle East.[8]

US MILITARY OBJECTIVES

In light of US interests and threats in the Middle East, the United States has established distinct military objectives in the region. These include the following:[9]

1. To preserve Israel's qualitative edge and help Israel to maintain a positive military balance against potential adversaries.

2. To deter and prevent aggression from Iran and Iraq against friendly states. As part of this objective, the United States seeks to keep Iran and Iraq from becoming significant conventional threats, and to prevent them from acquiring unconventional and advanced conventional military capabilities. To deter Iraq and defeat Iraqi aggression if necessary, the United States seeks to facilitate US deployments in the region. The United States also seeks to enhance interoperability with friendly states both to increase US capabilities and to enable these states to make a contribution to a coalition effort against aggression.

3. The United States also seeks to help friendly Arab states defend themselves against local threats, an effort which benefits America's own ability to operate in the region. In principle, the United States is pursuing a three-tiered approach: (a) encouraging national self-defense efforts, so that each nation bears primary responsibility for its own protection; (b) encouraging collective defense efforts such as through the Gulf Cooperation Council (GCC) so countries may work closely on collective defense and security arrangements; and (c) participating with other states from outside the region to meet threats to American allies. Given the rise in WMD threats and the lack of regional capabilities, this is one of the key areas of US focus.[10]

MEASURES TAKEN BY US TO ACHIEVE OBJECTIVES

The United States has pursued an extensive menu of measures to enable it to pursue the interests mentioned above.[11] American efforts have focused on strengthening Israel, deterring Iraq and Iran, and supporting friendly Arab states.

Israel
The United States has undertaken considerable efforts to ensure Israel's qualitative edge and that it maintains a favorable military

balance. The United States' most evident contribution is the foreign military financing (FMF) and economic support fund (ESF) assistance provided annually to Israel. The United States has provided Israel with over $70 billion in economic and military assistance since 1949. In fiscal year (FY) 2001, the US will provide Israel a total of $2.82 billion – $1.98 billion in military aid and $840 million in economic support funds. In addition, Israel will receive a portion of the $1.2 billion in aid funds approved following the Wye agreement between Israel and the Palestinians in late 1999. Israel is the largest recipient of bilateral American assistance. Israel's FMF represents about 26 per cent of its defense budget and is crucial to the country's ability to modernize its military forces. The money Israel receives in 2001, for example, will enable it to continue funding multi-year procurements and follow-on support for F-15 and F-16 fighters, Beech King B200T aircraft, AIM 120 AMRAAM missiles; Joint Direct Attack Munitions and Cobra and Apache/Longbow helicopter upgrades.[12]

Many Israelis train in the United States, including 533 students under the FMF program in FY 1999 at a cost of nearly $17 million (the FY 2000 program was about one third of this size). This training is designed to help Israel maintain its qualitative edge and to promote interoperability between the Israeli and American armed forces. In FY 1999, Israelis attended Air War College courses, International Officers School training, flight simulator training and avionic systems and armament maintenance training.[13]

The United States has built its formal relationship with the Israeli military under the umbrella of a number of political-level cooperative enterprises. As a major non-NATO ally, Israel participates in extensive technology-sharing arrangements with the United States, such as cooperative research and development programs. The United States and Israel have coordinated combined planning, prepositioning and exercises through the Joint Political Military Group (JPMG), established in 1983. The Defense Policy Advisory Group (DPAG), founded in 1999, took over some of the JPMG's functions and provides a body to coordinate formally between the US Defense Department and the Israeli ministry of defense, including on issues like theater missile defense. At the level of the US president and Israeli prime minister, a Joint Strategic Planning Committee was founded following the Wye agreement in 1998, and was then superseded by a Strategic Policy Planning Group (SPPG) under Prime Minister Ehud Barak and President Bill Clinton in 1999. During 2000, Barak and Clinton also examined the possibility of a formal upgrade of US–Israeli relations in the areas of deterrence and technology transfer.[14]

Under the rubrics of these formal mechanisms, the United States and Israel cooperate in a variety of defense arenas, ranging from intelligence exchanges to US armed forces procurement of Israeli military items developed in Israel. The United States has tried to help Israeli interaction with other regional militaries, such as by scheduling a trilateral naval exercise with Turkey and Israel (observed at times by Jordan). The United States has also explored the possibility of Israel's sharing early warning against missile threats with some of its neighbors. The United States has actively encouraged a dialogue between the Israeli and Egyptian military establishments.

The United States has also played an active role in peace-keeping efforts between Israel and its neighbors. The United States is the key player (providing up to 1,000 personnel) in the multinational force and observers mission in the Sinai, which monitors the status of the Egyptian–Israeli peace treaty. And American presidents have indicated a willingness to position US observers in the Golan Heights in the event of a peace agreement between Israel and Syria.

In the main, the United States has tried to isolate its efforts on behalf of Israel from its efforts to build ties in the Arab world. In a formal sense, the US military has placed Israel within the jurisdiction of its European Command, while virtually all other Middle East states are within the ambit of the US Central Command (USCENTCOM), founded in 1983. The commander of the US Central Command has never visited Israel, and support for Israel or the US–Israel military relationship is not routinely mentioned in CENTCOM documents. The US CENTCOM commander sought to avoid all cooperation with Israel during the Gulf War, for fear that such an open relationship would undermine the coalition effort.[15]

Deterring Iraq (and Iran)

The United States has undertaken extraordinary efforts to deter potential aggression from Iraq and/or Iran over the last decade, and to build the military capability presence necessary to defeat such aggression should it occur. A variety of tools have been fundamental to these efforts.

Troop Presence and Deployments The US armed forces has maintained a significant military presence, including a continual military presence in the Persian Gulf to enhance regional stability and support efforts to bring Iraq into compliance with UN Security Council (UNSC) resolutions. Some 20–25,000 US personnel were ordinarily present in the USCENTCOM region in the year 2000.[16] These include 4,000 service personnel based at Prince Sultan Air Base, about 60 miles south-east of Riyadh, Saudi Arabia, who carry out patrols of the no-fly zone over southern Iraq. The US navy has maintained a presence in Bahrain since 1949, where its 5th Fleet is headquartered. Today, the navy usually maintains a carrier battlegroup of about ten major warships with support craft in the area. The US army has hundreds of armored vehicles, artillery pieces and attack helicopters at Camp Doha in Kuwait, with approximately 3,000 troops deployed there. The American ground force presence in the region is maintained primarily through an extensive program of combined exercises with GCC states and other coalition partners. Under this program, US army and Marine combat units are rotated periodically through the region, obviating the need for the establishment of permanent bases.[17] The annual US deployment effort in the Gulf costs up to $2 billion a year. In 1998, GCC states contributed $511 million toward US costs, and $319.5 million in 1999.[18]

The United States has led efforts to enforce the no-fly zones over northern and southern Iraq essential to implement UN Security Council resolutions and to prevent Saddam Husayn from taking large-scale military action against Kuwait or against the Kurd and Shi'a minorities in Iraq. Since 1999, Iraq has begun firing anti-aircraft guns and surface-to-air missiles at American warplanes enforcing the no-fly zones; the United States has retaliated by striking these air defense targets. The US navy has participated in a continuous search of ships going to and from Iraq, in those instances where they have not complied with the required paperwork and proper cargo loading to facilitate safe inspection. The US navy, together with allied and coalition navies, has boarded and inspected over 12,320 ships since the inception of maritime intercept operations. More than 700 of these have been diverted for violations of the UN sanctions regime.[19]

To counter the potential Iraqi missile threat, the US army has deployed Patriot anti-missile missiles to key regional locations. And the United States has undertaken other military operations, such as Desert Thunder and Desert Fox in late 1998 to strike at Saddam Husayn's weapons production capabilities.

Deployments in the region have continued at an effort level that probably no one foresaw when they began. For example, Operation Southern Watch began on 26 August 1992. By May 2000, the US air force and its coalition partners had flown more than 200,000 sorties – exceeding the number flown in Desert Storm. The US air force has dedicated roughly 6,000 airmen and 120 aircraft to this operation. This commitment has not only been costly in dollars, but has led directly to readiness problems within the US air force and indirectly to the service's decision to reorganize its operational force structure into ten Aerospace Expeditionary Forces capable of handling regular, extended, temporary deployments.[20] The companion, Operation Northern Watch, has involved 16,000 sorties since the beginning of 1997.[21] The United States is maintaining a total of about 270 aircraft in the Persian Gulf region, excluding aircraft based in Turkey operating as part of Operation Northern Watch.[22]

Prepositioning Prepositioning accommodates the rapid deployment of forces to the region during crisis response and the subsequent sustaining of those forces. It advances regional access, encourages peacetime engagement and offers continuous deterrence. The United States has been prepositioning equipment in the Gulf region to enable a more rapid response in the event of a crisis with Iraq or Iran. The Defense Department already has placed equipment for a heavy brigade in Kuwait, with a second set warehoused in Qatar, and a third at sea aboard US navy ships. USCENTCOM plans in 1999 were to add equipment for a fourth brigade, in order to equip a 50,000-strong reinforced division of four heavy brigades.[23]

Arms Sales The Middle East has been the largest importer of arms in the world. Between 1950 and 1999, 38 per cent of US defense industry sales were to the USCENTCOM region, and between 1950 and 1995, about $125 billion in arms sales.[24] According to one study, the Middle East accounted for 46.3 per cent of all developing nations' arms transfer agreements in the 1996–99 period, and the United States has provided about half of these arms.[25] In selling them, the US has sought to enhance its influence in the Middle East and to increase the interoperability between American and friendly Arab forces.

Saudi Arabia has been the developing world's leading arms importer, and the United States has worked with Saudi Arabia on everything from infrastructure development to the provision of advanced equipment and advisers.[26] The US arms trade with friendly Arab states involves much in the way of sophisticated systems. The United States has provided or promised F-15s, F-16s (including Block 60), Apache, AMRAAM, HARM, Stinger, Patriot (PAC II and III), and other sophisticated platforms and weapons systems to the region.

Some American analysts have pointed out that arms sales of equipment common to US forces have functioned at times as prepositioning for US forces in the Middle East. The United States has frequently 'overbuilt' and sold weapons beyond the immediate requirements of its friends in the region. For example, US forces deploying to the Gulf during Desert Storm were able to take advantage of many of the stocks of weapons and munitions, and the service facilities, that the United States had previously sold to key states like Saudi Arabia. Three Gulf states in particular, Bahrain, Kuwait and Saudi Arabia, have largely standardized on US equipment since 1990.[27] The United Arab Emirates indicated that it may also move in that direction, with its recent decision to procure F-16 aircraft with AMRAAM missiles.

Infrastructure Development The US involvement in building the military infrastructure in Saudi Arabia goes back many decades. And these efforts in the Gulf, in Saudi Arabia and elsewhere continue today. For example, in October 1999 Secretary of Defense William Cohen announced that the United States would upgrade Camp Doha, the Ahmad al-Jaber and Ali al-Salem air bases in Kuwait, to enhance rapid deployment facilities in the event of future Gulf crises. Kuwait was expected to absorb a large part of the $173 million cost.[28]

Exercises The United States has an extensive exercise program planned within the USCENTCOM area of responsibility (AOR). These exercises are designed to accentuate access, strengthen military to military contact, improve interoperability, promote forward presence, hone combat skills, stimulate development of coalition warfighting procedures, develop professional, apolitical militaries focused on defending their countries from external threats, and encourage greater democratization.[29]

USCENTCOM scheduled 82 exercises in FY 1999, and successfully completed 62 per cent of these despite the disruption to the US military caused by the conflict in Kosovo. Bright Star 99/00 was the largest exercise, with 11 participating countries and over 70,000 troops. In General Zinni's words, the exercise 'trained US forces, validated deployment procedures, and established coalition interoperability while supporting regional stability and cultural interaction'.[30] However, owing to overall reductions within the Pentagon, budget exercises in the USCENTCOM region have been reduced by 36 per cent since 1996, and further reductions are likely.

Missile Defense One major new undertaking in the late 1990s was the Cooperative Defense Initiative (CDI) between the United States and Arab states in and around the Gulf.[31] The CDI has five pillars: active defense, passive defense, shared early warning, consequence management and medical countermeasures. The US objective is to work bilaterally and multilaterally with Saudi Arabia, Kuwait, the UAE (United Arab Emirates), Bahrain, Qatar, Oman, Egypt and Jordan to develop capabilities in each of the five initiative areas. Secretary of Defense Cohen explained in early 2000 that the objective was to 'alert the countries of the region to the nature of the threat and to explore ways in which our militaries can share information, share intelligence, share ways in which the threat can be deterred or minimized should it ever occur'.[32] Eagle

Resolve, a recurring exercise to validate CDI education and training, 'ensures that the political military requirements associated with managing coalition cohesion in the face of threatened or actual chemical or biological weapon use is met'.[33] Of course, the ability of local states to manage consequences in a chemical or biological warfare environment will also enhance the ability of US forces working with them to operate in such settings.

Helping Friendly Arab States
Apart from the overall effort to deter Iraq and Iran, the United States has strong bilateral relations with a number of Arab states and programs designed to meet their particular needs.

Foreign Military Financing (FMF) In FY 2001, the United States provided $1.3 billion in FMF to Egypt to continue its support for building a modern, well-trained Egyptian military. The stated purpose of such assistance is to help ensure regional stability, help Egypt to participate as a coalition partner, and help to maintain US access to the Suez canal and overland routes to support American forces in the Gulf. Most of these funds will be used to maintain and upgrade existing US equipment in service, but some will allow for new programs, including the co-production/purchase of M1-A1 Abrams tanks and procurement of 40 F-16 Block 40 aircraft. In recent years, US security assistance has funded 85 per cent of Egyptian purchases. Egypt also requests US assistance in the form of excess defense articles and special drawdown authority.

The United States trains over 1,000 Egyptian students annually, and trained 2,145 Egyptians at a cost of nearly $25 million under the FMF program in FY 1999. The US State Department has described training programs for Egypt in the following manner:

> Egypt's US-funded training program is exceptionally robust and vital to our relationship. Specifically, Egyptian training funded under the IMET and FMF programs enhance counter-terrorism training and improve Egypt's maintenance and supply capabilities. These funds have also been instrumental in improving the English language skills of the Egyptian officer corps, training military police, providing

logistics instruction, and teaching hostage negotiation techniques. FMF-funded training has improved the proficiency of Egyptian pilots and provides advanced leadership skill, logistics, maintenance, and operational training for members of each of its four services. FMF funds tuition for Egyptian students attending US military staff colleges and academies, thereby improving understanding between our militaries. All of these programs directly enhance joint training, as well as Egypt's value as a key coalition partner.[34]

The United States will also provide $75 million in FMF to help Jordan upgrade air defense systems and improve its command and control systems. The administration requested $1.5 million in FY 2001 to continue support for Jordan's humanitarian mine removal program in the Jordan Valley. In addition, the United States has small FMF programs in Tunisia and Morocco to redress equipment needs and enhance Morocco's ability to participate in joint exercises.[35]

Local training Over 1,000 US military personnel are involved in the US security assistance program in USCENTCOM's Central Region. US military and defense contractors are heavily involved in helping local militaries learn how to operate and maintain American weapons systems. The US is also engaged in training host nation military and civilian personnel in humanitarian mine removal operations.

International Military Education and Training (IMET) The IMET program seeks to expose the militaries of regional states to the American military and the concept of a professional force respectful of human rights and civil authority. IMET is also designed explicitly, in the case of Egypt, to ensure that the latter's defense forces are proficient in the use of newly acquired US military hardware and capable of supporting US operations. The US has also stressed training for mine removal operations in the Middle East.

Since there are no regional US military centers within the USCENTCOM AOR, about 2,500 students attend military courses, schools and colleges in the United States each year.[36] Jordan, Egypt, Morocco, Lebanon and Tunisia were among the largest IMET participants in FY 1999, with nearly 10 per cent of education dollars in the IMET program going to train military personnel from these five countries. Jordanian IMET funding ranks with that from Poland and Thailand as the world's highest. In FY 1999, Jordan had 196 students in the US under the IMET program, Egypt had 82, Morocco 50, Tunisia 118 and Lebanon 163. The US also has smaller programs for Algeria, Bahrain, Oman and Yemen. US proposals for fiscal years 2000 and 2001 were similar.[37]

Humanitarian Assistance Humanitarian projects include medical and dental screening, inoculations and veterinary care and mine removal operations.

MEASURING SUCCESS

American efforts have been largely successful in pursuing many government objectives, although numerous challenges remain and some of the problems appear impervious to a full solution.

Israel
While there is a debate about the extent of the positive military balance that Israel enjoys, no Arab state has challenged Israel militarily since Iraq's launching of Scud missiles against Israel during the Gulf War. Israel's military appears to be qualitatively superior to those of its Arab neighbors, particularly since some Arab states have not been able to maintain investment levels in their military during the last decade.

Israel has also made significant progress toward addressing the evolving threat posed by WMD in the hands of some Arab states and Iran. For example, Israeli–US cooperation has led to successes like the Arrow missile defense program, which was declared operational by the Israel air force in the fall of 2000.[38] Concern about terrorist threats from Lebanon has provided the impetus for another American–Israeli program – the Tactical High Energy Laser, which is designed for defense against rocket attacks.

These developments, coupled with successes in the peace process during the 1990s, enabled Israel to reduce the defense burden on its society. While defense spending grew somewhat during the decade, as a percentage of GDP it fell dramatically.

Yet, despite these apparent successes, concerns remain. Israel has no reasonable expectation of successful defense in the near term against the threats posed by advanced surface-to-surface missiles from neighboring states like Syria, and more distant threats from Iran, Iraq and Libya. Moreover, the prospective development of nuclear and biological weapons and delivery systems is even more daunting. Thus, while Israel has enjoyed an unprecedented period without a full-scale war with Arab states, the potential dangers to its existence may have mounted.

US policy has helped Israel move toward a solution to this dilemma, but the effort required for success will be great and continuing. Israel may look to the United States to provide assistance in the development of longer range systems to strike at missile threats (for example, Boost Phase Launch Intercept, which would enable Israel to destroy enemy missile launchers following an initial attack on Israel). More strikingly, Israel may ask the United States to extend its deterrent umbrella as a means of discouraging unconventional weapons attacks.

It appears that the United States has largely been able to manage its relationship with Israel so that it has not impeded the US military's ability to pursue an enhanced military relationship with Arab states in a variety of areas. Thus, the United States has been able to pursue increased prepositioning, arms sales and combined exercises and to maintain its efforts against Iraq. To the extent that the latter policy has come under challenge, this has largely been due to its perceived inefficiency and to Iraqi civilian suffering rather than US–Israeli relations. However, it remains an open question whether this assessment will be affected by the continuing Palestinian violence and its impact in the Arab world.

Iraq and Iran
Throughout the 1990s, the United States trumpeted its success in keeping Saddam Husayn within his 'box'. Iraq threatened on more than one occasion to undertake military operations against Kuwait, but backed down in the face of strong US opposition.

According to US officials, Operation Desert Fox did degrade

the threat posed by Iraqi WMD. USCENTCOM's conclusion was that the 'assessed impact of Operation Desert Fox, coupled with Operation Southern Watch and Operation Northern Watch, is that further development of Iraq's ballistic missile program has been delayed by several years'. But given the fact that there have been no inspections within Iraq for over two years, it is impossible to know with certainty whether American efforts continue to significantly delay Iraqi WMD activities. These doubts have been reinforced by reports from Iraqi defectors.

Equally worrisome for US officials is the perception that they have been losing the public relations war in the Arab world, and in Europe, with Saddam Husayn. Although many Arab leaders share the US assessment of the dangers posed by Saddam, both they and European states have begun to loosen their grip on sanctions' enforcement. In late 2000 it appeared that large elements of the sanctions regime were virtually on the brink of collapse, as Iraq improved its political and economic ties with Arab states and Turkey and many nations permitted humanitarian (and other) aircraft flights into Baghdad.

In the case of Iran, the United States also views its policy as having contributed to the democratic impulses witnessed in Iran over the past five years. And there have been positive signs from Iran in terms of calls for dialogue with the West, as well as a rapprochement with some of the southern Gulf States. But Iran's opposition to Arab–Israeli peace, its quest for WMD, and its support for terrorism have continued, and American policy to prevent this and bring Iran into a more cooperative relationship cannot yet be judged as successful.

Perhaps even more disturbing for US policy makers, many Gulf states are moving away from a public posture of concern about Iran's military capabilities to seek instead reconciliation with Iran. In 1999, the annual meeting of the Gulf Cooperation Council did not condemn Iran for occupying the United Arab Emirates three mid-Gulf islands, but merely urged a Saudi–Omani–Qatari committee to encourage direct negotiations between Iran and the UAE.

Friendly Arab States
Nonetheless, American efforts with its Arab friends have also had a number of important positive effects. Relations with the United

States have probably helped to ensure stability in Egypt and have aided transitions in the Jordanian and Moroccan monarchies following the deaths of King Husayn and King Hassan.

It is harder to assess with certainty the impact of American efforts to help build Arab capabilities to the level where they could make a significant contribution in the event of aggression from Iraq or Iran. Given the secretive nature of many Arab societies and armed forces, it is difficult to find useful, objective information in the public domain concerning the performance of their militaries. Generally, Western analysts believe that Arab fighting forces have been relatively ineffective in the modern era, and unable to translate the massive expenditures Arab societies have made for infrastructure, military equipment and training into first-rate forces.[39] Norvell De Atkine stresses the difficulties faced by well-meaning and talented American military advisers:

> It would be difficult to exaggerate the cultural gulf separating American and Arab military cultures. In every significant area, American military advisors find students who enthusiastically take in their lessons and then resolutely fail to apply them. The culture they return to – the culture of their own armies in their own countries – defeats the intentions with which they took leave of their American instructors.[40]

Of course, this was true earlier during the Gulf War. While from the political standpoint it was important to have Arab allies in the fight against Saddam, and critical to have access to Arab states, the military contribution they made could be considered marginal. To be sure, Egyptian forces played a key role in the land offensive through Kuwait as the leading element in Joint Forces Command-North. And Saudi forces, working closely with their American counterparts, gave a far more impressive acquittal of themselves than had been anticipated. But none of this was decisive in the battle.[41] Following the Gulf War, both Bahrain and the UAE dispatched forces to Kuwait in October 1994 in response to provocative Iraqi troop movements; but from a military perspective their contribution must be considered marginal.

Today, the Arab states do not appear able to do much in terms of carrying the burden of fighting for the United States, although their political and logistic support remain critical. Some states, like Saudi Arabia, have improved their defense capability (particularly their air force) since the Gulf War and may be able to deal with low intensity contingencies.

At the same time, the United States' Arab friends remain vulnerable to threats from larger rivals like Iran and Iraq. No individual Gulf Arab state can deal on its own with a potential threat from Iraq or Iran. The same is true from a region-wide perspective. When Iraq invaded Kuwait in 1990, the only region-wide defense capability was the token 'Peninsula Shield' defense force stationed at Hafr al-Batin in Saudi Arabia. Today, the Gulf Cooperation Council (GCC), despite many efforts, has made only limited progress in providing for regional defense and cannot be said to have developed a unified military strategy. Problems with effective standardization, interoperability and focus on key missions remain.[42] In a promising development, the GCC members signed a military cooperation agreement on 1 January 2001. But it is unclear whether this will have any real impact on enabling them to confront external security threats from Iran or Iraq for the foreseeable future.[43]

Simply put, friendly Arab states working either alone or together cannot bear most of the burden of their own defense. Instead, they would need strong foreign support to defend themselves against the real threats that they may one day face. In a sense, the Gulf War has left a heritage of Gulf dependence on US power projection capabilities. The Gulf states tend to cooperate more with the United States in the areas of prepositioning, deployment facilities, and exercises than they do among themselves in the GCC.[44] But even here, if threats were ambiguous, there could be difficulties that would militate against local leaders to act quickly and decisively to mount operations in the region.

BUILDING THE US DEFENSE CAPABILITY IN THE REGION

US military commanders assess that the United States' posture in the CENTCOM region has improved significantly in the last decade. As the retired former CENTCOM commander, General A. C. Zinni, put it:

> Our military posture in the Gulf region today is far stronger than it has ever been. Just a few short years ago, the current development of our military facilities and access throughout the Arabian Peninsula would have been unimaginable. In addition, our ability to deploy forces quickly through such instruments as rapidly deployable forces, prepositioning, and forward headquarters have been greatly improved. Our exercises with coalition partners have grown in quality and sophistication and enable us to test the force projection capabilities of US units, and give deployed units critical experience. Moreover, despite reports about strains in the coalition, our presence is welcomed by all the states of the Gulf Cooperation Council without exception.[45]

Some of the concrete areas of progress include the following:

Level of US Military Presence in the Region

The United States has far more assured access to the Gulf than ever before. Before the Gulf War, the US enjoyed significant prepositioning rights only in Oman – which was also the only GCC member that regularly participated in major combined operations with US forces. Since the war, four additional GCC members have signed defense cooperation agreements with the United States. Among these are Bahrain and Qatar; in addition to naval access, they have each hosted an Air Expeditionary Force for two-month rotations in support of Operation Southern Watch.

Despite this progress, it remains unlikely that US forces in the region would be able to thwart a quick concerted strike from Iraq. American air power could severely damage an invading Iraqi force. But to be sure of halting Iraq, the United States would still have to act decisively at early signs of tension and build up its forces in the region. This was the course taken by the US in Operation Vigilant Warrior following Iraq's provocative troop movements in October 1994. At that time, after the Iraqis massed two Republican Guard divisions on the Kuwaiti border, the United

States deployed a Marine expeditionary unit, elements of a heavy army division, a carrier task force and additional land-based aircraft. Former Defense Secretary Perry has explained this overall approach in the following manner:

> Peacetime force presence gives us the ability to respond immediately to threats and provocations and is the basis for an effective response to any large-scale military challenge. However, despite the fact that these forces are above the historic norm of US presence in the Middle East, they are not designed by themselves to meet a full-scale attack on our areas of vital interest. While they, working together with local forces, would provide the framework on which such an address would be built, a major regional conflict, such as another Iraqi invasion of Kuwait or Saudi Arabia, would require the dispatch of substantial US and coalition forces from outside the Gulf.[46]

Extent of Prepositioning
Stockpiling American material in the region is important for early defense requirements. It reduces the need for airlift and fast sealift, decreases deployment times for American forces, and provides sustainment early during the force build-up. The US has made substantial progress toward meeting its prepositioning objectives in the Persian Gulf.

In concrete terms, the Marine's Maritime Prepositioning Force Program is designed to support the deployment of a Marine Expeditionary Brigade. Comprised of Maritime Prepositioned Ship Squadrons 1, 2 and 3 afloat in the Indian Ocean, this program has maintained a high *matériel* readiness rate and supply attainment. The army's prepositioning program, with a goal to place a heavy division of equipment in the region, is partially completed. The brigade set at Camp Doha, Kuwait, is fully operational. The preposition site in Qatar, which will house the second brigade set and a division base set, is still under construction, with a completion date set for FY 2001. A combat brigade afloat set is complete and combat ready, while a second afloat brigade will augment the first one in FY 2002. The air force has prepositioned bare base sets. USCENTCOM believes that the US enjoys inter-operability and the ability to utilize Arab assets.[47]

Overflight/Naval Passage
Egypt and other friendly Arab states continue to provide the United States with assured access to the region to meet shared objectives. For example, one US official indicated that Egypt 'routinely expedites USAF [US air force] overflights via its airspace and US naval vessels and battle groups that transit the Suez Canal. Our military aircraft and vessels also regularly utilize Egyptian airfields and port facilities for en route support and maintenance'. According to an official paper produced by the government of Egypt, Egypt provided transit passage through the Suez Canal for 106 US warships and granted overflight permission for 31,463 flights (of which 5,881 were executed) in the period from 1 January 1999 to 31 July 2000.[48]

At the same time, there are limitations on the extent of US presence and the willingness to reach open agreements with the United States, especially in the case of Saudi Arabia. For example, despite allowing the US air force to operate out of Saudi Arabia to maintain the southern 'no-fly zone' in the wake of the Gulf War, Saudi Arabia would not allow the United States to preposition two division sets of equipment. Saudi officials indicated at that time that the US insistence on an open basing facility openly violated the royal family's pledge to the Islamic clergy that it would not grant bases to non-Muslim forces.[49]

Weapons of Mass Destruction
As noted above, significant organizational effort is underway both with Israel and with friendly Arab states. The United States has also deployed Patriot missiles and other assets to the region in crisis periods. But thus far the effort lags far behind the evolving threat.

CHALLENGES TO US POLICY

While the United States has been largely successful in meeting its core interests, US policy faces a number of challenges in the years ahead. Among these are the following:

Preserving Israel's Qualitative Edge and Positive Military Balance
The United States has built relations with friendly Arab states while enhancing its support for Israel. These efforts, taken in conjunction with progress in the peace process, have seen a period in which there was no major Arab–Israeli conventional war.

Nonetheless, Israel's leaders articulate concerns that their qualitative technological edge is eroding. They point out that America's Arab friends are procuring systems fully as sophisticated as those that the United States is selling to Israel. These include Egypt's acquisition of the ground-based AMRAAM, PAC III, F-16s and Abrams tanks, Saudi Arabia's purchase of AMRAAM and the UAE's procurement of Block 60 F-16s. Many of these systems have decreased requirements for man-in-the-loop, so that Israel's qualitative manpower edge may become less important in the battlefield setting.

At the same time, the United States is providing excellent and extensive training to its Arab friends.[50] Senior Israeli military leaders believe that the performance of Egypt's armed forces has improved significantly as a result. According to one report, a major Israel Defense Force (IDF) command-post exercise in January 2000 focused on a possible Egyptian intervention in an Israeli–Syrian war scenario. Israelis cite the historical unwillingness of Egypt's military to countenance a dialogue with their Israeli counterparts as an indication of the potential threat that Egypt could pose.[51]

Israel's worries have been exacerbated by the recent increase in oil prices. Increased oil revenues create the possibility for a renewed arms race in the region, as Arab states and Iran can afford to spend more money on buying new weapons systems and rebuilding their armies.

American officials tend to downplay Israeli concerns. They articulate a commitment to Israel's qualitative edge and claim that Israel continues to enjoy access to better technology and know-how than Arab states. They note that US aid to Arab states is designed to counter the threats posed by Iran and Iraq, and thereby helps to contain the threat they pose to Israel. They share the view of analysts who assert that Arab states are dependent on US technicians and technical support to keep their weapons working, and therefore could not undertake a campaign against Israel. For example, Anthony Cordesman asserts that the United States has limited sales of software optimized to attack US or Israeli air and air defense systems. He also describes in detail how the United States limited the capabilities and range of the F-15S aircraft it sold to Saudi Arabia in the late 1990s, in order to preserve Israel's military edge.[52]

But despite the overwhelming consensus that Arab armies have not performed well in the modern era, one would do well to heed the warning of De Atkine that 'it is particularly dangerous to make facile assumptions about abilities in warfare based on past performance'. After all, the Arab states did achieve surprise and some tactical success in the October 1973 war, forcing Israel to pay a very heavy price. And there appears to be little doubt that the United States is increasingly willing to sell much of its most advanced technology in the Middle East as a means of maintaining its defense industrial base. Balancing Israel's defense requirements with the desire to maintain Arab friendships and US markets will be a continuing challenge.

Maintaining the Coalition against Iraq/Preserving US Access in the Region

In recent days, Saddam Husayn has enjoyed a return to center stage in the Middle East. This was particularly evident with the participation of Iraq in an Arab summit in October 2000, for the first time since the Gulf War. There are increasing indications that, while Arab states continue not to trust Saddam Husayn, they may have difficulty in continuing their support for American efforts, particularly in maintaining the sanctions regime. We have witnessed a number of terrorist acts against American personnel, causing the violent deaths of 56 American troops or related personnel since the end of the Gulf War. These include the death of five Americans when a bomb was detonated at a Saudi National Guard office in Riyadh on 13 November 1995, the death of 19 airmen (and wounding of 500) from a massive truck bomb in Dharan on 25 June 1996, and the recent attack on the USS Cole. In such a setting, some Arab regimes may believe – as they did two decades ago – that an American presence on their soil could undermine their stability. These states may be more concerned with their domestic Islamic backlash against a US presence than with meeting the requirement of coalition efforts against prospective foes like Iraq. Such beliefs may make America's presence increasingly difficult to preserve. If these trends continue, it may be difficult for the US to limit Iraqi capabilities.

Improving the Military Capabilities of Friendly Arab States
The United States has invested considerable efforts in building cooperative activities with friendly Arab states. But most analysts continue to believe that the chance these states would make a significant combat contribution to an American-led coalition remains low. American efforts to help individual Arab states and the GCC bring their performance up to the level that would enable them to participate far more effectively in combat operations with the United States, remain a considerable challenge in the future. But as the United States has demonstrated for a long time, this need not be a significant impediment to the US ability to achieve its military objectives in the region.

NOTES

1. I wish to thank Davi Bernstein, who provided research assistance for this paper. I am also grateful for comments I received from Danny Sebright, Larry Hanauer, Tom Keaney, Charles Perkins, Sandra Charles, Rafi Danziger and Larry Velte. Any errors are my own.
2. The White House, 'A National Security Strategy for a New Century', 5 January 2000, www.defensedaily.com/reports/whitehouse.htm; General Anthony C. Zinni, Commander-in-Chief, US Central Command, 'Statement', House Armed Services Committee, 15 March 2000.
3. William J. Perry, *United States Security Strategy for the Middle East* (Washington, DC: Department of Defense, May 1995), pp. 5–10.
4. George Tenet, Director of Central Intelligence, Statement before the Senate Armed Services Committee on 'The Worldwide Threat in 2000: Global Realities of Our National Security', 21 March 2000; Vice-Admiral Thomas R. Wilson, Director, Defense Intelligence Agency, 'Military Threats and Security Challenges Through 2015', Statement for the Record, Senate Armed Services Committee, 2 February 2000; Director of Central Intelligence, 'Unclassified Report to Congress on the Acquisition of Technology Relating to Weapons of Mass Destruction and Advanced Conventional Munitions, 1 July Through 31 December 1999', www.cia.gov; Seth Carus, *Iran and Weapons of Mass Destruction* (New York: American Jewish Committee, June 2000).
5. Vice-Admiral Thomas R. Wilson, 'Military Threats and Security Challenges Through

2015', Statement for the Record before the Senate Armed Services Committee, 3 February 2000, p. 10.

6. General Henry H. Shelton, Chairman, Joint Chiefs of Staff, 'Posture Statement', before the Senate Armed Services Committee, 8 February 2000.

7. Thomas E. Ricks, 'US Bases in Mideast Placed on High Alert', *Washington Post*, 24 October 2000.

8. Deborah Sontag, 'Poll Shows Palestinians No Longer Back US-led Talks', *New York Times*, 15 November 2000.

9. One official indicated that the full set of US military interests include ensuring Israel's security, ensuring access to oil, safeguarding the security of American citizens, maintenance of sea (and air) lines of communication, non-proliferation of weapons of mass destruction and fostering regional stability.

10. For the discussion of a former commander of USCENTCOM, see J. H. Binford Peay III, 'The Five Pillars of Peace in the Central Region', *Joint Force Quarterly* (*JFQ*), Autumn (1995), pp. 32–9; Perry, *United States Security Strategy for the Middle East*, pp. 21–2.

11. For the discussion of a former commander of USCENTCOM, see Peay, 'The Five Pillars of Peace'. Peay's pillars for his theater strategy were power projection, forward presence, combined exercises, security assistance and the readiness to fight.

12. John D. Holum, Senior Advisor for Arms Control and International Security, 'Statement' before the House Appropriations Committee, Subcommittee on Foreign Operations, Export Financing and Related Programs, 6 April 2000; see also Office of the Secretary of State, 'Congressional Budget Justification for Foreign Operations, Fiscal Year 2001', 15 March 2000, www.state.gov/www/budget/fy2001/fn150/forops_ full/150fy01_ fo_near-east.html.

13. Department of State, 'Foreign Military Training Report FY 1999 and 2000', Joint Report to Congress, 1 March 2000, www.state.gov/www.global/arms/fmtrain/fpo_ nea_all.html.

14. See, for example, Aluf Benn, 'PM Hopes for Strategic Upgrade as a "Parting Gift"', *Ha'aretz*, 7 November 2000.

15. Dore Gold, 'The Gulf Crisis and US-Israel Relations', *War in the Gulf: Implications for Israel* (Jerusalem: Jerusalem Post, 1992), pp. 74–6.

16. See Thomas E. Ricks, 'Persian Gulf, US Danger Zone', *Washington Post*, 15 October 2000, p. A1, including map on p. A23 for a typical deployment. Anthony Cordesman found in 1998 that the US had about 7,500–12,000 Americans deployed permanently in the southern Gulf and at sea, with an ability to rapidly deploy some 30,000–35,000 in an emergency. Anthony Cordesman, 'US Policy, the Southern Gulf States, and the Changing Strategic Balance in the Gulf', www.csis.org/mideast/gulfspch.html, 16 March 1998.

17. Perry, *United States Security in the Middle East*, p. 30.

18. Zinni, 'Statement'. General Zinni anticipated that Saudi contributions would plateau, and perhaps decline, in the future.

19. Ibid.

20. James Kitfield, 'The Long Deployment', *Air Force*, July 2000. See Ricks, 'US Bases', for a listing of significant US offensive operations since the Gulf War.

21. Thomas E. Ricks, 'Containing Iraq: A Forgotten War', *Washington Post*, 25 October 2000, p. A1.

22. Gopal Rotnam, 'Persian Gulf Region's Security Remains Weak', *Defense News*, 27 November 2000, p. 3.

23. Ed Blanche, 'USA Looks to Put More Equipment in the Gulf', *Jane's Defense Weekly*, 27 October 1999.

24. For detailed information, see Comptroller, Defense Security Assistance Agency, *Foreign Military Sales, Foreign Military Construction, and Military Assistance Facts* (Washington, DC: Defense Security Cooperation Agency), 30 September 1999.

25. Richard F. Grimmett, 'Conventional Arms Transfers to Developing Nations, 1992–1999', Congressional Research Service, 18 August 2000, p. 10.
26. Andrew Rathmell, 'Saudi Arabia's Military Build-Up – An Extravagant Error?', *Jane's Intelligence Review*, Vol. 6, No. 11 (1 November 1994) p. 500.
27. Anthony Cordesman, *US Forces in the Middle East: Resources and Capabilities* (Boulder, CO: Westview, 1997), p. 84.
28. Ed Blanche, 'Kuwait Boosts Spending to Cover Allied Operations', *Jane's Defense Weekly*, 17 May 2000.
29. Peay, 'The Five Pillars of Peace'.
30. Zinni, 'Statement'.
31. Secretary Cohen has publicly indicated that the US conception was to also include Israel in the CDI, if it so chose.
32. Cited in 'Cohen out to "Recycle" the Gulf Arabs' Petrodollars', *Mideast Mirror*, 11 April 2000.
33. Jim Garamone, 'Cooperative Defense Initiative Seeks to Save Lives', *Armed Forces Information Service*, 10 April 2000; Zinni, 'Statement'; Secretary of Defense William Cohen, News Briefing, 22 October 1999.
34. Department of State, 'Foreign Military Training Report'.
35. Holum, 'Statement'; 'Congressional Presentation Document'.
36. In late 2000 the Defense Department launched a new Near East and South Asia Center located in Washington, DC.
37. Comptroller, Defense Security Assistance Agency (1999), pp. 101–15; Office of the Secretary of State, 'Congressional Budget Justification for Foreign Operations, Fiscal Year 2001'.
38. Marvin Feuerwerger, *The Arrow Next Time* (Washington, DC: Washington Institute for Near East Policy, 1991); Dore Gold, *War in the Gulf: Implications for Israel* (Boulder, CO: Westview, 1992), pp. 91–2.
39. See, for example, Norvell De Atkine, 'Why Arab Armies Lose Wars', in Barry Rubin and Thomas Keaney (eds), *Armed Forces in the Middle East* (London: Frank Cass, 2001), Chapter 2; Kenneth M. Pollack, 'Saudi Military Effectiveness in the 1990s', unpublished paper, 15 December 1998.
40. De Atkine, 'Why Arab Armies Lose Wars', p. 37 above.
41. Kenneth M. Pollack, 'The Sphinx and the Eagle: The Egyptian Armed Forces and Egyptian-American Military Ties', unpublished paper, 1 September 1998.
42. See Cordesman, 'US Policy', for an indictment of Gulf failures; see also Gopal Ratnam, 'Persian Gulf's Security Remains Weak', *Defense News*, 27 November 2000, p. 3.
43. Gopal Ratnam, 'Analysts: GCC Resolution Unlikely to Create Unified Force', *Defense News*, 5 February 2001, p. 8.
44. Anthony Cordesman, *After the Storm: The Changing Military Balance in the Middle East* (Boulder, CO: Westview, 1993), p. 597; Anthony Cordesman, *Saudi Arabia: Guarding the Desert Kingdom* (Boulder, CO: Westview, 1997), pp. 187–90; Anthony Cordesman and Abraham R. Wagner, *The Lessons of Modern War, Volume IV: The Gulf War* (Boulder, CO: Westview, 1996), pp. 183–99; Rathmell, 'Saudi Arabia'; Anthony Cordesman, 'The Changing Military Balance in the Gulf', *Middle East Policy*, June 1998.
45. United States Central Command, 'Theater Strategy: Shaping the Central Region for the 21st Century', undated, pp. 7–8.
46. Perry, *United States Security Strategy in the Middle East*, pp. 29–32.
47. Zinni, 'Statement'.
48. John D. Holum, Acting Undersecretary of State, 'Statement' before the House Appropriations Subcommittee on Foreign Operations, 25 February 1998; Government of Egypt, 'United States-Egyptian Military Cooperation: Egypt's FY 2001 Request for Military Assistance', undated paper.

49. Cordesman, *Saudi Arabia*, pp. 190–4.
50. See, for example, Barbara Opall-Rome, 'Israel Fears Erosion of US-Pledged Edge', *Defense News*, 29 May 2000; 'Pentagon to Back Sale of Raytheon's Top Missile to Saudi Arabia', Bloomberg.com, 24 July 2000; Arieh O'Sullivan, 'Is Egypt the New Enemy?', *Jerusalem Post*, 13 August 1999, p. 3B.
51. Aluf Benn, 'Egypt, Israel Anchor Region', *Defense News*, 18 December 2000, p. 31.
52. Cordesman, *After the Storm*, p. 593; Cordesman and Wagner, *Lessons of Modern War*, Vol. IV, pp. 192–3.

4

Russia's Military Involvement with the Middle East

OKSANA ANTONENKO[1]

From the mid-1950s until its dissolution four decades later, the Soviet Union played a key role in helping Arab states improve their military capabilities. Throughout the Cold War, the Soviet Union supplied advanced military equipment, trained officers in its military schools and provided in-country military advisers to regional allies such as Egypt (before 1972), Syria, Libya, Yemen, Algeria and Iraq. This assistance was provided in the context of US–Soviet competition for influence in the Middle East and therefore under very favorable conditions, often practically free of charge or under long-term loan arrangements that were never expected to be repaid.

For many Arab states, Soviet military assistance was important both in its geopolitical and military aspects. However, although Soviet military assistance provided some tactical advantage for its allies during the Arab–Israeli conflict, it failed to give them superiority.

There were a number of reasons for such low effectiveness. The main one is that the Soviet Union provided only inadequate and selective training to its clients, and therefore they had only a poor ability to absorb and use more advanced Soviet weapons. Although the Soviet Union supplied Syria and Egypt with MiG-21 and Su-7 fighters, T-55 tanks and other advanced equipment, these Arab states still suffered a humiliating defeat in the 1967 war with Israel.

Later, the Soviet Union provided Syria over $20 billion of

weapons, but the Syrian armed forces failed to absorb them due to their ongoing operations in Lebanon, preoccupation with internal security objectives and political problems. This was demonstrated during the 1982 Israeli invasion of Lebanon, when Syrian troops showed very limited capability, despite large shipments of weapons from the Soviet Union. Most improvements in Syrian capabilities are attributed to their improved skill in using old weapons, rather than new high-tech supplies from the Soviet Union. In fact, no Soviet military assistance could compensate for the fact that Israel possessed better-trained and better-equipped forces with much higher readiness levels and overall efficiency.

The second reason for the low impact of Soviet military assistance was Moscow's restraint in offering particular advanced weapons (including Weapons of Mass Destruction, or WMD) to its clients, fearing that escalation of the conflict would drag the Soviet Union and the United States into direct confrontation. While new equipment was supplied, the newest and most advanced weaponry, such as SS-1 'Scud' SSMs (surface-to-surface missiles), though promised, was held back. Soviet military cooperation with Arab states was provided as long as the main Cold War bargain cheap weapons supplies for political influence – benefited both sides. However, even during the Cold War, the Soviet Union could not completely restrain its clients' actions, which limited its political influence. Moreover, once the bargain was no longer acceptable, both sides used the termination of military assistance as a geopolitical signal. In 1972, Egypt cut off all military ties with the Soviet Union, while the Soviet Union did not provide any military assistance to Iraq during the Iran–Iraq or Gulf Wars.

After the end of the Cold War and the dissolution of the Soviet Union, Russia's military cooperation with regional states underwent a significant transition from the two previous main principles of Soviet military cooperation.

On the one hand, Russia was no longer in the position to offer large-scale financial donations, in the form of weapons supplies, in exchange for illusory political influence over traditional Soviet allies. Moreover, until recently it was unclear whether reasserting its political role in the Middle East was indeed among the priorities of Russia's foreign and security policy (political statements were rarely backed by real actions).

On the other hand, Russia was no longer prepared to exercise self-restraint in its arms sales to the region as long as financial arrangements were beneficial for the Russian defense industry, which over the past decade had grown to depend on arms exports for its survival. All arms sales were seen as purely commercial projects, often driven by individual Russian arms-producing or arms-exporting companies. This was clearly demonstrated in Russia's military cooperation program with Iran, which was continued despite active US pressure, including sanctions. A similar lack of restraint is demonstrated in Russia's proposals to Syria and Libya, as well as declared plans to restore active military cooperation with Iraq, once sanctions are lifted.

As a result of these two changes, Russia's military cooperation with Middle East states, while reduced in scale, may potentially have a much greater impact on regional security if it included such weapons as missiles. Moreover, Russia's desperate attempts to penetrate the world's largest arms market in the Middle East now faces competition from other suppliers – such as Ukraine, Belarus, east European states, China and North Korea – all offering used and older models of equipment and modernization of ex-Soviet equipment for lower prices. This places the sale of advanced weapons systems at the top of Russia's arms marketing strategy for the Middle East.

Finally, the most significant feature of Russia's new post-Cold War foreign military assistance is that it is more and more often provided by private Russian actors operating without state sanction, or in some cases in violation of Russia's declared policy. The most striking case of such assistance is the training of Iranian scientists, including those dealing with ballistic missile technology, in Russian universities and scientific institutions. There is also the possibility of Russian scientists moving to Iran and Iraq, to take up highly paid positions.

Another category of Russia's private actors is military advisers who worked in the Middle East during the Soviet period, many of whom continue to do so in a private capacity, after they have left the Russian armed forces, by signing individual contracts with the former host country. From the 1950s onward, the Soviet Union sent over 80,000 military advisers to the Middle East and trained over 55,000 officers from Middle East countries in its military schools and academies. According to Russian sources, at present only around 360 Russian military specialists officially work in the Middle East, and 270 officers from the region are being educated in Russian military schools.[2]

STRATEGIES FOR MILITARY COOPERATION

The main strategies for Russia's military cooperation with Middle East states now include:[3]

- arms sales on platforms and components, as well as used equipment;
- technical cooperation on upgrades, repairs and modernization of ex-Soviet equipment and production of ammunition;
- providing Russian military in-country advisers and educating officers from Middle East armies in Russian military schools and academies, as well as training specialists to operate Russian-made equipment;
- joint projects for modernization of Russia's equipment for sale to third countries;
- high-level political and military exchanges and promotion of Russian weapons systems through participation in arms exhibitions in the Middle East.

With the exception of modernization of Russian equipment for export to third countries, all the above strategies are similar to those pursued by the former Soviet Union. However, the scale of Russia's cooperation with Middle East armies in all the traditional spheres has declined drastically over the past decade. In addition to financial constraints and growing competition from ex-Soviet and private arms suppliers, there are a number of more fundamental reasons why Russia's offers of military cooperation are no longer readily accepted in the region, unless they include services and assistance which cannot be acquired from other sources.

The main factor is the decline of Russia's influence in the world as a whole, and particularly in the Middle East. Russia's voluntary and abrupt withdrawal from the region left ex-Soviet allies in strategic limbo, with a great sense of vulnerability and uncertainty. While the Russian government was busy developing relations with the United States and Europe, Arab states sought to diversify their military and strategic relations. By the time the Russian government, under Foreign Minister Yevgeny Primakov, decided to re-focus more attention upon the Middle East, it quickly discovered that it has lost credibility and is no longer perceived as a major regional power. Moreover, many states understand that Russia is desperately trying to obtain superpower status symbols while being unwilling to provide funds to support its influence.

Thus, Russia's initial attempts to revitalize ex-Soviet alliances in the Middle East were met with a great deal of skepticism practically everywhere in the region. Many states, like Syria, Yemen and Libya (after the sanctions were lifted) are now seeking to use arms sales as a vehicle to gain more leverage over European and US policies. Moreover, many states are acutely aware of Russia's desperate dependence on arms exports, and try to lengthen negotiations in order to secure better financial conditions. Unlike the United States, which continues to provide financial assistance to Egypt, Israel and Jordan for acquiring its equipment and offers training, Russia is no longer in the position to do so.

Thus the only two states with which Russia did manage to link military cooperation to political relations were Iran and Iraq. Iraq needed Russia's support to lift sanctions and hopes to use its assistance to eventually rebuild its military capability. Iran needs Russia to provide military equipment not available from Western sources. However, Russia's alliance with Iran and Iraq did little to improve its role in the Middle East; it became a constant source of concern throughout the region, as well as in both Teheran and Baghdad.

Another factor for the loss of Russia's credibility as a reliable military partner for Arab states can be found in Russia's domestic policies. During the 1990s, continual tensions and rivalry between the foreign ministry, defense ministry and various arms-exporting agencies (which were reorganized nine times between 1995 and

2000), significantly undermined both the trust in Russia's supplies and their effectiveness. Each of the agencies pursues its own agenda in the region. Therefore, despite many high-level visits to the region by various Russian officials, practically no significant contracts were signed. Moreover, different agencies within Russia often leak information about negotiated arms export deals in the press in order to expose their domestic rivals, thereby complicating negotiations and preventing finalization of major arms export deals.

Finally, the most important factor that has undermined the effectiveness of Russia's military cooperation is the deterioration in the quality of services and equipment. The decline of Russia's armed forces in the 1990s is well known to its potential clients in the Middle East. Although the Russian armed forces are still better equipped and trained to operate equipment than most Arab armed forces, their expertise has significantly declined. Many of the best specialists who work as military advisers and have language skills left the armed forces to find employment in the commercial sector. Those who remain in the army lose their technical skills, owing to shortage of funds for regular training and military exercises. The quality of military education is inadequate to address the challenges of modern warfare. Moreover, many in-country advisers, working on modernization of their clients' equipment, experience delays and poor quality in supply of spare parts.

Despite uncertain and inferior service, Russia continues to seek US levels of compensation for its specialists' work, while other ex-Soviet states like Ukraine and Belarus are happy to provide similar service for a fraction of the price. And finally, in many traditional Soviet client states in the Middle East, such as Syria, Libya, Algeria and Yemen, there is a gradual change in the political and military elites. While the old generation was primarily educated in the Soviet Union and speaks Russian, the new generation is often pro-Western and prefers to receive education in Europe.

Despite these problems, Russia managed to preserve and in some cases expand its military-technical cooperation with Middle East countries. Table 4.1 summarizes Russia's arms sales to the region since 1992.

TABLE 4.1:
RUSSIAN ARMS DELIVERIES TO THE MIDDLE EAST IN THE 1990s

State	1992	1993	1994	1995	1996	1997	1998	1999–2000
Iran	One Kilo-class SSK, 10 Su-24, 8 MiG-29	80 ACV,* One Kilo-class SSK	200+ T-72 delivered up to 1994,* 94 AAM		2 T-72 MBT 2 BMP-1 ACV	One Kilo-class SSK, Aircraft engine license, (2 An-74T Ukraine)	100 T-72 kits, 200 BMP-2 kits[4]	
UAE	80 BMP-3 ACV	95 BMP-3 ACV*	118 BMP-3 ACV	122 BMP-3 ACV	25 BMP-3 ACV	69 BMP-3 ACV	4 Il-76 ac, 82 BMP-3 ACV	
Kuwait			30 SA-18 SAM	9 9A52 MRL, 100 BMP-3[5]	18 9A52 MRL[6]			
Egypt					SA2/3/6 upgrade	20 Mi-17 upgrade		SA-3 upgrade
Syria						200 T-55MV from Ukraine	1000 AT-14 ATGM	
Yemen				4 Su-22 from Ukraine				31 T-72
Jordan				126 BMP-3 ACV				50 BTR94 ACV Ukraine
Oman	6 MBT[7]							

Source: IISS *Military Balance*, UN Conventional Arms Register (CAR), others.
Abbreviations:
AAM = Air to Air Missile
ACV = Armored Combat Vehicle
ATGM = Anti-Tank Guided Missile
MBT = Main Battle Tank
MRL = Multiple Rocket Launchers
SAM = Surface to Air Missile
SSK = attack submarine
Note: * = without ammunition.

The sales in Table 4.1 show three main trends: low volume with a focus on modernization, diversification from traditional to new markets, and Russia's failure to prevail in competition with ex-Soviet as well as Western suppliers in different markets. These trends have a major effect on Russia's military cooperation with each Middle Eastern state.

IRAN

Over the past decade, Russia's military cooperation arrangements with Iran have been the most extensive of these efforts. Iran has been the third-largest Russian arms exports client after China and India. Since the two countries signed a bilateral military-technical cooperation agreement in 1989 (signed with the Soviet Union and inherited by Russia), Russia has supplied Iran with equipment and services worth over $4 billion. According to some reports, Iran paid two-thirds in cash and one-third in goods for Russian military supplies, making it among one of Moscow's most profitable customers.[8]

Amongst all Russia's Middle East clients, Russian–Iranian cooperation is the most advanced in the range of weapons systems sold to Iran by Russia and in the scale of technical cooperation. Between 1992 and 2000, Russia sold Iran 3 Kilo-class submarines, over 200 T-72 tanks, 10 Su-24 and 8 MiG-29 aircraft. Moreover, Iran has acquired licenses for the production of T-72C and BMP-2 armored fighting vehicles. Russia has also provided Iran with a large number of military advisers who have trained its military – including submarine crews – to operate these advanced weapons systems and helped set up licensed production arrangements. A number of Iranian military officers are attending Russian military schools. There are also many private Russian citizens (some estimate more than 500) who are working in Iran and suspected of providing military technology-related expertise.

Russian–Iranian military cooperation is supported by close bilateral relations that amount to a strategic alliance based on common strategic interests in containing US and Turkish influence in the Caspian region.[9] Moreover, Russian–Iranian bilateral military cooperation is complemented by cooperation in other areas, such as civilian nuclear energy, oil and gas exploration and commercial trade, which has exceeded $500 million a year.

However, Russia's military and civilian nuclear cooperation with Iran has become a source of constant concern and tension in Russia's relations with Israel and the United States. The US government has applied consistent pressure on Russia to reduce, or even cancel, some of its projects. In 1995, Russia and the United States reached an agreement in the framework of the Gore–Chernomyrdin Commission, under which Russia agreed not to complete new arms deals with Iran after fulfilling all its current contractual obligations, in exchange for lifting some US restrictions on high-technology exports to Russia. This agreement was controversial in both countries. Russian officials argued that the agreement covered only Russia's obligation in the field of nuclear and missile technologies. Republicans in the US Congress questioned the Clinton administration's judgment in agreeing that Moscow could complete the sale of arms to Iran (including tanks, armored personnel carriers and Kilo-class submarines). The Clinton administration responded by pointing out that arms transfers allowed under the agreement did not provide Iran with new weapons capabilities or alter the military balance of power in the Persian Gulf.[10] However, a number of states, including Israel, expressed concerns over the content and the scale of Russian arms transfers to Iran.

The Putin government, however, decided to abrogate the Gore–Chernomyrdin understanding and failed to halt arms sales to Iran. It appears that in early November 2000 Russia informed Washington that it was to withdraw from its commitments not to supply Iran with conventional weapons, probably because of the profits to be made from further sales to Iran.[11] The legal status of this agreement had always been in dispute. It seems likely that Russia will not supply new platforms, but will continue to supply spare parts and compete for modernization of Iranian Soviet-made equipment. Russia fears losing the Iranian arms market, which is increasingly targeted by other states, including China, North Korea and even France.

Russian experts called on Russian arms export agencies to

make Russia the main supplier for Iran's 25-year program to modernize its armed forces.[12] Iran reportedly expressed interest in acquiring Russia's used Su-25 planes, MI-17-1B helicopters, and T-72 tanks; the new air defense system S-300 PMU1 and the RLS (Rocket Launching System) 'Defense-14' as well as a licensing agreement for the production of the Tu-334 civil airliner. Some Russian experts also suggested that parts might be exported to Syria, and thence from Syria to Iran, even if Russia abides by its moratorium on future military supplies to Iran. Russian commentators have speculated that the contracts with Iran could be worth as much as $7 to $8 billion.

A particular concern is over any Russian assistance that might help Iran obtain nuclear and missile technology.[13] Russian experts deny Russian governmental assistance, though the United States claims that Russian institutions, companies and individual scientists – frequently without direct sanction from the government – often provide assistance. The Israeli government declared in 1999 that Russia's arms export control system has begun to erode further. Although President Putin has tried to reinforce the effectiveness of federal government controls, particularly in the sensitive military and other technology transfer fields, more measures will be required to dispel US and Israeli concerns.

US–Russian tensions over cooperation with Iran were most heightened when Russia began to provide assistance to construct the nuclear power plant at Bushehr, which the United States claims can assist the Iranian nuclear weapons program. Russia is providing four reactors and turbines. The United States claims that this project could assist Iran to advance its military nuclear program, and was successful in halting Ukrainian participation in it. The Russian government views American pressure as commercially rather then security motivated. Further, Russia refuses to acknowledge these accusations, claiming that it has supplied to Iran technology similar to what the United States agreed to supply to North Korea as part of agreements to stop that country's development of nuclear weapons. Russia also states that Iran is ready to open the Bushehr plant for intrusive inspections by the International Atomic Energy Agency (IAEA). So far, these disagreements have not been resolved and Russian personnel continue to work at Bushehr. There are also suspicions that Russia provides direct support to the Iranian nuclear program (which is not linked with Bushehr), but there is no clear evidence that Russian nuclear scientists working in Iran are authorized by the Russian government.

Another aspect of US and Israeli concern is suspected Russian assistance to Iran in the development of ballistic missile technology. Some US intelligence reports claim that Russia has transferred unspecified SS-4 SSM technology to Iran, as well as assisting Iran with the development of a national communications satellite with dual-use technology.[14] The Missile Technology Control Regime (MTCR), to which the Russian Federation belongs, while only a voluntary arrangement and not a treaty, presumes that the sale of complete rockets and certain complete subsystems will not be permitted by its members. However, Category II material – covering a wide range of parts, components and subsystems such as propellants, structural materials, test equipment and facilities and flight instruments – may be exported at the discretion of the MTCR partner government on a case-by-case basis for acceptable end-uses. In the absence of further information, it is difficult to assess whether MTCR guidelines were breached by any Russian technology transfer.

In February 1998 the Russian ministry of defense released an official statement that it has neither agreements nor contacts with Iran or other Middle East countries covering missile technology. Moreover, it has recognized that proliferation of missiles and missile technology constitute a serious threat to Russia. However, in 1998, on the basis of intelligence reports, the United States imposed sanctions on several Russian institutes which train Iranian scientists. Despite Russia's outrage at these sanctions, it had to acknowledge that some programs could potentially compromise its non-proliferation commitments. Since that time, Russia has announced new measures to reinforce its export control policies and has stopped some of the more controversial training programs.

The United States continues to express concern over the potential leakage of Russian technical expertise to Iran. In March 1999, Israel's then Minister of Trade and Industry, Natan Sharansky, charged that Russia was not doing enough to stop the leakage of missile technologies to Iran.[15] Israeli concerns have resulted in the cancellation of its agreement with Russia for the sale of natural gas. Russian officials claim that the United States and Israel have provided no proof for their allegations that Russian military specialists and defense institutes are continuing to leak sensitive technologies to Iran.

A sign of intensified Russian–Iranian military cooperation came in July 2000 when the first Russian military delegation, led by the head of Russian Ministry of Defense Department of International Cooperation, General Leonid Ivashov, visited Tehran. The result of this visit was an agreement to organize regular consultations between the two ministries of defense on military and political issues of common concern. According to some reports, the three areas of common concern (or perceived common threats) included expanded US and NATO involvement in the south Caucasus, the existing balance of power in the Middle East, and uncertain developments in Afghanistan.[16] Putin considers its relations with Iran as an important factor in his strategy to increase Russia's influence in the Middle East.

SYRIA

Unlike the case of Iran, where the Soviet Union began military cooperation only in 1989, Soviet–Syrian military cooperation dates back to the mid-1950s. This cooperation covered all spheres, including massive arms supply, training of Syrian officers and provision of a large network of Soviet in-country military advisers. From 1980 to 1991, the Soviet Union supplied Syria with military equipment worth over $26 billion, including 65 launchers for tactical and sub-strategic missile systems, about 5,000 tanks, 1,200 aircraft, 4,200 artillery pieces and mortars and 70 warships.[17] The Soviet Union also assisted Syria with the construction of more than 100 military facilities. During the same period, at least 9,600 Syrian officers were trained in Soviet military schools.[18] Over 90 per cent of Syrian military equipment is Soviet-made though much of it – an estimated 500 aircraft and 4,000 tanks – requires modernization.

Between 1990 and 1991, Soviet arms transfers to Syria dropped from $1.47 billion to $1.05 billion,[19] as Russia started to demand hard currency payment for its supplies. Since 1991, military supplies were practically frozen with the exception of a contract for T-72A tanks in 1992–93 at a total cost of $270 million. In 1997, Russia supplied Syria only with spare parts worth $1 million.

According to a number of Russian analysts and officials, Syria is viewed as a priority customer for Russian military cooperation and arms sales in the Middle East, and is thought to have the potential to become the third largest Russian arms customer (after China and India).[20] However, Syria's weak economic position, unresolved debt issues and fears of competition from Ukrainian and Belorussian companies have prevented Russia and Syria from substantially expanding their military-technical cooperation.

In the past, Syrian officials have repeatedly expressed interest in considering Russia as a potential candidate for modernizing its armed forces. In 1996, a special bilateral Russian–Syrian commission on military-technical cooperation developed a draft agreement, under which Russia was supposed to supply Syria with a large consignment of AKS-74U and AK-74M rifles and ammunition, 9M117M guided missiles, 9M113 missiles for Konkurs anti-tank missile systems, PG-7VL rockets for RPG-7 rocket launchers and PRG-29 grenade launchers with night-vision equipment. In addition, Russia was to modernize Syria's T-72 and T-55 tanks. The contract was expected to be worth $2 billion.

However, disagreements over the Syrian debt to Russia, and Syria's insistence on lower prices and extended payment schemes for future purchases, led to a failure to sign any comprehensive contract. Syria refused to recognize its $11 billion debt to Russia and proposed to postpone repayment indefinitely. Russia had high expectations for a breakthrough in Russian–Syrian military-technical cooperation during the visit of President Hafiz al-Asad to Moscow in summer 1999. In order to reach this breakthrough, Moscow announced before the visit that it was ready to remove the linkage between debt negotiations and new arms supplies agreements. However, no agreement was reached. Asad insisted on a long-term payment schedule for a $2 billion contract, while Moscow was opposed to any new loans to Syria.

In the meantime, other ex-Soviet states offered more attractive conditions to Damascus. A Ukrainian tank-repair plant at Kiev won a contract for the modernization of Syria's T-55 tanks. The plant also hoped to win the next contract for the modernization of 300 T-72 tanks.

So far, Russia and Syria have signed one major arms export contract for the supply of 1,000 Metis-M (NATO designation AT-13) and Kornet-E (AT-14) anti-tank missiles worth $138 million ($73 million and $65 million respectively). This deal caused a lot of concern in both the US and Israel. In 1999, the United States introduced sanctions against three Russian institutes and arms producers (the Instrument-Making Design Bureau in Tula, the Volsk mechanical plant and the Central Institute of Machine-Building), which were planning to supply more advanced anti-tank weapons to Syria. Moreover, the Clinton administration linked any Russian supplies of advanced weapons for Syria with continued US aid to Russia. The Russian government expressed outrage over these sanctions and the missiles were reportedly delivered to Syria in 1999.

Israel expressed concern over the sale of the AT-14 Kornet third-generation anti-tank guided missiles to Syria. According to *Jane's Defense Weekly*, the AT-14 Kornet is designed mainly for the export market, and has an outstanding 5,000-meter range. The use of laser beam-riding technology for guidance enables simpler operation by operators with only limited training. While the Kornet does not pose a new challenge to Israeli main battle tanks, it presents a more serious threat in a static battlefield, such as southern Lebanon or the Golan Heights demilitarized zone, where its accuracy allows lethal attacks against fortified positions or medium-protected vehicles.[21] These characteristics make Kornet a source of potential threat to Israel.

Moreover, the sale of such equipment to Syria violates the pledge that Russia would only sell 'defensive weapons and spare parts for arms sold to Syria under previous contracts. Russia does not sell offensive weapons to anyone'.[22] By contrast, in October 1999 the Russian ambassador to Syria stated that 'Russia will sell to Syria any modern weapons which it may require because Syria is not threatening any state's security and is not subject to international sanctions.'[23] This statement demonstrates that the Russian government was determined to capture the Syrian arms market, despite strong opposition from the US and Israel.

Syria continues to experience difficulties in providing cash payments for the new arms contracts with Russia. There were reports that Saudi Arabia and even Iran might provide financial assistance to Syria to help modernize its weapons systems, but there is no sign such help will actually be given. However, Russian arms exporters have formulated proposals for Syria. During Russian Defense Minister Marshall Igor Sergeev's visit to Damascus, he offered to supply Su-27 aircraft, T-80 tanks and the S-300 air defense system, as well as to modernize MiG-21 and MiG-23 aircraft and T-72 tanks.[24] Experts suggested that projects might include 20 Su-27 or MiG-29SMT aircraft, a large shipment of T-90 tanks and the upgrade of over 100 MiG-23s and MiG-21s and also T-90 tanks.[25] There are reports Russia has negotiated with Syria on the sale of S-300 surface to air missiles, as well as TOR-M1 and BUK-M-1.2 air defense missile systems.

Syria also reportedly expressed interest in expanding military-to-military contacts with Russia, which do not involve large payments. Syria is planning to increase the number of its military officers educated in Russian military schools (including at the Air Force Academy). Russia is seeking to expand such cooperative arrangements as joint exercises. Syria has already participated in exercises at the Transbaikal Military District, using S-200B air defense systems. Such joint exercises are expected to continue and be expanded. There were also unconfirmed reports that Syria and Russia are discussing establishing a Russian naval base on the Syrian Mediterranean coast.[26] The number of Russian military advisers in Syria is also set to increase.

However, these expectations of Russian arms export companies may never become reality. Although Russia's arms export officials continue to speak with optimism of a Syrian arms deal, there has been little to suggest that the two sides have resolved their differences. While arms sales are no longer linked with the resolution of the debt dispute, Russian officials in Putin's administration continue to insist that any deliveries to Syria be made under strict commercial conditions. Equally, the Syrian side understands that

Russia is asking for a higher price than Ukraine, Belarus, China or North Korea. Syria also believes that Moscow's wish for greater influence in the region may provide leverage, if it waits to obtain better payment terms for any future Russian arms supplies. Finally, there is uncertainty about whether President Bashar al-Asad, educated in the West, will be as committed to close relations with Russia as was his father.

Under certain circumstances, Russia–Syria military cooperation and arms sales could vastly increase, though this is by no means certain. Ultimately, the regional situation might force Syria to accept at least some Russian offers, since there is no other state likely to supply Syria with large amounts of arms. This deal could be made possible if wealthy Arab states finally provide Syria with financial assistance. But any supply of modern weapons to Syria by Russia under the current conditions is bound to intensify tensions between Moscow and Washington, as well as between Russia and Israel.

LIBYA

Russian officials repeatedly declared that they view both Libya and Iraq, after the lifting of international sanctions, as major markets for Russian arms exports. However, in the Libyan case, an end to sanctions failed to bring Russia many dividends. As with Syria, Russia's arms exports are hampered by unresolved disputes inherited from Soviet contracts and by intense competition from other ex-Soviet states such as Ukraine, Belarus and Kazakhstan, as well as China and North Korea.

Between 1970 and 1991 Russia supplied $19 billion of military equipment to the Libyan armed forces. More than 90 per cent of Libyan military equipment is Soviet- or Russian-made. Since the introduction of sanctions in 1991, Russia has lost potential sales worth approximately $7.5 billion. In particular, sanctions destroyed a large-scale Libyan Air Force modernization program, which would have included the delivery of MiG-29 fighters worth billions of dollars. After sanctions were lifted in 1999, Russia sought to renew its arms sales, including platforms, spare parts and modernization contracts for Libyan equipment. However, Russia's hopes on major contracts with the Libyan armed forces so far remain unfulfilled, due to unsettled debts – the largest being $3 billion for contracts unfulfilled because of sanctions. Libya also insists that Russia should compensate it for losses incurred when Russia joined the international sanctions regime and terminated the implementation of previously signed contracts.

Although Libya hired Russian experts to undertake the assessment of modernization requirements for its Soviet-made weapons systems (mainly Su-17 and Su-24 aircraft), it is reluctant to give Russia preference for the implementation of actual modernization contracts. This can be explained by aggressive competition from Ukraine, Belarus and a number of other east European states for such contracts. Ukraine offers more attractive financial conditions for modernization than Russia (monthly salary for Ukrainian military specialists working in Libya is approximately $350–$400, while Russian specialists charge over $1,000 for the same work). Moreover, the spare parts market for ex-Soviet equipment is very big, and includes a number of Warsaw Pact countries seeking to sell excess equipment and spare parts still held by their armed forces under very good conditions.

As a result, out of 40 projected modernization contracts, Russia has so far won only one, for the supply of ammunition and spare parts for $100 million to the Promeksport company. It is likely that Ukraine and Belarus will receive a much bigger share of modernization contracts. In August 2000, the Russian vice-premier in charge of the military-industrial structure, Ilya Klebanov, announced that Russia's expectations towards military-technical cooperation with Libya so far have not been realized, because 'Tripoli has not taken the political decision to develop large-scale military cooperation with Russia'.[27]

As far as sales of new equipment are concerned, Russia has offered Libya a number of systems, but may be facing competition from Western arms suppliers. According to Yuri Rodin-Sova, the president of the Russian financial-industrial group, Oboronitel'nye Sistemy, which markets Russian air-defense systems such as S-300, Russia offered to develop the Libyan air defense system on the basis of the S-300PMU1 and S-300PMU2. This would use some older air defense systems that Libya acquired from the Soviet Union. However, these negotiations were far from complete. It appears likely that, in case of complete removal of political sanctions toward Libya by European states, the Libyan government, which possesses significant financial resources for modernization of its armed forces, is likely to look to the West for major new arms import contracts.

The example of military cooperation with Libya demonstrates that, in the future, Russia will have problems increasing its positions even in the so-called 'traditional Soviet markets'. Russia's marketing strategies face many obstacles: first, unsettled disputes over past contracts undermined Libya's trust in Russia as a reliable ally. Second, Russia's inability to compete with financial terms offered by other ex-Soviet states and by China and North Korea, damages Moscow's chances. Finally, realization of Russia's declining role has removed the strategic rationale for regional states to pursue contracts with Russia, regardless of financial problems.

Similar problems are likely to torpedo Russia's high expectations about modernization of the Iraqi armed forces after the removal of sanctions. If, however, European states continue to enforce self-imposed restriction against arms sales to Iraq (as they do toward Iran and China), Russia may have less difficulty capturing the Iraqi arms market. There are some reports that Russian officials are already discussing prospects for the upgrade of the Iraqi air defense system, reports which were denied by the Russian government.

THE UNITED ARAB EMIRATES (UAE)

Although the UAE does not belong to Russia's traditional markets in the Middle East, Russian–UAE military cooperation developed quite rapidly in the 1990s. In 1998, the UAE was the fourth biggest Russian arms customer after China, India and Iran. The fact that Russia and the UAE do not have any disputes left from Soviet times, and that the UAE is interested in purchasing new equipment for cash, make it one of the key targets for Russian arms export agencies. From 1992 to 2000, the UAE purchased 591 Russian BMP-3 Armored Combat Vehicles for $800,000 each. In May 2000, Russia delivered several sets of dynamic protection equipment and splinter-proof screens to modernize the BMP-3 previously sold to the UAE (this was the first time Russia undertook modernization of BMP-3).[28] Russia also leased 4 IL-76 transport aircraft to the UAE in 1998.

Russia is expecting further expansion of such sales. On 24 May 2000, Russia announced a $500 million deal (other sources reported it is worth $734 million) for the supply of the Panzir-S1 anti-aircraft system. This system is among the most advanced air defense systems produced by Russia to protect strategic facilities from tactical aircraft, attack helicopters, ballistic and guided missiles, guided bombs and other high-precision weapons. The range of its missiles is from 1,000 meters to 20 kilometers and its artillery fire from 200 to 4,000 meters.[29] The deal was reportedly negotiated by the Tula Design Bureau, which builds the system, and is said to be among the largest contracts ever concluded by a Russia defense enterprise.[30] This is only the second time in the history of Russia's arms exports that a recipient country has signed a contract under which the Russian company must first complete the R&D (research and development) of the most advanced technology equipment. The UAE paid 30 per cent of the contract in advance to cover the R&D phase. Russia will be offering the UAE other advanced systems, such as the MiG-31M interceptor aircraft, Ka-50 attack helicopter and T-90 MBT.[31]

OTHER MIDDLE EAST AND ARAB STATES MARKETS

Russia has established extensive military cooperation with Kuwait, which in 1995–96 bought 27 9A52 Smerch multiple rocket launchers. The contract was estimated to be worth over $48 million.[32] Russia is also supplying Kuwait with 100 BMP-3 Armored Combat Vehicles, and has started to build a plant for repairing and servicing of these vehicles.

At the same time, Russia is developing military cooperation with Yemen. Yemen was a long-standing Soviet client, but financial problems, combined with Russia's insistence on immediate cash payments, practically terminated bilateral military cooperation. In July 2000, Russia made the first delivery of military equipment to Yemen since 1990, consisting of 30 T-72 tanks. Following this delivery, Russian Defense Minister Igor Sergeev visited Yemen to promote further military cooperation. However, it is unlikely that bilateral military cooperation will develop more dynamically in the near future. Yemen is seeking cheaper supplies from other ex-Soviet states. In 1995, for example, it acquired four Su-22 attack aircraft from Ukraine for a very low price.

Similar tactics are being practiced by Jordan, which is conducting negotiations with practically all potential suppliers of used equipment from ex-Soviet states and eastern Europe. Jordan established military-technical cooperation with the Soviet Union in 1982, and sales exceeded $1 billion by the time of the USSR's collapse. Although Jordan purchased 126 BMP-3 Armored Combat Vehicles from Russia in 1995, bilateral military cooperation between the two countries has been practically frozen since then. Jordan has made a few acquisitions from Russia's competitors, including 50 BTR-94s from Ukraine in 1999. In August 2000, the Russian *Independent Military Review* reported that Jordan and a Georgian aviation plant are developing plans for joint upgrade of Su-25s that might be sold to third countries.[33] Russian arms export officials and experts view Jordan as potentially a very attractive market, emphasizing, on one hand, Jordan's political motives to use Russian and other east European supplies to balance its dependence on US military aid and, on the other, Jordan's requirements for modernization of ex-Soviet equipment. However, no major contracts between Russia and Jordan are expected in the near future.

Russia's military cooperation with Egypt started in 1955 and was practically terminated by 1973. During that period, the Soviet Union supplied Egypt with military equipment worth over $8.5 billion. Since the collapse of the Soviet Union, Russia has actively targeted Egypt for contracts to modernize its ex-Soviet equipment. According to Russian estimates, over 70 per cent of air defense systems, 40 per cent of aircraft, 85 per cent of artillery systems and 45 per cent of tanks and BTRs, which Egypt received from the Soviet Union, require modernization.[34] Russia's expectation for large contracts was not fulfilled, however, because of the reorientation of Egyptian armed forces to US equipment, which is supplied under favorable financial conditions. Finally, in 1998, Egypt and Russia signed a contract for the supply of spare parts and electronic components which was worth an estimated $2.7 million. Russia also supplied 20 Mi-17 helicopters and undertook upgrades of surface-to-air missile complexes for additional $125 million. Given that Egypt was generally satisfied with the quality of services and equipment provided by Russia, it is likely to continue using Russian companies for modernization of ex-Soviet equipment.

One of the more extensive examples of Russia's military-technical cooperation with Arab states can be found in Algeria. Since 1962, the Soviet Union has supplied over $11 billion worth of military equipment to Algeria. In 1996, the Algerian government made a political decision to develop strategic cooperation with Russia to modernize its armed forces. Since that time, Russia and Algeria have concluded a number of agreements for the development of a system for radio-electronic warfare and electronic intelligence-gathering. Moreover, Algeria has expressed interest in the modernization of its air defense system, on the basis of the Russian S-300PMU-1 surface-to-air missile system and the upgrade of the old Soviet air defense systems, as well as purchasing Su-24M aircraft and modernizing MiG-21 aircraft.[35] Moscow is also conducting negotiations on upgrading Algerian surface ships and developing a coastguard system. Russian experts assess the value of potential contacts as up to $4 billion. While Russian–Algerian military cooperation has a good chance of expanding further, there are several problems, in particular Algeria's $4 billion debt to Russia, as well as increasing competition from Ukrainian and Belorussian firms for the upgrade of Soviet equipment. The Algerian leadership is exploiting this competition to reduce prices to a level that is no longer attractive for Russian suppliers.

ISRAEL

Since December 1995, when Israeli Prime Minister Shimon Peres and Russian Defense Minister Pavel Grachev signed a five-year bilateral agreement for military-technical cooperation (which was extended in 2000), Russia and Israel have pursued military co-operation. Unlike other Middle East and Arab states, Russia and Israel work together to upgrade Russian equipment, mainly for exports to third countries. Moreover, Israel has developed the know-how and has managed to capture unilaterally a large share of the market for the upgrade of ex-Soviet equipment. Russia and Israel cooperate on upgrades of aircraft, sold by Russia to India and China, as well as those for central European and African markets. Many former Soviet scientists, who were working in the military-industrial complex before emigrating to Israel, provided the basis for this know-how. This cooperation is strategically important to Russia, which is seeking ways to compete for arms sales in the developed markets in Europe and in east Asia, practically impossible without foreign electronics. While Russian companies continue to lobby the Russian government to maintain the principle of full self-sufficiency for all arms exports, many of their clients specifically request foreign electronic sub-systems as a prerequisite for purchasing Russian weapons systems, particularly Russian aircraft.

Although Russia's cooperation with Israel is very important for Russia's global arms export ambitions, a number of concerns are repeatedly voiced in Russia about it. Many Russian experts claim that Israel received a disproportionately large share of profit from the sale of upgraded equipment.[36] Others claim that Russia's military cooperation with Israel could undermine Russia's plans to expand military cooperation with other Middle East and Arab states. And finally, there are claims that Russia cannot consider Israel as a reliable strategic partner for future upgrades, because of US influence over Israel which could sabotage future contracts.

Concerns over the reliability of Israeli cooperation were tested in April 2000, when the United States pressured Israel to cancel its contract to install the Elta Phalcon phased-array radar (Air-borne Early Warning (AEW) system) on the Russian A-50 air-frame for export to China. US Secretary of Defense William Cohen announced that this system could change the balance of forces in the Taiwan Straits and endanger American troops.[37] Cohen also warned that China could sell the Israeli technology to Iran and Iraq. Under continued strong US pressure, Israeli Prime

Minister Ehud Barak cancelled the sale on 10 July 2000.[38] It now appears that Russia will exploit the failure of that contract to sell China A-50s with Russian avionics.[39]

Unless the situation in the Middle East escalates further into a prolonged new conflict, and despite the failed AEW deal, Russian–Israeli military-technical cooperation is likely to develop further. This cooperation is clearly mutually beneficial and strategically important for the Russian defense industry, which is unlikely to significantly improve the reputation of its electronic sub-systems, while continuing to depend on exports for survival.

For Israel, this cooperation is likely to bring significant profits as Russia expands its exports to both traditional and new markets. However, Israel remains concerned over potential transfer of its technology to adversaries in the Arab states, which maintain close military cooperation with Russia.

CONCLUSIONS

Although Russia's military cooperation with Middle East states declined significantly after the end of the Cold War and the collapse of the Soviet Union, it continued to maintain a presence in traditional Soviet markets. Moscow has developed cooperation with new clients such as Israel, the UAE and Kuwait. Although Russia's military supplies were mainly oriented towards the upgrade and modernization of Soviet equipment, a number of contracts have shifted the military balance among different armed forces in the region. These include, for example, the sale of three Kilo-class submarines to Iran, as well as the contract for supply of anti-tank missiles to Syria and advanced air defense systems to the United Arab Emirates. Additional deals of the same significance have so far been delayed by financial difficulties on the part of Russia's clients in the region. But a number of contracts under negotiation between Russia and Syria, Libya, Algeria and Iran may be completed and thus significantly alter the regional balance of forces.

Despite continuous pressure on Russia from the United States and Israel, Moscow is determined to expand its military sales to the region. Aside from economic needs, Moscow's determination is further reinforced by its perception that the United States is trying to marginalize Russia's regional role. In an environment of mistrust and deteriorating US–Russian relations, Washington will have little leverage to pressure Moscow to abandon these efforts, as instances of Russian technology transfer to Iran and Syria – despite America's threats of sanctions – have demonstrated. Russian–Israeli military cooperation represents a more effective alternative to sanctions-driven policies. As long as Russia sees economic benefits from alternative military cooperation programs, it is more likely to exercise restraint in its military transfers.

NOTES

1. Research for this article was conducted by Colin Robinson, Research Assistant for the Russia and Eurasia Programme at the International Institute for Strategic Studies.
2. Yuri Morozov, 'Strategiya Rossii v oblasti voenno-technicheskogo sotrudnichestva so stranami blizhnego vostoka' (Russia's Strategies for Military-Technical Cooperation with the Middle East), *Arms Export Journal*, published by Russia's AST Centre, No. 3, 2000, p. 18.
3. Ibid.
4. Four T-72, three BMP-2, two 140mm artillery pieces, and two unspecified missiles and missile launchers were also listed as imported by Iran in 1998.
5. UN CAR (Conventional Arms Register) gives 91 BMP-3s. IISS also shows delivery of unspecified number of BMP-2s. Currently, Kuwait holds 46 BMP-2s and 55 BMP-3s. (*The Military Balance 2000–2001*, p. 145.)
6. UN CAR shows a transfer of 27 ACV not confirmed by *The Military Balance*.
7. Not reported in *The Military Balance*.
8. Andrei Volpin, *Russian Arms Sales Policy towards the Middle East* (Washington Institute for Near East Policy Report, October 1993), p. 14.
9. The deputy chairman of the State Duma Defense Committee said that 'apart from commercial interests, Iran is a regional partner and our cooperation with Iran is long term'. *Jane's Defense Weekly*, Vol. 33, Issue 16 (19 April 2000), p. 17.
10. Statement by John Baker, Deputy Assistant Secretary of State, *Washington Post*, 26 October 2000.
11. *RFE/RL Newsline*, Part I, 27 November 2000, p. 2, quoting *Vremya Novostei* and *Nezavisimaya Gazeta*.
12. Morozov, 'Strategiya Rossii', p. 15.
13. Steve Rodan, 'Secret Israeli Data Reveals Iran Can Make Missile in Year', *Defense News*, 6–12 October 1997, cited in Stephen Blank, *The Spirit of Eternal Negation: Russia's Hour in the Middle East* (report published by the Conflict Studies Research Centre, November 1998), p. 22.
14. Sources cited in Blank, *Spirit of Eternal Negation*, p. 22.
15. *The Jamestown Monitor*, www.jamestown.org/pubs/view/mon/005/052_002.htm.
16. Paul Goble, 'A Russian–Iranian Rapprochement', *RFE/RL*, www.rferl.org/nca/features/2000/07/f.ru.000703124557.html.
17. Vadim Kozyulin, 'Russia and Syria: Military-Technical Bargaining', *Yadernyi Kontrol*

Digest, Vol. 5, No. 3 (15) (Summer 2000), electronic version, www.pircenter.org.
18. Morozov, 'Strategiya Rossii', p. 14.
19. Volpin, *Russian Arms Sales*, p. 13.
20. Morozov, 'Strategiya Rossii', pp. 14–15.
21. *Jane's Defense Weekly*, Vol. 30, Issue 5 (5 August 1998), p. 8.
22. David Hurst, 'Russia Agrees to Sell Arms to Syria', *Guardian*, 29 April 1994.
23. *Independent Military Review*, 29 October 1999, http://nvo.ng.ru/wars/1999-10-29/1_korotko.html.
24. Kozyulin, 'Russia and Syria: Military-Technical Bargaining'.
25. Morozov, 'Strategiya Rossii', p. 15
26. 'Damascus Reportedly Offers Use of Naval Base to Russian Fleet in the Mediterranean', *Al-Quds*, 2 April 1999 (cited in the BBC Summary of World Broadcasts [SWB] 6 April 1999).
27. *Independent Military Review*, No. 28 (4 August 2000), electronic version at http://news.mosinfo.ru/news/2000/NVO.
28. 'Russia Modernises United Arab Emirates' Infantry Combat Vehicles', SWB, SU/3833 S1/1 (6 May 2000).
29. *Independent Military Review*, No. 21 (16 June 2000).
30. *The Jamestown Foundation Monitor*, Vol. 6, Issue 105, http://www.jamestown.org/pubs/view/mon/006/105_001.htm.
31. Morozov, 'Strategiya Rossii', p. 17.
32. Derived from *Jane's World Armies'* figures. Charles Heyman (ed.), *Jane's World Armies* (Issue 8) (Jane's Information Group, Coulsdon, Surrey, 2000), p. 409.
33. *Independent Military Review*, No. 30 (18 August 2000).
34. Morozov, 'Strategiya Rossii', p. 16.
35. Ibid., p. 15
36. Ibid., p. 17
37. *Jane's Defense Weekly*, Vol. 33, Issue 16 (19 April 2000), p. 2.
38. 'China's Foreign Conventional Arms Acquisitions: Background and Analysis', *CRS Report for Congress*, 10 October 2000, Congressional Research Service, pp. CRS-20.
39. 'Russia to Sell Radar Planes to China', ITAR-TASS, 31 October 2000, SWB/3987.

5

Guns and Butter in the Egyptian Army

HILLEL FRISCH[1]

The Egyptian army seems to possess the characteristics of a modern army (in the 1950s sense, when nationalism and patriotism unquestionably prevailed in military establishments) in a post-modern age. While the post-modern army is often seen as being professionally small, the Egyptian army remains rather large. While the post-modern army is typified by increasing civilian–military integration, the Egyptian army has constructed at least 17 military cities to isolate the military from the civilian population.[2]

Bernard Boëne claims that Western militaries in the post-modern age are peripheral in the value structure of the societies within which they operate, but are increasingly physically integrated into civil society as a result of professional wives, who want to integrate into civilian society.[3] In Egypt, by contrast, the values held by the armed forces are assumed to be the values still cherished by Egyptian society. Even the sections devoted to women and family in *al-Nasr*, the official army journal, depict wives in the Egyptian military, however worldly, who still fill the role of mothers. In short, the ethos and discourse of the Egyptian armed forces resembles the style of the early and mid-twentieth century. The army continues to be the repository of military values and the defender of the state and nation, forever on guard to protect its independence and integrity.

This first glance, however, does not give a complete picture of the situation. Upon closer examination, the armed forces are shown to be under criticism for being too expensive.[4] In *al-Ahram*, Ahmad Ibrahim Mahmud writes, 'Since the mid-1970s Egypt has focused on giving complete first priority to domestic development to confront its growing economic problems.'[5] In a more subtle reference to this fact, Abd al-Mun'im Sa'id, director of Egypt's prestigious al-Ahram Center for Political and Strategic Studies, praises the benefits of US civilian aid compared to its military aid, though more money is earmarked for the latter category.[6] Newspapers devote many articles to praising the army's 'civilian' and development-oriented services, as if to defend its contribution to the nation on this more important front.[7]

This tension between supporting a large military while coming to grips with the acute, almost insurmountable, social problems facing Egypt, is a central factor in analyzing the mission and political status of the Egyptian armed forces. There is a clear contradiction on this issue. On the one hand, both the Egyptian military and outside experts agree that the Egyptian armed forces have become more professional and have radically modernized their force, structure and equipment, while maintaining a strength level of about 420,000 men. On the other hand, the armed forces' estimated real budget fell by nearly half in the last two decades of the twentieth century.[8] Meanwhile, US military aid, a hefty $1.3 billion annually which is not included in the military budget, fell in real terms by 50 per cent.[9]

How can this combination of factors be possible? Sophisticated equipment – including items needed for new command, control, communication and intelligence systems – means increased operating costs as well as requiring more and better quality commissioned and non-commissioned officers.[10] US military aid does not cover these expenses.[11] In order to balance the accounts, the army must either sacrifice quantity for quality or slash military salaries severely. The February 1986 rebellion in the Central Security Forces to protest low wages suggests that salary reduction is not politically feasible.[12] Such a solution is all the more untenable in the face of rising Islamic fundamentalism. This chapter will attempt to solve this apparent riddle, while analyzing the Egyptian military's mission, force structure, capabilities and relationship to civil society.

94

FIGURE 5.1:
DEFENSE EXPENDITURES, 1978–98

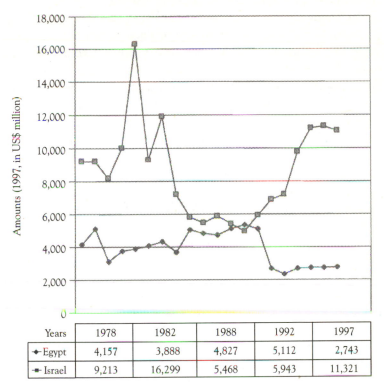

Years	1978	1982	1988	1992	1997
◆ Egypt	4,157	3,888	4,827	5,112	2,743
▪ Israel	9,213	16,299	5,468	5,943	11,321

THE EGYPTIAN ARMED FORCES' MISSION

The Egyptian military's mission, as defined by political leaders and senior officers, is to defend Egypt and achieve Egyptian national interests. The stress on defense rather than offense, and peace rather than war, resonates in almost every public address issued by Egypt's senior politicians and ministers, including the minister of defense. In a November 1995 speech, President Husni Mubarak stated that 'in general, the level of our armed forces is a source of pride for us all, and [they] are capable of deterring any danger threatening our national security'. When asked about criticism from other states that Egypt is expanding its military power, he replied, 'The call to weaken the Egyptian army is misleading. We

95

have to maintain a military power capable of deterring at the same time we work for peace'.[13]

In October 1996, Mubarak linked Egyptian deterrence with the need to preserve the Arab–Israeli peace process, saying that a strong Egyptian army helped preserve regional stability and the chance of reaching peace. According to the official summary of the statement, 'History has taught us that the cause behind many wars is the weakness of one side and the increase and growth of military power of the other side. This prompts the second side to attack, as has happened and is happening around us now. Therefore, peace and stability must exist under the umbrella of a military force that protects and preserves them.'[14]

Similar statements were made consistently by Minister of Defense and War Production, Field Marshal Muhammad Husayn Tantawi, 'Peace does not mean relaxation. The endless development of military systems and the arms race prove that survival is only assured by the strongest and that military strength will always be necessary. Military strength has grown to be a prerequisite of peace. Any threat to any Arab or African country is a threat to Egypt's national security.'[15]

This basic position was voiced slightly differently by Major General Muhammad Seif Eddin Galal, commander of the Third Field Army, upon completion of the Jabal Pharon exercises in April 1998, 'The exercise affirms to the world the effective role of the Egyptian armed forces, to lighten the path of Egyptian diplomacy to impose the peace of the strong which began on October 6 [the beginning of the 1973 war with Israel].'[16] Even when assessing the capabilities of the Egyptian air force, its commander makes clear its basic defensive mission when in an interview in 1999, he concluded, 'We cannot be taken lightly. We cannot be beaten.'[17]

However, much as these statements stress deterrence, they equally emphasize that this can only be achieved through efforts to enhance offensive capabilities, commensurate with the potential foe's strength. Nor can war with Israel be entirely ruled out. In his article stressing Egypt's commitment to social and economic development, Mahmud points out that 'the Egyptian military school of thought, in its strategic assessment, believes that there are a cluster of factors that are likely ... to push either in the direction of war or in the direction of peace ... The probabilities of armed conflict breaking out between Egypt and Israel or not breaking out depends on the following main factors: the fuzziness or lack of information regarding Israeli intentions ... Israeli military capabilities and their development, the size and type of the Israeli armed forces, [and] the military alliances and axis which Israel maintains with other countries ... Therefore the transparency of [Israeli] intentions and plans ... for military development and the development of military capabilities [and] moving forward in the Arab–Israeli settlement will help a great deal in avoiding the outbreak of armed conflict in the area and the opposite is true.'[18]

STRUCTURE, CAPABILITIES AND BATTLE-READINESS

President Anwar Sadat's prescient decision in the early 1970s to abandon the Soviet patron for the United States laid the foundation for the Egyptian army's radical transformation 'from [an] armed forces consisting of an army that relied mainly on infantry, a weak air force, and an essentially defensive navy, to an Egyptian armed forces that now reflect an offensive orientation ...'[19] The United States has contributed nearly $28 billion in military aid, since it first became available in 1975 in the form of weapon sales, training and mutual exercises with US forces. In 1998, Sa'id summarized this relationship: 'The modernization of the Egyptian armed forces in the past two decades has in large measure relied on American military aid.'[20]

The radical transformation of the armed forces is reflected in changes in the overall structure of its ground forces. Between 1973 and 1983, Egyptian ground forces consisted of ten divisions, five of them armored or mechanized. By the late 1990s, the Egyptian army had 12 divisions, of which all but one were armored or mechanized.[21] Perhaps even more significant is the increasingly Westernized and modern equipment these divisions operate. An estimated 70 per cent of Egypt's active tanks are of Western design, including 400 of 512 planned M-1 A-1 Abrams battle tanks (with a 'hit/kill ratio' that equals or surpasses any main battle tank armament in the world), equivalent to Israel's Merkava-3. Egypt is also converting M-60 A1 tanks to A3s, has been upgrading Russian T-62s, produces and operates 24 SPH 122 mm self-propelled guns, and is in the process of absorbing 600 new YPR-765 armored personnel carriers (APCs) from Holland.

To counter enemy armor, the Egyptians have at their disposal vast amounts of anti-tank missiles that proved their effectiveness in the 1991 Gulf War. During 1997 alone, the Egyptian army received 540 TOW-2 launchers, French Hot-3 missiles and 1,000 Hellfire-2 laser-guided anti-tank missiles.[22] Both the quality and mobility of the tanks and anti-tank missiles and launchers enhance substantially the offensive capabilities of Egyptian ground forces. The contribution of the United States to this transformation has been overwhelming.

The growing influence of American-made equipment is evidenced to an even greater extent by Egypt's air force, which, since the early 1980s, has integrated 160 F-16 jet fighters into its force structure, roughly two-thirds the number of these fighters possessed by Israel. Eight of 21 fighter squadrons are equipped with these planes, capable of carrying GBU-15 glide bombs and smart weapons such the AFM-84 Harpoon. Within the next few years, 220 of its 500 fighters will be composed of F-16s, the same planes that are the mainstay of Israeli air force offensive capabilities.[23]

To enhance combined ground-air operations, the Egyptians have purchased and integrated 36 ultra-advanced AH-64A Apache attack helicopters, all of which will be upgraded to the improved D model, equipped with a Long Bow radar that can locate both ground and air targets. Older helicopters, such as the SA-342 Gazelle, and the Naval Westland Sea King Mk-47 and SH-2G helicopters, make up the rest of the combat squadron.[24] As Sa'id notes, this transformation could never have taken place without massive US aid and training.[25]

Despite its emphasis on offensive air power, Egypt remains committed to enhancing its air-defense system, where it has been traditionally strong. Tradition is reflected in the fact that Air Defense Command is an autonomous branch, separate from the air force, reporting directly to the minister of defense and war production rather than to the commander of the air force or even to the chief-of-staff.[26] Surface-to-air missiles (SAMs), including the 1998 sale of 1,000 Stinger missiles (the world's most advanced personal anti-aircraft weapons) and advanced warning systems (such as five Grumman Hawkeye planes) have been increasingly of American make.[27] According to military expert Shmuel Gordon, 'The Egyptian air arm, the pivot of an Arab war coalition, is completing a long process of transformation to Western systems and technologies. It has procured various modern systems, such as aircraft, attack helicopters, air-to-air and air-to-ground guided munitions, early-warning systems, and electronic warfare systems.'[28]

Even the Egyptian navy, long the Achilles heel in the country's military, has seen substantial change. Once again, this development can be attributed mainly to United States aid. In the past 20 years, the navy has undergone significant restructuring. But the new advanced equipment and technology from several Western nations also poses a problem. While Egypt's naval forces are significantly more modernized than they were in the 1970s, the navy's major weakness now lies in the poor quality of its personnel. This is primarily due to the difficulty in effectively training personnel to operate a large number of different ships from different countries that operate on different technology levels.[29]

In the 1980s, Egypt's navy began to replace Soviet ships with more modernized Western equipment, including British-made Ramadan-class missile boats and Spanish-made Descubierta-class missile frigates, and attempted to upgrade older vessels with Western radar and electronic warfare systems. The purchase of four new Chinese-made Romeo-class submarines and American supplied state-of-the-art weapons and detection systems, including underwater-to-surface Harpoon missiles, was the most successful attempt to alleviate this problem.[30]

In the 1990s, in response to Israeli naval upgrades, the Egyptian navy went through a decade-long modernization process to replace outdated Soviet vessels with modernized Western ships and technology, relying on the United States as its major source of equipment and training. The US was ready to help, partly because it wants to maintain a strong, friendly naval force between the Persian Gulf and the Mediterranean Sea to secure oil exports and trade routes. Egypt completed these transactions in 1996, with the acquisition of four modern Oliver Hazard Perry-class frigates and ten Super Sea Sprite helicopters. Egypt plans to overhaul its submarine fleet with vessels from the United States, the Netherlands or Germany. Owing to this long-term restructuring, Egypt's navy has grown from an inconsequential force to a powerful military presence.[31]

Because US military aid has become so important to the military balance in the Middle East, it is important to take a look at how the aid has comparatively benefited Egypt and its most serious adversary, Israel. In general, the United States was the only country that refused to export its most advanced military technologies. This changed with President Clinton's decision to sell the AIM-120 AMRAAM missile to the UAE. The missile, which increases pilot survivability by letting the pilot break away immediately after launch and engage other targets, is the most advanced air-to-air missile in the US arsenal. Egypt's requests to purchase the AMRAAM, however, have continually been rejected by the Pentagon due to strong Israeli objections. Instead it has received less advanced but still formidable weapons, such as the flare-resistance air-to-air missiles (AIM-9-M), electromagnetic AAM (AIM-7-M), night-vision navigation systems (Path Finder), laser-designator pods (Sharp Shooter) and vehicle-mounted Stinger Avengers.[32]

While both Egypt and Israel have received a sizable quantity of advanced combat aircraft from the United States, American defense cooperation with Israel has proven to be a greater force multiplier. The US supported Israel's Arrow anti-ballistic missile program through funding about 70 per cent of development costs and providing $156 million for deployment of a third battery of Arrow missiles. In addition, a quick channel for sending emergency assistance (Air Mark) was set up, and Israel was directly connected to an early-warning system to detect SSM launches with a hotline between the US secretary of defense and the Israeli defense minister.[33]

Due to the acquisition of the most advanced American aircraft and tanks, such as the Apache-64A attack helicopters, the F-16 Fighting Falcon combat planes and the M-1 A-1 Abrams battle tanks, it can be argued that Egypt's weaponry is on par, or nearly on par, with Israel's military. Nevertheless, Israel's great advantage over Egypt lies in its ability to develop and manufacture weapons and munitions indigenously, using the most advanced technologies, although financial constraints prevent it from producing large quantities of these systems.[34] Egyptian analysts are also convinced that the United States maintains a technology gap in Israel's favor.[35]

Westernization of the Egyptian armed forces is hardly limited to weapons or force structure, but includes training as well. Joint exercises with the United States and its allies are important components of such training. The large-scale 'Bright Star' exercises, initiated in 1981, take place every two years. The October 1999 maneuvers involved 66,000 military personnel from 11 countries, including Egypt, the United States, France, Britain, Italy, Greece and Kuwait. The commanding officer was a US army general.[36]

Assuring high-quality manpower is an essential characteristic of modernizing armies. Egypt has gone to great lengths to improve the quality of its recruits. Radical transformation in the quality of officers and soldiers took place even before the October 1973 war, when an estimated 60 per cent of those who fought had been high-school or university students.[37] Ostensibly, Egypt should not find it difficult to maintain and perhaps even improve on these figures. Over 250,000 high-school students graduate every year, and roughly half graduate from the universities, which also serve as a pool for recruitment, especially for officers. Meanwhile, the armed forces recruit or conscript 80,000 youth and young men each year.[38] It was not surprising that *al-Ahram* reported in 1994 that 70 per cent of army personnel had attained at least a secondary education.[39]

Theoretically, the armed forces should be able to choose selectively from this pool. However, there is some evidence that both the readiness to join and the quality of those joining does not fully meet expectations. For example, in 1996 the Egyptian armed forces sent two delegations to promote conscription amongst Egypt's sizeable expatriate community – an expensive undertaking which could be justified only if the local educational system was not yielding the quality of soldiers the armed forces thought necessary for an increasingly sophisticated military.[40]

An article on the military colleges in *al-Nasr* also suggests that the Egyptian military does not always recruit at the level it would like. The 1996 article urged high-school achievers to consider a military career, by arguing that the military colleges in which they were to be educated and trained were better than their civilian counterparts. It provided strong evidence of competition from the engineering and computer programs in Egypt's top universities.[41] From the photos and the cadets interviewed, though, it is clear they are not succeeding in recruiting Egypt's urban and Western-ized elite. While the armed forces is an avenue for upward mobility in Egypt, the type of people who use this route are usually less educated and more rural in origin. An analysis on Egyptian educa-tion in the English-language *al-Ahram Weekly* reported that the average expenditure on rural students in the state school system was only 28.5 per cent of that expended on urban students.[42]

WHO IS THE ENEMY?

Almost all of Egypt's capabilities, equipment, and deployment of forces are concentrated on one front, to engage one opponent only: the Israel Defense Force. The Egyptians have made this explicit since the Badr-96 exercises in 1996, in which they specifically named Israel as the training target.[43] In the early 1990s, the target was left unnamed. According to an official description, the Badr-96 exercises in Safajeh took place over the course of ten days, beginning with a mechanized infantry battalion landing on a beach supported by navy, air force and air defense operations. As the battalion penetrated the hinterland, it was augmented by border guards, shock troops, paratroopers and specialized units from the engineering, chemical and electronic warfare corps.[44] According to Amos Gilboa, 'The Badr-96 exercise held in summer of 1996 reflects both the state of Egyptian battle-readiness and the target for such extensive operations. The exercise was supposed to be a response to an [Israeli] attack on the Egyptian front in which the Egyptian army first engages in a defensive battle and then switches to a counterattack, and finally takes over the whole of the Sinai including limited penetration over the international border.'[45]

Another large-scale operation, the Jabal Pharon exercises, conducted on 22 April 1998, was also focused on improving assault capabilities against Israeli forces. It was carried out by the Third Field Army, positioned along the central and southern part of the Suez canal. Air, navy, air defense, paratroopers and specialized forces participated in the exercises. The project focused on fighting in desert, mountainous and coastal areas, a combination of topographic features found mainly in the Sinai.[46]

DEVELOPING NON-CONVENTIONAL WEAPONS

Egypt's linkage between the arms build-up and the Israeli front is even more pronounced in its efforts at enhancing its non-conventional capabilities. In the conventional sphere, Egypt can, at least partially, justify its enhancement of rapid deployment capabilities on the need to project power in the Gulf in conjunction with other forces. Abd al-Mun'im Sa'id has even placed this goal within a broader Egyptian foreign policy transition that stresses geoeconomic rather than geostrategic concerns. He argued that since the 1991 Gulf War, Egypt must project its power in the region to assure Egyptian economic interests related to oil, employment and remittances.[47] An attempt to create a joint Egyptian–Syrian security umbrella for the Arab Gulf states along these lines in the 1992 Damascus Protocol failed.

This is not the case for non-conventional weapons. Egyptian sources make almost no mention of non-conventional capabilities and stress that Egypt is mainly focused on achieving at least deterrence, if not conventional parity, with Israel. There is, however, a danger that US aid frees resources for developing non-conventional weapons. Egypt has chemical warfare plants, is cooperating with North Korea in developing ballistic missiles, and has purchased from North Korea Scud-C missiles with a range of 600 km, placing most of Israel in their reach.[48] Egypt, along with Syria, has consistently refused to sign the Chemical Weapons

Convention as long as Israel refuses to sign the Nuclear Non-Proliferation Treaty.[49]

CIVIL–MILITARY RELATIONS: THE MILITARY AND THE FUNDAMENTALISTS

According to Phillipe Droz-Vincent, the Egyptian military – or at least its higher echelons and front-line troops – are a privileged elite for good reason: 'In Egypt, among the centers of power possessed by the regime, the police and the army are often the sole recourse.'[50] Egypt's president relied on the army in 1981, when Sadat was assassinated, and again in 1986, when the poorly paid and poorly armed Central Security Forces (CSF) mutinied. The CSF itself was established in 1977 in the wake of the food riots in January that year – the most serious popular rebellion against the Egyptian regime since the army came to power in the 1952 coup. Mubarak has built up the CSF significantly, hoping it would counterbalance the military's power.[51]

During the 1980s and 1990s, Egypt witnessed extreme acts of religiously inspired violence. Over 1,000 people were killed between 1991 and 1996 alone. The most infamous, though hardly the bloodiest, event was the fundamentalist attack on tourists in Luxor in November 1997, in which 58 people were killed.[52] The army has played only a minor part in the fight against these fundamentalists. For example, in the Luxor incident its role was limited to the evacuation of 14 wounded to Cairo in army transports, from which they were transferred to a military hospital by army helicopters.[53] The fight against terrorism is not, therefore, perceived as a task that the armed forces must address directly. Nevertheless, senior military officials frequently warn that during waves of increasing violence, the armed forces might become engaged.[54] The Egyptian armed forces' role has thus far mainly concentrated on providing a decisive deterrent force positioned in the background.

The regime's cautiousness is hardly puzzling. Involvement in suppressing growing Islamic fundamentalist violence risks exposing the army as well to fundamentalist infiltration. President

Sadat's assassins included a colonel on active service, as well as a reserve lieutenant-colonel. While Mubarak has built up the CSF significantly, he was forced in the wake of the February 1986 riots to dismiss 20,000 of its members, probably due to Islamist infiltration. The assassination of a high-level undercover agent, Major General Rauf Khayrat, during the riots could have only been possible through the complicity of high-ranking officers.[55]

The Egyptian military has gone to great pains, chiefly through the establishment of military cities, to isolate military personnel from civilian society in the hope of stemming such infiltration. Journals brought out by the military attempt to delegitimize fundamentalist ideologies and the groups that voice them. 'The Extremists Commit Major Sins in Order to Avoid Small Ones', reads the title of one article by General Muhammad Shabal, the retired general and Islamic commentator in *al-Nasr*. In the article, he attempted to demonstrate that the fundamentalists are willing to kill over minor matters such as the separation between men and women in the universities and women's dress.[56] The article claims that the doctrine of the extremists in Algeria and Egypt is identical. Another article condemned on religious grounds the use of religion in inciting communal hatred against the Copts, affirming that those doing so 'are neither Muslims nor Egyptians'.[57]

Although the army is kept in the background, the regime has made sure to implicate it in the struggle against the fundamentalists by trying such prisoners in military courts.[58]

SOLVING THE PUZZLE – THE MILITARY AND THE ECONOMY

How, then, does Egypt solve the problem of improving the quality of personnel and equipment at a time of declining budgets? Part of the answer lies with the military's ability to find alternative sources of income. As Picard noted already in the 1980s, the reduction of military budgets in the Arab world led to a search for funding through privileged, often monopolistic, activities in the marketplace. The actors could be military organizations,

military-owned companies, or senior and retired military personnel engaged in businesses with a connection to the armed forces.[59]
The military justified this role as both seeking self-sufficiency (al-
iktifa'a al-thati) and the armed forces' need to supplement civil
institutions in working to 'institutionalize' (taqnin) the state.[60]
Both motivations were considered in keeping with the widely
accepted tendency to expand the meaning of national security to
include economic and social welfare. While in the West this often
reflected the importance of private economic actors within the
state, at the expense of allocations to the military, in Egypt, the
new more economically oriented concept of national security was
manipulated to enhance its privileged role in the state and the
economy.

These underpinnings can be examined in the relationship
between the military and arms production, over which the state
has an exclusive monopoly. In the words of former Minister of
State for Military Production, Muhammad al-Ghamwari: 'The
state will not permit any sector to own military industry because
of its role in producing military material for the armed forces.'[61]
The military's monopoly over military production is moreover
guaranteed by emergency legislation that effectively prevents any
possibility of monitoring the industry by the legislature and the
press. In October 1999, the People's Assembly extended Law No.
49, passed in 1974, for another three years,[62] despite the vociferous
objections of opposition parties. In addition, there is no legislative
oversight whatsoever in regard to the military budget.

The government facilitated military expansion in the economic sphere well beyond these limits through the Administration
of National Service Projects, created in January 1979.[63] By 1994,
this organization ran 16 factories employing 75,000 workers, with
40 per cent of its production geared to the civilian market in the
form of agricultural machines, fodder, cables, medications, pumps
and ovens. Companies owned by the military expanded into areas
such as water management and the production of electricity, to
the chagrin of civil ministries.[64]

As Egypt's cities expanded outward, the military made big
profits by selling land formerly used for army bases or developed
by using soldiers as cheap labor. According to Akhbar al-Yawm, by

1994 the army had made one billion Egyptian pounds from land development deals in the Suez area alone. The military has also been accused of smuggling, through the two free trade zones under its control in Suez and Port Said.[65] In addition, the army is paid by the government for its work combating illiteracy in the desert periphery, educating the inhabitants of Upper Egypt, organizing medical expeditions to the western desert, providing water to nomads and producing and distributing medicines.

The military's economic mandate has effectively been extended since the early 1990s. In 1996, the minister of state considered development projects to include the military's manufacturing equipment for water purification, desalination for waste water treatment, and garbage disposal.[66] Three years later the mandate was extended to 'productive sections particularly in … high-precision industries, which are difficult for other than the military production to manufacture', in addition to the 'basic needs of man, agriculture, irrigation, land reclamation and other pursuits'.[67]

By far the most important of the new areas of activity was land reclamation, or, more specifically, the military's role in the two biggest land reclamation and urban resettlement projects ever undertaken by the state. Egypt hopes that the implementation of two huge and highly contested 30-year projects, centered around the northern Sinai and the southernmost reaches of the western desert, will let Egypt disperse the country's population over 20 per cent of its land mass, compared to 5 per cent at present.

The al-Salam canal, which will feed Nile water into the Sinai peninsula, is the most advanced of the two schemes, with 420,000 acres scheduled to be reclaimed. Half the reclaimed land will go to settlement and agro-industry and the remaining half to agriculture and flower growing.[68] The Egyptian government hopes to increase the population in the Sinai to three million inhabitants, an almost ten-fold growth from its present level.

An even more ambitious venture is the New or Southern Valley project situated in the southern reaches of the western desert. The first stage of the Southern Valley project (scheduled for completion in 2017) involves canal construction, massive irrigation, agricultural infrastructure, the establishment of six large-scale cities and four free-trade zones, at a total estimated cost of 300 billion Egyptian pounds. About 35 per cent of investment will involve agriculture, with the remainder allocated to tourism and industry, especially the metallurgical and mineral sectors.[69] Water will be carried in the Toshke canal from Lake Nasser, to reach the Farafra Oasis 500 km away. The military will be responsible for planning, canal construction and earth removal.

Critics fault the projects for focusing on agriculture, in which Egypt has no significant comparative advantage.[70] Even more alarming is the diversion of water that will soon be necessary to meet Egypt's current demands, to desert areas characterized by high evaporation levels.[71] The project also pushes the lower classes for relocation, though they can rarely afford or succeed in this effort. Critics feel that the Southern Valley, especially, is far too distant and inhospitable to make population dispersion worthwhile. Doubts about this project's feasibility can be documented by the slow pace of progress regarding the more hospitable and accessible Sinai. The Egyptian authorities had hoped to increase the Sinai population in the past 20 years by one million inhabitants, but succeeded in attracting only one fifth that amount. Moreover, the authorities themselves fear that creating large urban centers in southern Sinai might facilitate fundamentalist activity, and thus harm tourism in the area.

Ostensibly, the military's participation in the project is justified on strategic grounds. Israel's successful assaults through vast stretches of wilderness have demonstrated that desert stretches, once considered an obstacle to invasion, no longer act as natural barriers.[72] The collaboration of Sinai Beduin with the Israeli administration when Sinai was under Israeli rule suggested that Egypt's security would be enhanced by settling non-Beduin Egyptians there. Incidentally, the Sinai scheme also demonstrates Egypt's defensive posture, since it would not be inclined to invest such huge amounts for civilian development and resettlement in areas where it intended to launch a military attack.

Whatever the true motives behind the grand national projects, there is no doubt that they offer ideal opportunities for the military to obtain more funds and strengthen its position within the state. Of course, the military's importance as a pillar of the regime also means that the president's oversight of that institution remains strong. He supervises the filling of senior positions and ensures that the armed forces don't get too much credit for achievements. Officers are frequently rotated and discouraged from interfering in civilian policy issues, even when these affect the military's interests.[73] In a one-month study of prime time coverage by the official television station, the military was mentioned as a news item only once. In Jordan, by contrast, the army was deemed newsworthy on 14 of 30 days. Coverage of the Egyptian military in the official Egyptian press is also scarce. This may be due to the widespread belief in the virtues of secrecy that so characterized the October 1973 war, Egypt's greatest military achievement in the twentieth century.

CONCLUSION

The Egyptian military's relationship to the political sphere represents a sobering reminder to the social scientist of just how difficult the task is of theorizing civil–military relations in the Middle East. The differences among Arab armies as institutions and fighting organizations are quite extensive.

Equally, Egypt's armed forces have elements of both modern and post-modern armies. For example, they continue to be large, yet are becoming rapidly more professional.[74] Western armies are normatively peripheral, but sociologically fused with mainstream society due to reliance on professional and technological training, professional wives and tendencies to live in civilian areas. In the Egyptian military, by contrast, there is growing physical segregation alongside a functional and economic expansion into civilian roles.

At first glance, growing physical segregation and economic role expansion should be perceived as contradictory trends: the first suggesting the modern army of yesteryear, while the latter should be seen as a characteristic of the post-modern army. The expansion of the Egyptian military into civilian, industrial and technological spheres, however, has nothing to do with the fiercely individual nature of career choices or role transformation characterizing post-modern states and their militaries. This is very much a reflection of the previous modern state and army era, and probably also reflects its earlier stages. While not quite the status of the military's involvement in the economy under Muhammad Ali, it is not radically different either.

A rent-seeking military the size of the Egyptian army suggests that the Egyptian state is a long way from making the transition to the post-modern, globally oriented service-state.[75] Egypt's poor economic prospects might not necessarily reduce the military's privileges, but at some point they could weigh heavily against its long-term prospects of keeping up with the technological advances amongst Egypt's military competitors. In the event of a conventional interstate war, this could prove to be crucial, especially against the potential Israeli foe.

NOTES

1. I would like to thank Steve Glicksman for his excellent research assistance.
2. Charles Moskos, 'Towards a Postmodern Military', in Stuart A. Cohen (ed.), *Democratic Societies and Their Armed Forces* (London: Frank Cass, 1999), p. 18. Regarding the military cities see interview with Field Marshal Muhammad Husayn Tantawi, Armed Forces Commander-in-Chief and Minister of Defense, MENA, 6 October 1994, in FBIS-NES-94-195.
3. Bernard Boëne, 'Trends in the Political Control of Post-Cold War Armed Forces', in Cohen (ed.), *Democratic Societies*, pp. 75–6.
4. Phillipe Droz-Vincent, 'Le militaire et le politique en Egypte', *Monde Arabe Maghreb-Machreq*, 162 (July–September 1999), p. 26.
5. Ahmad Ibrahim Mahmud, 'Al-Quwat al-Musallaha wal-Siyasa al-Kharijia lil Misr' (The Armed Forces and Egypt's Foreign Policy), *Al-Siyasa Al-Dawliyya*, 139 (January 2000), pp. 62–9; in a speech at the Third Field Army headquarters, Tantawi placed the president's interest in social and economic advancement before Egypt's commitment to the peace process. 'The President is keen to provide job opportunities for young people, raise the standard of living of citizens and upgrade services (health, education, food) develop utilities (water, sanitary drainage, transportation, housing) and create a new society in which new generations may enjoy security, safety and prosperity'. 'Defense Minister Notes Mubarak's Work for Development', *FBIS-NES* 1999-09-11, 11 September 1999.
6. Dr 'Abd al-Mun'im Sa'id, 'Limatha al-Hawar al-Istratiji al-Masri al-Amariki?' (Why an Egyptian–United States Strategic Dialogue?), *Al-Siyasa al-Dawliyya*, 134 (October 1998), p. 114.
7. In June 1999 alone, *al-Ahram* reported on the opening of the military hospital in Al-Arish, describing it as a 'gift to the people of Sinai' (6 June 1999), the army's contribution in the fight against illiteracy in Jiza (21 June 1999), and three articles on Egypt's peacekeeping forces on the occasion of Mubarak's visit to central Africa (24 June 1999 and 26 June 1999). In fact, five of the 15 articles published in that month in the newspaper were devoted to these matters.

8. Droz-Vincent 'Le militaire et le politique en Egypte', p. 17.
9. '1998 Annual Report on Military Expenditures – Egypt', submitted to the Committee on Appropriations of the US House of Representatives by the Department of State, on 19 February 1999, www.state.gov./www/ global/arms/98-amiex1.html.
10. For a very thorough and detailed critique of the veracity of existing budget estimates and reports by analyzing operations and operating costs, see Shawn Pine, *The Egyptian Threat and the Prospects for War in the Middle East* (Sha'arei Tikva, Israel: Ariel Center for Policy Research, 2000), pp. 31–45.
11. Anthony H. Cordesman, *After the Storm: The Changing Military Balance in the Middle East* (Boulder, CO and San Francisco, CA: Westview Press, 1993), p. 21.
12. Joseph Kechichian and Jeanne Nazimek, 'Challenges to the Military in Egypt', *Middle East Policy*, Vol. 5, No. 3 (September 1997), p. 129.
13. 3 *FBIS-NES* 95-087, 14 November 1995.
14. *FBIS-TAC-96-010.* MENA broadcast, 5 October 1996.
15. 'Egyptian Defense Minister Addresses People's Assembly Committee', *FBIS-NES-96-026*, 6 February 1996.
16. 'Egypt: Egyptian Defense Minister Attends Military Exercises', *FBIS-NES-98-112*, MENA broadcast, 22 April 1998.
17. Mahmud, 'Al-Quwat al-Musallaha', pp. 62–9.
18. Ibid., p. 84.
19. Amos Gilboa, 'Challenges to the Military in Egypt', in Mark Heller and Yiftach Shapir (eds), *The Middle East Military Balance – 1997* (New York: Columbia University Press, 1999), p. 50.
20. Sa'id, 'Limatha al-Hawar', p. 114.
21. 'Egypt's War Preparations Viewed', *Hatzofeh*, 25 September 1998, in FBIS 98-320, 11 November 1998,
22. Amos Gilboa, 'Challenge to the Military in Egypt', p. 47,
23. Ed Blanche, 'The Old and the New – Changing the Face of Middle East Airpower', *Jane's Defense Weekly*, 10 November 1999, p. 10.
24. Interview with General Ahmad Shafiq, Commander of the Egyptian Air Force, FBIS-NES 1199-1031, 20 November 1999; from *al-Musawwar*, in Arabic, 22 October 1999.
25. Sa'id, 'Limatha al-Hawar', p. 114.
26. John Keegan, 'Egypt', *World Armies* (London: Macmillan, 1983), p. 168.
27. *Hatzofeh*, 28 September 1998, Weekly Supplement, p. 6.
28. Shmuel Gordon, 'The Balance of Air Forces', in Shlomo Brom and Yiftah Shapir (eds), *The Middle East Military Balance 1999–2000* (Cambridge, MA: MIT Press, 1999), p. 60.
29. Gilboa, 'Challenge to the Military in Egypt', p. 49.
30. Eli Oren, 'The Balance of Naval Forces', in Brom and Shapir (eds), *The Middle East Military Balance: 1999–2000*, p. 85.
31. Ibid., p. 86.
32. Gilboa, 'Challenge to the Military in Egypt', p. 32.
33. Ibid., p. 54.
34. Ibid., p. 31.
35. Sa'id, 'Limatha al-Hawar', p. 115.
36. 'The Armed Forces is the Supreme School of Nationalism: MENA reports on Progress of "Bright Star 99" Exercise', *FBIS*, 1999-1021, 21 October 1999.
37. Kechichian and Nazimek, 'Challenges to the Military in Egypt', p. 126.
38. Droz-Vincent, 'Le militaire et le politique en Egypte', p. 17.
39. *al-Ahram*, 21 October 1994, cited in ibid., p. 18.
40. *al-Nasr*, 691 (January 1997), p. 7.
41. Muhammad Nabil, 'Tahqiq: Al-Kulliyat al-'Askariyya Tastaqbilu Shabab Misr wal-'Arab' (Report: The Military Colleges Enroll the Youth of Egypt and the Arabs), *al-Nasr*, 702 (December 1997), p. 5.
42. 'Dream Dropouts', *al-Ahram Weekly On-Line*, 21–27 September 2000, p. 2, www.

    ahram.org.eg/weekly/2000/500/dev3.htm.
43. Gilboa, 'Challenge to the Military in Egypt', p. 48.
44. FBIS-NES 96-176, 10 September 1996.
45. Gilboa, 'Challenge to the Military in Egypt', p. 48.
46. 'Egypt: Egyptian Defense Minister Attends Military Exercises', *FBIS-NES*-98-112, MENA broadcast, 22 April 1998.
47. Abd-Mun'im Sa'id Aly, 'From Geopolitics to Geo-Economics: Egyptian National Security Perceptions', in *National Threat Perceptions in the Middle East* (New York: UNIDIR, 1965), pp. 24–5.
48. Pine, *The Egyptian Threat*, pp. 27–8.
49. Ephraim Dubek, *Uvechol Zot Shalom: Yehasei Israel-Mitzraim* (Peace Nevertheless: Israeli–Egyptian Relations) (Tel Aviv: *Yedi'ot Aharonot*, 1998), pp. 308–9.
50. Droz-Vincent, 'Le militaire et le politique en Egypte', p. 27.
51. Kechichian and Nazimek, 'Challenges to the Military in Egypt', p. 128.
52. Meir Hatina, 'Egypt', *Middle East Contemporary Survey – 1997* (Tel Aviv: Westview Press and the Dayan Center of Middle East and North African Studies, 1999), Vol. 22, p. 306.
53. *al-Nasr*, 702 (December 1997), p. 61.
54. Droz-Vincent, 'Le militaire et le politique en Egypte', p. 24.
55. Kechichian and Nazimek, 'Challenges to the Military in Egypt', p. 128.
56. Muhammad Shabal, 'Al-Mutatarafun Yartakibun al-Kaba'ir li-Yamna'u al-Sagha'ir' (The Extremists Commit Major Sins to Prevent Minor Ones), *al-Nasr*, 673 (July 1995), p. 62.
57. Muhammad Shabal, 'Laisu Muslimun … Laisu Misriyyun' (Neither Muslims Nor Egyptians), *al-Nasr*, 704 (February 1998), p. 22.
58. Kechichian and Namizek, 'Challenges to the Military in Egypt', p. 131.
59. Elizabeth Picard, 'Arab Military in Politics: From Revolutionary Plot to Authoritarian State', in Adeed Dawisha and I. William Zartman (eds), *Beyond Coercion* (London: Croom Helm, 1988), pp. 142–5.
60. Droz-Vincent, 'Le militaire et le politique en Egypte', p. 21.
61. *FBIS-NES*-96-112, 8 June 1996.
62. *Al-Musawwar*, 19 October 1999.
63. Ahmed Y. Zohny, 'Towards an Apolitical Role for the Egyptian Military in the Management of Development', *Orient*, 4 (1987), p. 548.
64. Droz-Vincent, 'Le militaire et le politique en Egypte', p. 21.
65. Ibid., p. 28.
66. 'Egypt: Mubarak Authorized to Issue Decrees With Force of Law', FB-98-105, MENA broadcast, 15 April 1998.
67. 'New State Minister for Military Production Interviewed', *FBIS-NES*-1999-1020, *al-Musawwar*, 19 October 1999.
68. Barbara Smith, 'A Survey of Egypt: Making the Desert Bloom', *Economist*, 20 March 1999.
69. 'New State Minister for Military Production Interviewed', *FBIS-NES*-1999-1020, *al-Musawwar*, 19 October 1999.
70. Habib Ayab, 'L'eau et les politiques d'amenagement du territoire en Egypte', *Monde Arab Maghreb-Machrek*, 162 (October–December 1998), p. 77.
71. Ibid., pp. 72, 77.
72. Ibid., p. 73.
73. Droz-Vincent, 'Le militaire et le politique en Egypte', p. 25.
74. Boëne, 'Trends in the Political Control of Post-Cold War Armed Forces', pp. 74–5.
75. For a devastating but excellent account of Egypt's economic malaise, see Timothy Mitchell, 'No Factories, No Problems: The Logic of Neo-liberalism in Egypt', *Review of African Political Economy* (December 1999): 1–12 (internet version, http://proquest. umi.com).

6

The Syrian Army on the Domestic and External Fronts

EYAL ZISSER

On the evening of 10 June 2000, Syria's citizens were told that Hafiz al-Asad, who had been their leader for 30 years, had passed away. Asad was the President of the Syrian Republic, secretary-general of the ruling Ba'th Party, and head of the National Progressive Front (the formal framework for any permitted political activity in Syria, which includes the Ba'th party and six other small parties). But among the plethora of titles he carried and functions he fulfilled, Asad was also General Commander (al-Qa'id al-'Amm) of the Syrian army, holding the rank of *fariq* (lieutenant general).

The following evening, Sunday, 11 June 2000, Vice-President 'Abd-al Halim Khaddam, serving as temporary acting president, promulgated two decrees, announcing the appointment of Bashar al-Asad, the late president's son, as the general commander of the Syrian army in addition to his promotion to the rank of *fariq*, the most senior rank in the army, which his father had held.[1] Several hours later, Bashar received members of the senior officers' corps, headed by Defense Minister Mustafa Talas and Chief of the General Staff (CGS) 'Ali Aslan. They had come to offer their condolences on the death of his father, and to pledge their loyalty and complete support.[2]

The appointment of Bashar al-Asad as general commander of the army, and his subsequent election as president, marked the completion in the grooming of a man who had held only the rank of lieutenant (*mulazim awwal*) when he returned to Syria in

January 1994, following the death of his brother, Basil, in a car accident. This process was conducted under the guidance of his late father. It included rapid promotion and such accelerated military training courses as those for tank battalion commanders, and the command and staff course for senior officers.[3] Alongside this, the late president and his son effected unprecedented changes in the senior army command echelons, removing several veteran officers, members of Hafiz al-Asad's generation. These were the men who for decades had been charged with ensuring the stability and very existence of the Syrian regime. They were replaced by younger officers, mostly 'Alawis, apparently closely associated with Bashar.[4]

Hafiz al-Asad's efforts to ensure this son's standing as his heir were concentrated, at least in the initial stages, on the military. This demonstrated that the army, especially a loyal base of support within the officers' corps, remained a key source for legitimacy and political support for any Syrian leader.

Indeed, since Syria gained independence in April 1946, its history has been accompanied by the continual involvement of the military in the country's political life. In the 'Corrective Revolution' of November 1970, which brought Asad to power, military intervention of the Syrian army in the country's affairs had ostensibly reached its peak. It had been a victory for the army and for the senior officers' echelon over their rivals in the Ba'th Party institutions, the governmental apparatus, and within the Syrian public in general. However, this time this revolution was a kind of victory of the army over itself. After all, for the first time, the army stood in solid unanimity behind its commander, Hafiz al-Asad – as opposed to the military coups of the 1950s and 1960s, when army units and their commanders fought each other as a result of discord within their ranks. Asad's base in the military was reinforced by personal, familial, regional, ethnic and mainly ideological factors.

Nevertheless, a study of the period of Asad's rule (1970–2000) reveals that the Corrective Revolution was not only the peak of military involvement, but also largely the end – at least thus far – of this involvement. Indeed, in the course of the 30 years Asad was in power, he successfully subordinated the army to his rule and distanced it from involvement in the day-to-day affairs of Syrian political life. The regime was thus able to maintain prolonged political stability, with the army focusing on its military duties and becoming a more professional army. The need for professionalism became more acute with the increasing awareness on the part of the decision makers in Damascus, especially following 1967, of what they perceived as a real Israeli threat to Syria's national security.

In the course of Asad's rule, therefore, the army became an instrument in the hands of the regime not only for stabilizing its rule at home, but also for promoting Syrian national interests in the region: in Lebanon and vis-à-vis Jordan, Turkey, Iraq and mainly Israel.

The death of Hafiz al-Asad, and the rise of his son as his successor, once more raised the question of the army's role in present-day Syria. Is it indeed to be the trained, obedient watchdog of the Asad family, enabling it to maintain its rule in the country, or rather an independent locus of power, holding the key to the country's future in its own hands? Actually, when the moment of truth did arrive, the senior officers' echelon of the Syrian army stood unanimously and firmly behind Bashar. Nevertheless, many – both inside and outside Syria – cast doubt as to whether this demonstration of loyalty and support would continue for any length of time. Uri Lubrani, who served as coordinator of the Israeli activity in Lebanon for 20 years, was rather blunt in his assessment: 'They [the Syrians] have crowned a 34-year-old fellow. They made him the military commander overnight. [It is not hard to guess] what the generals in the Syrian army are thinking. I would say that he has barely a 50 per cent chance of survival.'[5]

The very fact that these doubts have surfaced bears witness to the fact that the army – trained and obedient as it may be – has remained the main player in Syrian politics. With the demise of the man who had been its master for three decades, it could sooner or later resume its previous role in the country's politics. This process might have implications for the army's capabilities in confronting the Israeli army, as well as for Syria's regional standing and, especially, its standing in Lebanon. In any event, the Syrian army, as indeed the entire Syrian state, is now at a crossroads.

THE SYRIAN ARMY – THE ROAD TO THE TOP
(1946–70)

The Syrian army began as the 'Syrian Legion', established by the French in the course of the First World War. In 1923, the French established the 'Special Forces (Troupes Specials) of the Levant' to help maintain law and order in the territories of the Levant under their control. On 1 August 1945, these forces were turned over to the governments of Syria and Lebanon and became their national armies. Ever since, these countries commemorate Army Day on this date.[6]

The French recruited volunteers for the Special Forces from among members of the minority communities and the lower classes of society. They hoped to gain from the separatist tenden-cies that had existed at that time within the minority communi-ties. The latter, for their part, as well as members of the Sunni community from the rural areas and the periphery, tended to enlist in the ranks of the Special Forces to improve their socioeconomic situation and overcome the limits of their ethnic status and con-straining communities.[7] The biography of Hafiz al-Asad provides a good example of this process. When young Asad had completed his secondary education, he wanted to study medicine in Beirut, but because his family was unable to finance his studies, he was forced to opt for a military career.[8]

Thus, the Special Forces, and later the Syrian army, became the main route of social mobility for large portions of Syrian society which, until then, had been on the sidelines of the existing socioeconomic and political order. It may also be claimed that the Syrian army became the melting pot which brought together – and to a certain degree even fused together – groups of various different backgrounds who formed personal and political alliances crossing ethnic, regional and family lines. In the course of their army service, the recruits even acquired new world-views – pan-Arab, Ba'thist, pan-Syrian views and even Communist – which they shared with other recruits from different origins and back-grounds.[9]

Given the Syrian state's weakness in the early years of its independence, the army's involvement in Syria's political life was inevitable, as happened in neighboring Arab states. There were those who viewed this involvement as unavoidable in states devoid of societal or civilian frameworks, and largely lacking an educated, politically conscious middle class capable of filling the vacuum created by the end of colonial rule. Under these circumstances, the army stood out as a modern institution, whose core – the officers' echelon – was often characterized by professional unity, ideology and a desire for change.[10]

In his book, *The Policy of Social Change in the Middle East and North Africa*, Manfred Halpern portrayed the officers' corps as representing the new salaried middle class that had emerged in the Arab world as the result of the modernization process. This class also includes teachers, administrators in the civil service and government apparatus, technicians, high school and university professors, journalists, lawyers and others. This explanation helps, at least in part, in understanding the Ba'th Revolution of 8 March 1963, which brought the Ba'th Party to power in Syria, and the Ba'th officers' echelon to rule. These officers had come from a defined social stratum, as members of minority ethnic groups, mainly 'Alawis, and Sunnis from the rural areas and the periphery. They had enlisted in the army in massive numbers, risen through its ranks, gained control of it and on that basis seized power over the entire country.[11]

Although in the 1950s and the 1960s the army did succeed in successive military coups and seized power in Syria, it just as often failed to maintain rule for any length of time. This was mainly because the joint experience gained through military service, which was to have created a common denominator for the officers and serve as a binding and unifying element, was constantly over-shadowed by power struggles within the military based on ideological, and sometimes ethnic and personal, differences. From this aspect, the army genuinely reflected the general situation of the Syrian society as being divided into factions and groups on the basis of family, ethnic affiliation and – in those years – ideology as well. The army was unable to maintain unity, since it lacked an effective hierarchy at whose apex was a commander able to enforce his will on the army's units.[12]

The Corrective Revolution which brought Asad to power in November 1970, was the first coup in which the army stood united behind its commander. However, Asad deliberately refrained from establishing a military regime, i.e., from handing the regime's institutions entirely over to army officers. He may have been motivated by doubts as to their ability to conduct the state's affairs and he may possibly have been of the opinion that military support for his regime was insufficient to confer legitimacy. Therefore, Asad preferred to base his rule on a broad political and even socioeconomic coalition. This coalition centered around the members of his own 'Alawite community, to which Asad added members of other ethnic minorities and members of the Sunni community from rural areas and the periphery.[13]

In effect, Asad established his regime as a personal, familial and even tribal and ethnicity-oriented regime. This was a regime based on ties of loyalty, mainly blood ties, between Asad and members of his family, tribe and ethnic group who had been granted key positions in the military-security apparatus. There were also patron-client ties between Asad and the members of his tribe and his community, as well as supporters from other ethnic communities who were integrated into the ruling leadership. Thus, while the army and the security forces were viewed as an important element in Asad's regime, the loyalty of the army units and senior officers to Asad was not automatic support for the military commander by a unified professional group of officers. Rather, it was the support of individuals for Asad, based on blood or patron–client ties.[14]

THE SYRIAN ARMY: ASAD'S ARMY

Despite Hafiz al-Asad's efforts to distance the army from involvement in the state's politics, ever since he took over the army had been called on repeatedly to ensure the regime's stability and even existence. Thus, for example, it was called in during the years 1976–82, in order to put down the Islamic revolt. This revolt, which at its peak at the beginning of 1980 presented a palpable challenge to the Syrian Ba'th regime, was finally quelled through the use of army and security forces. In February 1982, toward the end of the revolt, army units were sent to the northern town of Hama to suppress the uprising there. The unrest was crushed by artillery and armored units and combat helicopters, which destroyed considerable parts of the town, causing thousands of casualties among its residents.[15] A year later, toward the end of 1983, army units were used by Hafiz al-Asad to address the threat from his brother, Rif'at al-Asad, who wanted to take advantage of the president's November 1983 heart attack to ensure his status as heir. After Hafiz al-Asad recovered from the heart attack and expressed open dissatisfaction with his brother's moves, Rif'at threatened to use the elite force under his command, the 'Defense Companies' (*Saraya al-Difa*), against the president. However, Hafiz al-Asad succeeded in recruiting most of the army commanders to his side, thus forcing Rif'at to give up his efforts.[16]

Asad thus succeeded in making the army a loyal and obedient watchdog. His success was due to a number of political moves. First, he bolstered the 'Alawite presence, and even control, in the army. Most of the senior officers were 'Alawite and some were even members of his tribe, the *Kalabiyya*. Indeed, at the time of Asad's death more than 90 per cent of officers carrying the rank of general were of the 'Alawite community.[17] It seems that the military has remained the preferred path for social mobilization for members of the 'Alawi community, although some have found their way into other state or party institutions. It should also be noted that, in certain cases, for example in the wake of Asad's heart attack in 1983, the 'Alawite generals banded together in order to protect their personal and even ethnic community interests. It was this that resulted in igniting the flame which led to the struggle between Rif'at and his brother. It seems that even after Asad's death a consensus was reached among the senior officers regarding support for Bashar al-Asad, as his father's heir.[18]

Second, Hafiz al-Asad established a network of patron-client ties, whose aim was to ensure the complete loyalty and support of the army generals, mainly the 'Alawis, for him as their commander. These generals were well rewarded and even allowed to turn their units into political and economic fiefdoms, providing them with secure power and substantial financial earnings.[19] These sources of income were essential, in view of the fact that the average salary of a senior Syrian officer during the 1990s was around Syrian Pounds 8,000 ($150) a month, a very modest sum even in Syrian terms, certainly for people charged with the country's fate.[20]

Third, Asad established several security apparatuses, which strike fear into the hearts of all Syrians, but focused on the senior officers' echelon in the army. These included the Air Force Security Administration, headed by Ibrahim Khuwayji, as well as the Military Security Department, headed, since February 2000, by Hasan Khalil, who replaced 'Ali Duba who had served as head of this department since 1974.[21] Alongside these internal security apparatuses, the regime established strike forces whose task was to ensure its existence and defend it from any threat coming from within the army's own ranks or from opponents inside Syria. These units had been granted the best military equipment and personnel, almost exclusively members of the 'Alawite community. They were subordinated directly to President Asad and not to the army command. One of these had been Rif'at al-Asad's Defense Companies unit. However, after Rif'at had tried to use this unit to promote his own standing, against his brother's will, it was converted into a regular army division and subordinated to the army general command. It was replaced by the Republican Guard Division, which was established in the mid-1980s under the command of 'Adnan Makhluf, a relative of Asad's wife's, Anisa. Both of Asad's older sons, Basil and Bashar, served in this division, as now does Bashar's younger brother, Mahir. In the course of his path to becoming Syrian president, Bashar dismissed Makhluf as the division's commander, replacing him with 'Ali Hasan, an 'Alawite officer close to Bashar.[22]

Worthy of note is the care taken by Asad to integrate senior army officers into the Ba'th Party institutions, because he was aware of the importance of the role of these institutions as a meeting point between members from the different apparatuses on which his regime was based. The party provides an ideological and organizational base common to all the forces which play a role in Syrian politics: the bureaucrats of the party, government and civil service, as well as senior army officers. It has branches in the army units and security forces, which send representatives to the senior party institutions. Senior army officers are members in such institutions as the Central Committee (*al-Lajna al-Markaziyya*) and Regional Command (*al-Qiyada al-Qutriyya*), alongside party bureaucrats.[23]

These steps were sufficient to ensure Asad's control over the army and establish his rule in Syria for decades. Towards this end, he was prepared to compromise on everything having to do with the army being a professional institution. Appointments were made on the basis of political and personal convenience. Asad appointed as high army commanders his close associates, family members and sometimes personal friends on whose loyalty he could depend. Among appointments of special note was Asad's colleague from his pilot course, Naji Jamil, who served as air force commander from 1970 to 1978, although he never finished the flying course.[24] Another prominent political appointment was that of Muhammad al-Khulil, as air force commander, in the spring of 1993 – a man who in the past had been a security officer but not a pilot.[25]

This category of political appointments also included Mustafa Talas, who has served as defense minister since 1972. Talas is viewed as a ceremonial figure and has long since lost any connection to the day-to-day professional management of the army. Despite the fact that he became a frequent source of embarrassment to the regime, he remained firmly ensconced in his position, as a repayment to a loyal friend who had known Asad since 1953, when they spent several weeks together in preparation for a flying course.[26]

Another outstanding characteristic of the manner in which Asad managed things as the commander of the army was his tendency to allow officers to retain their positions for long periods. This may have had its roots in his desire to allow his senior officers to acquire professional depth and experience, but in reality was based on retaining those who had shown personal loyalty. Thus a considerable number of senior officers remained firmly fixed in their positions for a decade or more. For example, 'Ali Duba served in his post as head of Military Security from 1974–2000, Hikmat Shihabi served as Chief of General Staff (CGS), 1974–98. Such longevity became a source of stagnation for the armed forces in professional terms.

THE SYRIAN ARMY ON THE EXTERNAL FRONTS

For years, and certainly after Asad's rise to power, the Syrian regime vacillated between the need to continue relying on the army's support in ensuring its stability, and its desire to build a professional army capable of promoting Syria's national interests, mainly on the Israeli front. Internal security considerations have remained the regime's principal concern, although Asad did manage to strike some balance between these two missions.

For example, the increase in the army's size during Asad's rule – to 500,000 in the year 2000 – served the regime's domestic needs, while arising as well from the long-standing confrontation with Israel.[27] It also appears that one of the things motivating Asad to refrain from deepening the army's involvement in Syrian politics was his feeling that it had to focus more and more on the struggle against Israel. That had been the main lesson that Asad drew from the 1967 war, a defeat that greatly shaped his thinking. This war taught him that the Israeli threat was very real and demanded the recruitment of all the national resources, both Syrian and those of other Arab countries.[28]

On the eve of the war, the Syrian army numbered about 50,000 men, while on the eve of the 1973 war, it already numbered 170,000 men.[29] It was this increase in the strength of the Syrian army that allowed Asad to start the October 1973 war on the basis of an ambitious operational plan, whose aim was to occupy the entire Golan Heights. This goal was not attained in the end, but nevertheless, in the war's early days, Syria enjoyed some impressive – though temporary – achievements in penetrating the Israeli defense lines, gaining control over considerable parts of the Golan Heights and capturing the Mount Hermon post on the first day of the war. However, the end of the war was less spectacular. Israel, which gave the northern front priority because of its proximity to concentrations of population in Israel, repulsed the Syrians on the Golan Heights, pushing them towards Damascus.[30] Moreover, the war did not lead to the creation of a united Arab front, but rather shattered it. Indeed, in the wake of the signing of the Israeli–Egyptian peace agreement in March 1979, a central element in Syria's security concept collapsed: the concept of inter-Arab co-operation and coordination. Asad's efforts to establish an eastern front based on an Iraqi–Syrian axis as an alternative to the Egyptian–Syrian axis failed, and Syria quickly found itself standing alone in its struggle with Israel.[31]

Israel did not wait very long before exploiting the new regional reality created with the signing of the Israeli–Egyptian peace agreement. It quickly initiated moves designed to push Syria out of Lebanon, exploiting the domestic turmoil in Syria at the time (the Islamic revolt), in its June 1982 operation in Lebanon.[32] This war served to strengthen the feeling in Damascus that Israel posed a real threat, resulting in an unprecedented build-up of Syrian military strength. The Syrians quickly revised their concept of strategic parity. Inter-Arab coordination and cooperation was to be replaced by the building of a national strength that would allow the Syrians to fight Israel alone, with no assistance or aid from other Arab countries. Damascus's ambitious goal to achieve strategic parity with Israel was expressed in the slogan *al-Sumud wal-Tasddi* (standing fast and meeting the challenge). This slogan symbolized the two steps that the Syrian army had to take. One was achieving a defense capability that would allow it to repulse any Israeli attack. The other was mounting an attack that would enable Syria to defeat Israel.[33]

In the years following the 1982 war, the Syrian army grew considerably, almost doubling from about 300,000 men in 1983 to about 500,000 in 1985. New divisions were formed and the army was equipped with advanced Soviet weapons: fighter planes, improved long-range surface-to-surface and surface-to-air missiles and electronic war and air defense systems. These moves were meant to close, or at least narrow, the qualitative gap between Israel and Syria, which was blamed for the defeat in Lebanon.[34]

However, Syria's build-up efforts exacted a price. It demanded increasing political reliance on the Soviet Union as the sole source of weapons and political backing. More serious, this build-up effort created a substantial increase in defense spending, which Syria found difficult to maintain. In previous years, military expenditures had amounted to almost half the Syrian GNP, far beyond the officially published budget allocations. The Syrian build-up from 1982 onward to achieve strategic parity with Israel increased military expenditures even beyond this. It resulted in a severe economic crisis, which brought the Syrian economy at the end of 1985 to the brink of collapse.[35]

Asad's lesson from the economic crises of the mid-1980s was clear: Syria's resources were not sufficient for it to engage in a process of unlimited military build-up, a process necessary and even imperative if Syria wanted to continue the military struggle against Israel. The truth of this conclusion became even more evident with the collapse of the Soviet Union toward the end of the 1980s, which seriously eroded one of the main components in the Syrian national security concept. The USSR could not be relied on as the sole source of weapons and as protector when needed against Israel and its ally, the United States.[36]

During 1991, Syria participated in the war over Kuwait, playing a minor role in a coalition led by the United States against its Arab 'brother', Iraq. Despite Syria's insignificant contribution to this war, it provided the Syrian army with excellent experience on the modern battlefield, on which it was liable to find itself in a future military confrontation with Israel. One of the main lessons Syria learned was that it needed to gain a defense capability against Israel's air power.[37] As a result, Syria procured Scud-C surface-to-surface missiles from North Korea and then worked on the development of the Scud-D with North Korean and Iranian assistance. These missiles have a range that covers most of Israel's territory (600–700 kilometers) and can carry chemical or biological warheads. Thus, for the first time in the history of the conflict, the Syrians had the capability of hitting populated areas deep inside Israeli territory.[38]

When Moshe Arens became Israel's minister of defense in March 1999, on the eve of the May 1999 elections in Israel, he began promoting the concept that the Syrian army had ceased to pose a serious threat to Israel. Arens argued that, since the Syrian economy was on the brink of collapse, the Syrian army became incapable of procuring new and advanced equipment or even basic logistic items. Furthermore, this army also failed to address the technological developments and other changes that took place in the modern battlefield, thus enabling the Israeli army to increase its military and technological superiority over the Syrian army.[39] The military establishment in Israel, led by officers of the intelligence branch, came out strongly against Arens's ideas by arguing that Syrian society was better able to absorb loss of life and economic damage.[40]

Despite the growing technological gap between the Israeli and the Syrian army, the latter has invested considerable efforts in improving its capability in those areas in which it enjoys a relative advantage, or at least parity, in relation to the Israeli army, while also upgrading its training and professionalism. The Syrian army strengthened its conventional warfare capability through the procurement of advanced Russian tanks and anti-tank missiles, which can deal successfully with Israel's advanced tanks. It has also equipped itself with surface-to-surface missiles of the Scud-C and Scud-D models, in addition to which it is working on the development of biological and chemical warfare. This strengthens Syria's deterrent against Israel, neutralizing the latter's strategic advantage in nuclear weapons and long-range aircraft.[41] On the political level, Syria succeeded in preserving and increasing its strategic alliance with Iran, while at the same time taking steps to improve relations with Iraq. These other two countries are on the brink of obtaining nuclear weapons, and might – in an emergency – lend Syria the strategic depth, which it so very much lacks.[42]

As a result, however, there arose some feeling of complacency in the Syrian army despite its technological inferiority to Israel and awareness that it would lose a war against Israel. During the 1990s, for example, Syria's army tried to obtain the capability to mount a limited surprise attack against Israel on the Golan Heights, perhaps as a means to gain Israeli concessions on that territory.[43]

The fact that the Syrian army, despite its weakness, is a difficult opponent for Israel, gave Asad the ability to promote Syrian regional interests. He was able to take control over Lebanon in the mid-1980s and use Hizballah against Israel without fearing that the latter would turn its weapons against Syria. Nevertheless, when in the fall of 1998 tensions between Syria and Turkey intensified, the limitations of the Syrian army became all too apparent. It could not deploy itself and prepare to deal with Turkey, as well as Israel. The result was Syria's total capitulation to Ankara's demands to stop its assistance to the Kurdish PKK forces operating against Turkey.[44] This is a clear indication that although Syria considers all of its neighbors – Turkey, Iraq and Jordan – as posing potential threats to its national interests and to its internal stability, it still views Israel as its major enemy and most threatening neighbor.

An interesting issue is what the future role of the Syrian army might be in the event that the country would some day make peace with Israel. Worthy of mention, in this connection, are reports that several high-ranking generals opposed Syria's signing a peace agreement with Israel for fear that such an agreement would diminish the army's role in Syrian politics.[45] According to these reports, the then commander of the Syrian Special Forces, 'Ali Haydar, expressed his opposition to such an agreement in the summer of 1994, challenging President Asad. Haydar was dismissed from his post and even arrested. However, it seems that the army in general did not oppose Asad's policy, and that the Haydar episode had to do with a personal dispute between 'Ali Haydar and Asad's family.[46] Moreover, it may be assumed that even in the event of an Israeli–Syrian peace agreement being signed, the regime would continue to rely on the support of the army in order to preserve its stability and ensure its continued existence.

Syrian generals might also note how the Egyptian army became stronger after the 1979 peace agreement with Israel, obtaining advanced equipment from the United States. They can assess, however, clear reluctance on the part of American leaders to become Syria's main source of aid and weapons. At any rate, even a peace agreement with Israel would not mean any change in the view of that country as a threat. Similarly, it may be assumed that there would be no change in the way Syria looks at its regional environment, and that it will continue developing and strengthening its army.[47]

CONCLUSION

The involvement of the army in political life in Syria went along with its becoming an independent state. This involvement constantly increased, until it brought army officers into power. The rise of army officers to power reflected the emergence, as a dominant force in Syrian politics, of a socioeconomic as well as political coalition based on members of the 'Alawite community, together with members of other ethnic minorities and Sunnis from rural areas and the periphery. Army officers quite often behaved as a social stratum with a definite ethnic identity.

In the long years of Hafiz al-Asad's rule, the army, which had been the nightmare of Syrian politicians in the 1950s and the 1960s, became the lapdog of the Asad family, did its master's bidding and bared its teeth to the enemy. Asad's powerful control over the army allowed him to focus most, even if not all, of the army's efforts towards external fronts, mainly the struggle against Israel and efforts to consolidate Syria's hold over Lebanon. The Syrian army acquired professional and operational skills and considerably increased its strength and capabilities. This was not sufficient for it to be able to defeat Israel. Nevertheless, the army has apparently succeeded in coming to terms with its disadvantages, lack of funding and technological backwardness. The answers that it found in overcoming its limitations in comparison with Israel, for example the procurement of a 'poor man's' non-conventional combat means (biological and chemical weapons and surface-to-surface missiles), made it an enemy considered by Israel as posing a real threat, despite the obvious weakness that even the Syrians themselves were willing to admit.[48]

In any event, the Syrian army will continue to be a key pillar for the government and will continue to be used as an instrument in promoting the regime's interests on the domestic as well as external fronts. The question is how the armed forces will adjust to the era following the demise of Hafiz al-Asad, who enjoyed the personal loyalty of its commanders.

NOTES

1. *Tishrin*, 12 June 2000.
2. Syrian TV, 11 June 2000; see also *al-Hayat* (London), 12 June 2000; *al-Sharq al-Awsat*, 13 June 2000.
3. The official name of this course is Command and Staff (*Qiyada wArkan*). See Eyal Zisser, *Asad's Legacy: Syria in Transition* (New York: New York University Press, 2000),

p. 160; see also *al-Ba'th*, 17 April 1996; *al-Wasat*, 14 August 1997; *al-Hayat* (London), 3, 5 January 1998.

4. See Eyal Zisser, *Asad's Legacy*, pp. 160–75; Eyal Zisser, 'Will Bashar al-Asad Last', *MEQ (Middle East Quarterly)*, Vol. 2, No. 3 (September 1995) pp. 3–12; *al-Watan al-'Arabi*, 18 February, 17 March 2000.

5. *Yedi'ot Aharonot*, 23 June 2000; see also an interview with Uri Lubrani by the author, Tel Aviv, 29 August 2000.

6. For more on the establishment of the 'Troupes Specials', see Philip S. Khoury, *Syria and the French Mandate: The Politics of Arab Nationalism, 1920–1945* (Princeton, NJ: Princeton University Press, 1988), pp. 170–2, 430, 617. See also N. E. Bou-Nacklie, 'Les Troupes Specials: Religious and Ethnic Recruitment, 1916–46', *IJMES (International Journal of Middle Eastern Studies)*, 25 (1993), pp. 645–60.

7. See Bou-Nacklie, 'Les Troupes Specials', pp. 645–60.

8. See Patrick Seale, *Asad of Syria: The Struggle for the Middle East* (London: I. B. Tauris, 1988), pp. 11–13, 24–40.

9. For more, see Patrick Seale, *The Struggle for Syria: A Study of Post-War Arab Politics, 1945–1958* (London: Oxford University Press, 1965); Andrew Rathmell, *Secret War in the Middle East: The Covert Struggle for Syria, 1949–1961* (London: I. B. Tauris, 1995). See also Michael H. Van Dusen, 'Intra- and Inter-Generational Conflict in the Syrian Army' (unpublished thesis, Johns Hopkins University, 1971).

10. See Eliezer Be'eri, *Army Officers in Arab Politics and Society* (Jerusalem: Israel Universities Press, 1969).

11. See Manfred Halpern, *The Politics of Social Change in the Middle East and North Africa* (Princeton, NJ: Princeton University Press, 1963); see also Daniel Lerner, *The Passing of Traditional Society* (Glencoe, IL: The Free Press, 1959). For more on the social background of the Syrian officers, see Hanna Batatu, *Syria's Peasantry, the Descendants of its Lesser Rural Notables and their Politics* (Princeton, NJ: Princeton University Press, 1999).

12. For more, see Itamar Rabinovich, *Syria under the Ba'th, 1963–66: The Army–Party Symbiosis* (Jerusalem: Israel Universities Press, 1972); Nikolaos Van Dam, *The Struggle for Power in Syria* (London: I. B. Tauris, 1996); Van Dusen, 'Intra- and Inter-Generational Conflict'.

13. See Seale, *Asad*; Moshe Ma'oz, *Asad, the Sphinx of Damascus* (London: Weidenfeld & Nicolson, 1988); Raymond A. Hinnebusch, *Authoritarian Power and State Formation in Ba'thist Syria: Army, Party and Peasant* (Boulder, CO: Westview Press, 1990); see also Eyal Zisser, *Asad's Legacy*, pp. 25–35.

14. Seale, *Asad*, pp. 439–60; see also Zisser, *Asad's Legacy*, pp. 28–35; Eyal Zisser, *Decision Making in Asad's Syria* (Washington, DC: Washington Institute for Near East Policy, 1998), pp. 17–27.

15. See Umar F. Abdallah, *The Islamic Struggle in Syria* (Berkeley, CA: Mizan Press, 1987), pp. 88–103; see also Seale, *Asad*, pp. 316–38.

16. See Seale, *Asad*, pp. 421–40; see also Zisser, *Asad's Legacy*, pp. 155–8.

17. See Zisser, *Decision Making in Asad's Syria*, pp. 21–5.

18. See Zisser, 'Will Bashar al-Asad Last'.

19. See Zisser, *Decision Making in Asad's Syria*, pp. 17–21; Middle East Watch, *Syria Unmasked, the Suppression of Human Rights by the Asad Regime* (New Haven, CT: Yale University Press, 1991), pp. 38–53.

20. For the average salaries in Syria see, for example, *Tishrin*, 20 April 2000.

21. See Zisser, *Asad's Legacy*, p. 166; Eyal Zisser, 'The Succession Struggle in Damascus', *MEQ*, Vol. 2, No. 3 (September 1995), p. 59.

22. See Zisser, *Asad's Legacy*, pp. 160, 162.

23. For the list of new members of these committees see *al-Ba'th*, 20 June 2000; see also Middle East Watch, *Syria Unmasked*, pp. 22–53.

24. See Seale, *Asad*, pp. 323–4; Zisser, *Asad's Legacy*, pp. 34–5.

25. See Seale, *Asad*, pp. 164, 181. See also Zisser, *Asad's Legacy*, p. 166; Zisser, 'Succession Struggle', pp. 58–9.
26. See Mustafa Talas, *Mir'at Hayati* (The Story of my Life) (Damascus: Dar Talas lil-Dirasat wal-Tarjama wal-Nashr, 1992), Vol. I, pp. 264–71.
27. See Fred H. Lawson, *Why Syria Goes to War: Thirty Years of Confrontation* (Ithaca, NY: Cornell University Press, 1996); see also Yaacov Bar-Siman Tov, *Linkage Politics in the Middle East: Syria Between Domestic and External Conflict, 1961–1970* (Boulder, CO: Westview, 1983).
28. See Seale, *Asad*, pp. 117–41. See also Eyal Zisser, ' Between Syria and Israel: the Six-Day War and its Aftermath', *Iyunim Bitkumat Israel*, Vol. 8 (1998) (Hebrew), pp. 205–52.
29. See Moshe Ma'oz, *Asad*, pp. 93–113; see also Ze'ev Ma'oz, 'The Evolution of Syrian Power, 1948–1984', in Moshe Ma'oz and Avner Yaniv (eds), *Syria under Assad* (London: Croom Helm, 1986), pp. 69–82; Ze'ev Eytan, 'The Syrian Army', in Avner Yaniv, Moshe Ma'oz and Avi Kover (eds), *Syria and Israel's National Security* (Tel Aviv: Ma'arachot, 1990) (Hebrew), pp. 155–70.
30. See Seale, *Asad*, pp. 202–25.
31. Ibid, pp. 290–315; Ma'oz, *Asad*, pp. 121–42.
32. See Itamar Rabinovich, *The War for Lebanon, 1970–1985* (Ithaca, NY: Cornell University Press, 1986). See also Ze'ev Schiff and Ehud Ya'ari, *Israel's Lebanon War* (New York: Simon & Schuster, 1984). See also Mustafa Talas, *al-Ghazw al-Isra'ili liLubnan* (The Israeli Invasion of Lebanon) (Arabic) (Damascus: Mu'assasat Tishrin lil-Nashr, 1983).
33. See Amos Gilboa, 'Syria's National Security Concept', in Yaniv *et al.*, *Syria and Israel's National Security*, pp. 143–54. See also Asad's speeches during the 1980s, *Tishrin*, 9 March 1987, 9 March 1988, 9 March 1989, 9 March 1990.
34. See Ze'ev Eytan, 'The Syrian Army', in Yaniv *et al.*, *Syria and Israel's National Security*, pp. 155–70; see also Shlomo Brom and Yiftah Shapir (eds), *The Middle East Military Balance* (Tel Aviv: Jaffee Center for Strategic Studies, 2000), pp. 345–57.
35. See Eliyahu Kanovski, *What's Behind Syria's Current Economic Problems* (Tel Aviv, Moshe Dayan Center for Middle Eastern and African Studies, 1985).
36. See Zisser, *Asad's Legacy*, pp. 37–51.
37. Ibid., pp. 52–65.
38. See *Ha'aretz*, 10 November 2000.
39. *Ha'aretz*, 9 April 1999; see also interview by the author with Moshe Arens, Tel Aviv, 17 May 2000.
40. See *Ha'aretz*, 9 April 1999; see also an interview with Maj. General Amos Malka, head of the IDF's Intelligence, *Bamachane*, 9 July 1999.
41. See *Ha'aretz*, 21 July, 10 November 2000.
42. See Eyal Zisser, 'Syria', in Bruce Maddy-Weitzman (ed.), *MECS* (*Middle East Contemporary Survey*), Vol. XXI (1997) (Boulder, CO: Westview Press, 1999), pp. 674–6.
43. See *Ha'aretz*, 18, 22 August 1996, 10 November 2000; *Yedi'ot Aharonot*, 23, 30 August 1996, 10 November 2000.
44. See Eyal Zisser, 'Syria', in Bruce Maddy-Weitzman (ed.), *MECS* (*Middle East Contemporary Survey*), Vol. XXII (1998) (Boulder, CO: Westview Press, 2001).
45. *Ma'ariv*, 4 September 1994; *al-Hayat* (London), 25 October 1994; *Yedi'ot Aharonot*, 25 November 1994.
46. *Yedi'ot Aharonot*, 25 November 1994; see also Batatu, *Syria's Peasantry*, pp. 237–8.
47. See *Ha'aretz*, 24 August 1999; *Yedi'ot Aharonot*, 24 December 1999; see also 'Adil Hafiz, *Hafiz al-Asad, Qa'id wa'Umma* (Hafiz al-Asad – the Leader and the Nation) (Arabic) (Damascus: al-Markaz al-Dawli lil-Nashr wal-I'lam, 1994).
48. See a statement by Faruq al-Shar' in February 2000, *al-Safir*, 12 February 2000; see also al-Jazira TV, 24 May 2000.

7

Soldiers without Fortune: Palestinian Militarization in the Post-Statehood Era

GAL LUFT

If and when there is a Palestinian state, it will already have an operational military force. This chapter discusses the extent to which the Palestinians will invest their scarce resources in a regular army, its mission and capabilities, and the likely relations between that army and the projected state.

By 1998, it was clear that the 'Palestinian police' was a hybrid, too complex and overstaffed to be the police force designed only to preserve law and order in the Palestinian territories, yet still lacking the infrastructure required for a regular standing army.[1] The Palestinian Authority (PA), however, continued to take steps toward militarization, despite signing the October 1998 Wye River agreement, which called for reduction of the size of the Palestinian police and collection of illegal weapons. The number of firearms in the possession of the Palestinians increased, through continual efforts to smuggle weapons and ammunition from Lebanon, Egypt, Jordan and Israel into Palestinian-controlled territories.

New fighting tactics were also introduced and training improved considerably, with Palestinian company and battalion commanders taking professional courses in Egypt, Yemen, Algeria and Pakistan. In 1998, the training of Palestinian security forces was limited to small units such as platoons and companies. But by the beginning of 2000, the PA started training battalion-sized formations in combat scenarios, including gaining control of an area of land and mock attacks on Israeli army (Israel Defense Force, or IDF) posts and Jewish settlements.[2] In addition, the uprising beginning in October 2000 let many Palestinian servicemen improve their combat skills by participating in gunfire battles against the IDF and drawing important tactical lessons. This experience would be useful for the training of future Palestinian recruits.

The Palestinian legislature also contributed to the foundation of a military. In May 1998, the Palestinian Legislative Council passed the Firearms and Ammunition Law, a law enabling the production of weapons and ammunition in the Palestinian-controlled territories thus laying the foundation for an indigenous defense industry capable of producing light arms and ammunition. The Civil Defense Law regulates the activities of some of the non-uniformed apparatuses in case of national emergency. There was also discussion of a National Service Law, a euphemism for mandatory conscription.

The official position of Israeli governments has been that there could be no Palestinian army west of the Jordan River, even in the framework of a comprehensive peace deal. 'The Palestinian state will be demilitarized', wrote Ze'ev Schiff, doyen of Israeli defense analysts, '… prohibited from acquiring, developing, purchasing, or deploying major weapon systems … A constitutional cap will be put on the amount of money the Palestinian state can spend on defense and armed forces … The Palestinian state will be prohibited from having a standing army, mandatory military service, national militia or a military reserve system … The force will be prohibited from conducting military training at any level beyond that of a platoon.'[3] These stipulations reflect an unrealistic attitude. Most of Schiff's proposed preconditions have already been violated and the army of Palestine is, in fact, in the making.

PALESTINIAN MILITARY ASPIRATIONS

Aware of Israeli sensitivity on the issue, Palestinians refrained from publicly discussing their plans. Chairman Yasir Arafat's secretiveness and centralist style of governing, as well as the tense relations among Palestinian security chiefs, prevented formation of a forum to discuss Palestine's long-term security needs. But there are patterns of behavior indicating that the Palestinian strategy is to promote militarization and advance the formation of a conventional armed force, even at the expense of violating provisions of future Israeli–Palestinian peace accord.

Increased Threat Perception
The Palestinians feel a sense of powerlessness vis-à-vis the mighty state of Israel and are likely to continue to perceive Israel as their main threat, even if a state of peace exists. The Palestinians' primary fear is that of an Israeli reoccupation. Several factors are given as a basis for such concerns. For example, the Palestinians know that an invading force of an Arab coalition via Jordan has traditionally been one of Israel's primary security concerns. Israel invoked this contingency to justify the need to maintain Israeli military presence in the Jordan River valley and at the border checkpoints with Jordan. In the event of an Arab coalition threatening or implementing an attack on Israel from the east, Palestine could be invaded by IDF armored formations moving to secure the passes along the Jordan River as part of an Israeli pre-emptive attack.

Palestine's dependency on the Israeli economy is also a source of inherent weakness. In the event of deterioration in Israeli–Palestinian relations, Israel could potentially strike at the Palestinian economy simply by refusing to employ Palestinian workers, or by obstructing the movement of goods and services into Palestine by an air and sea blockade. Another perceived threat is of Israel cutting the connection between Gaza and the West Bank, the two interdependent blocks of Palestine. For the Palestinians, such action would be a case for a military response.

A second set of threats that concerns the Palestinians is domestic. Maintaining domestic stability and countering potential opposition to Arafat are the primary responsibilities of the Palestinian security forces. No fewer than five intelligence bodies are involved in intelligence gathering and spying on Palestinian government officials, competing security forces and members of the Islamic opposition. Extensive intelligence efforts are also directed toward members of Palestinian militia groups and Fatah activists abroad. In the event that an agreement with Israel grants Palestine control over joint borders with either Jordan or Egypt, the Palestinian army will have to prevent cross-border infiltration of insurgents attempting to undermine the regime.

The collective threat perception of the Palestinian society is likely to enhance their desire for a formidable military body to protect their nascent country and its regime.

The Militarization of Palestinian Society

Since the establishment of the PA in 1994, the 'uniform' culture has pervaded every sector of Palestinian society. Yasir Arafat, dressed in military fatigues and carrying a firearm, has become a military as well as civilian leader of a nation in arms. Members of the security services are very visible and one out of every 50 PA residents is affiliated with the security establishment. Military parades and ceremonies are common, and the Palestinian media regularly show pictures of the armed forces in action.

The most striking indicator of the militarized society is the mobilization of the younger generation. Palestinian scout groups and the Fatah youth movement, the Shabiba, include semi-military activities, like parades, marching drills and martial arts in their programs. Summer camps run by the PA offer teenagers experiences such as handling and firing light weapons, planning and executing mock attacks on IDF posts, and training in first aid.[4]

Young Palestinians are led to believe that a Palestinian army is in the making and that it is the historic role of their generation to serve in it. It is most likely that the establishment of a standing army and the introduction of general conscription will be viewed favorably by the public.

Bad Record of Compliance

From the very beginning of the Israeli–Palestinian peace process, it was clear to both sides that the right of self-government would include the right to bear arms. Agreements signed between Israel and the Palestinian Authority – the 1994 Cairo Agreement, the 1995 Interim Agreement (Oslo II) – provided for the establishment of a Palestinian police force but also imposed strict limitations on its size, structure, responsibilities and weapons. These limits, how-ever, were constantly violated. The 1995 Interim Agreement (Oslo II) allowed the PA to employ no more than 30,000 police officers. In reality, the number of men in the Palestinian security services ranges between 41,000 and 45,000. The agreement also set a 15,240 limit on the number of firearms owned by the police. Here, too, the PA has a bad record of compliance. It is hard to determine precisely the number of weapons in the PA, but it is estimated to be four times the permitted number. Some of the weapons are held by civilian members of the Tanzim group of Fatah activists. The Tanzim often acts outside any control by the official security forces, as was seen in the riots beginning in 2000, when armed civilians opened fire at IDF troops and Israeli civilian targets.

Severe discrepancies also exist between the types of light weapons allowed by the agreement – including pistols, rifles and machine guns of 0.3" or 0.5" caliber – and the weapons that the PA actually held. The Palestinians have reportedly obtained anti-armor missiles, rocket propelled grenades, light mortars, land mines and hand grenades. It is also asserted that the Palestin-ians obtained shoulder-launched anti-aircraft missiles and truck mounted anti-aircraft guns.[5]

The structure and composition of the Palestinian security services are likewise incompatible with the provisions of Oslo. Israel acknowledged the need for a civil police to deal with pure law enforcement, a public security service to perform security related missions such as joint patrols, a preventive security service to prevent acts of harassment, violence and retribution, a presi-dential security force to protect Yasir Arafat and other VIPs, an intelligence service to combat terrorism and prevent incitement to violence, and emergency rescue services. In addition, Israel allowed the PA to establish a coastal police. Although only seven services are recognized by the agreement (see Table 7.1), the PA employs at least 12 security apparatuses, including military police, aerial police, military intelligence and an enigmatic special security force specializing in special operations. The proliferation of security forces applies Arafat's long-standing strategy of 'divide and rule'. By and large, the security services are hostile to one another and expend endless effort spying on and monitoring each other. This system ensures that no security chief obtains too much power to endanger Arafat's regime.

TABLE 7.1:
PALESTINIAN AUTHORITY SECURITY APPARATUSES

Force	Estimated Troops	Function
National Security Force*	14,000	Border control and joint patrols
Civil Police*	10,000	Law enforcement and riot control
Preventive Security Force*	5,000	Gather information on Israel and opposition movements
Presidential Security*	3,000	Protecting Arafat and other VIP and installations
General Intelligence*	3,000	Counter-espionage, counter-terrorism
Military Intelligence	Several hundred	Monitoring opposition activists
Military Police	Several hundred	Prison maintenance, security for VIPs, law enforcement
Special Security Force	Several hundred	Information-gathering on PA security forces
Coastal Police*	1,000	Protecting Gaza's territorial water
Civil Defense*	Several hundred	Rescue operations, first aid training
Customs and Excise Police Force	Few hundred	Controlling incoming goods and commercial fraud
University Security Service	Few hundred	Preserving law and order in campuses
Air Force	Few hundred	Maintenance and operation of aircraft

Note: *Services allowed by the Cairo Agreement.

The PA's bad record of compliance with security-related provisions is a harbinger of things to come. It shows that, on matters related to their own security, the Palestinians do not see themselves bound by signed agreements, and there is no indication that this behavior will change once the Palestinians achieve statehood.

Disproportional Defense Spending

The PA's conduct indicates that it is not only inclined to invest more resources in security than were prescribed by the agreements, but much more than most countries in a similar stage of development are willing to invest. The size and structure of the Palestinian security forces impose a heavy burden on the Palestinian economy. Almost one-third of the $1 billion annual budget of the PA is spent on salaries for security personnel. The percentage of the PA's defense expenditure as part of its gross domestic product surpasses that of most Middle Eastern countries, including Lebanon, Syria, Egypt and Iran.[6] This level of expenditure does not leave enough resources for infrastructure, health, welfare and education. It reflects national priorities rather than real security needs.

Demographic-Economic Incentives

The Palestinian population is one of the youngest in the world; 73 per cent of the population of the West Bank and Gaza is younger than 35 years old. More than 100,000 Palestinians are between 18 and 22 years old and the struggling Palestinian economy cannot offer them employment opportunities. Unable to find jobs, young frustrated Palestinians could join opposition movements and threaten the stability of the regime. Many Palestinians, among them speaker of the Palestinian Legislative Council, Ahmed Qurie (Abu Ala), believe that a large armed force will be a major job provider and that the only way to contain the resentment of the unemployed masses, keeping them off the streets, is by drafting them and instilling in them discipline and ideology.[7]

WHAT KIND OF ARMY?

The December 2000 round of Palestinian–Israeli negotiations in Washington demonstrated the different approaches that Americans, Israelis and Palestinians have to Palestinian militarization. Whereas President Clinton referred to the future state of Palestine as a 'non-militarized state', and the Israelis used the term 'demilitarized state', the Palestinians insisted on the more confining definition of 'a state with limited arms'. These are not differences of semantics, but of substance.

Palestinian legislators, diplomats, security chiefs and academics seem to be in agreement about the symbolic, as well as the functional, necessity of some form of a Palestinian army after statehood is proclaimed. 'A state', said police chief General Ghazi Jabali, 'is not worth anything without an army that protects its civilians'.[8]

There is little agreement among Palestinians, however, on the military's purpose, its size, functions and structure, nor on the organization and the nature of civil–military relations. Those who object to the establishment of a strong, heavily equipped army are mainly concerned that an oversized army will become a liability on the Palestinian economy, sapping resources for economic development. Another cause for concern is the conduct of the Palestinian security forces: their abuse of power, human rights violations, and involvement in crime and corruption. The behavior of the security apparatuses has caused many Palestinians to feel they are living in a police state. This raises concerns among many that a concentration of power in the hands of a dominant armed force could undermine any hope for Palestinian democracy.

'As a nation heading toward independence, I don't think that we need a military power in the traditional sense', said General Nasr Yusuf, director general of Palestinian Public Security and Police Forces, 'because our state will never enter into an arms race with Israel.'[9] Most Palestinians agree with this assertion. They realize that no matter how strong the Palestinian army will become, it will never be as strong as the IDF. The PA's expenditure on defense is only 3 per cent of Israel's. Any attempt to enter an arms race with Israel would be detrimental for the Palestinian economy. The size, the organization and the strength of the Palestinian army will therefore be designed to address the specific threats Palestine faces.

There are different views on what would constitute the acceptable force structure for the Palestinians. Yezid Sayigh suggested that, since maintaining both a defense force and a police force might prove too costly, the Palestinians should study options for a single formation, such as a national guard with responsibility both for law enforcement and for border security.[10] Some officials insist that Palestine should have, in addition to a ground force, an air transportation wing and a small navy to secure lines of communication and protect Gaza's territorial water.

One of the dilemmas the Palestinians will face is whether to equip their army with heavy weapons, such as tanks and artillery, or to keep it equipped strictly with light arms, as Israel demands. From the economic point of view, procurement of heavy arms would be a considerable burden. A first-class tank comparable to the Israeli Merkava 3 costs $3–5 million. Tank ammunition costs $750–2,500 per round. Maintenance and training costs are also onerous. Low-grade equipment will not match the IDF's capabilities and would still place a heavy toll on the Palestinian economy. The total Palestinian expenditure on defense in the year 2000, for example, is equivalent to what Israel pays to purchase, maintain and train one top-of-the-line tank battalion or three sophisticated F-15I jets. With such a disparity of military and economic power, the Palestinians are likely to have little incentive to invest in the development of an armored corps.

In addition to the relatively high costs of heavy weapons and the political implications of violating the agreement with Israel in such a way, there is another obstacle to establishing a heavily equipped military. The Palestinians suffer a scarcity of training grounds for heavy formations. Tank and artillery ranges require a lot of vacant space, such as the densely populated Gaza Strip and the mountainous West Bank lack. Without sufficient training, it is doubtful whether the Palestinians would ever be able to develop meaningful fighting capabilities of heavy formations. It is possible, however, that the Palestinian army will strive to obtain long-range weapons such as howitzers, mortars and rocket launchers. For the Palestinians, artillery pieces are somewhat strategic weapons that would enable them to threaten strategic targets in Israel and deter it from attacking Palestine, in the event of rising tension between the two countries.

The same limitations that apply on the ground apply to a greater degree in the air and at sea. Currently, the PA has a small aerial unit that operates a tiny fleet of seven transport aircraft and helicopters. Although about 200 Palestinians have reportedly undergone training as fighter and helicopter pilots, only a small fraction of them are young and fit enough to serve as pilots in a Palestinian air force. The only airfield, at Dahaniya in the Gaza Strip, is too small to accommodate a large air fleet. Following independence, Palestine is not likely to enjoy full sovereignty over its air space, as it is used by and considered essential for the training of the Israeli air force. It is very unlikely that Palestine will develop a significant air force, even in the long run. It is likely, however, that over time, the extent of civil air transportation will increase. Some of the civilian planes could serve military purposes, such as aerial photography and delivering military articles between the West Bank and Gaza (assuming that an air strip will be constructed in the West Bank).

At sea, it seems that Palestine is not likely to make serious progress toward building a significant naval force. The 13 craft owned by *Shurta Bahariyya*, the PA's coast guard, are mostly small Zodiac boats with no fighting capability. The Palestinians' first priority after independence would more likely be to invest in a commercial fleet, rather than a maritime force. In the longer run, Palestine is likely to opt for patrol boats and frigates. Arab countries in the process of modernizing their fleets may provide Palestine with vessels taken out of service. Since air and sea platforms cannot be hidden from the IDF's intelligence gatherers, it is unlikely that Palestine will be engaged in serious effort to challenge Israel in these domains.

DEVELOPING MEANS OF DETERRENCE

Owing to their tactical inferiority, the Palestinians realize that they are likely to fare poorly in an all-out one-on-one confrontation with Israel. The Palestinians are likely to adopt a defensive doctrine, the main pillar of which would be the emphasis on deterrence capability vis-à-vis Israel. Instead of investing in measures to prevail over Israel in the battlefield, the Palestinians are likely to seek means to deter Israel from using force against them. The following options are some of the main means of deterrence Palestine might consider:

1. Entering into defense treaties with fellow Arab nations. By entering into defense treaties with Arab nations, the Palestinians would send a message to Israel that a military attack on Palestine would automatically invite intervention by other militaries. Knowing that an attack on Palestine would result in a regional confrontation could well deter Israel from using force against its weak Palestinian neighbor. On the negative side, however, such agreements could trigger an Israeli response.

2. Developing long-range capabilities. The cheapest, most effective way to deter Israel from attacking Palestine would be to develop military capabilities that could inflict damage on a variety of strategic targets in Israel. The proximity to Israel's population centers would enable the Palestinians, even with primitive artillery pieces, to cover major Israeli cities. In addition, Palestinian artillery could reach strategic targets, such as critical road junctions, oil and gas farms, communication installations, power stations, industrial complexes, IDF bases and headquarters, government buildings, cultural centers and, most importantly, Israel's sea and air ports. The development of a Palestinian artillery corps would be the most cost-effective step. Artillery pieces such as 122 mm and 130 mm towed guns, katyusha rocket launchers, and 120 mm and 160 mm heavy mortars are easily obtained and cheaply maintained. Israel would naturally take into consideration the heavy price its civilian population might pay in the event it were to attack Palestine.

3. Acquiring non-conventional capabilities. Even an impressive build-up of artillery forces would not suffice to offset the Palestinian inferiority in firepower vis-à-vis the IDF. Palestine is not likely to be able to develop an air force, while the Israeli air force could inflict heavy damage on Palestine. In addition, Israel is known to have developed a nuclear arsenal to be used as a weapon of last resort. The logic of developing a non-conventional capability could also apply to Palestine. Several incentives could influence the Palestinians to introduce non-conventional weapons. First, their availability. Artillery shells and 122 mm rockets armed with chemical warheads have been

developed and are being produced by Arab countries like Syria and Iraq. This ammunition is easily transferred and cheaply stored and maintained. The Palestinians could smuggle such ammunition into their territory and store it in underground warehouses. Second, their versatility. Chemical ammunition can be launched from standard artillery pieces and does not require the extra cost of procuring launchers. Third, medium-range artillery pieces cannot be intercepted by Israel's ballistic missile defense system, the Arrow, that is being developed to counter non-conventional threats from distant countries like Iran and Iraq. The 1991 Gulf War, in which Iraq used missiles – albeit ineffectively – against Israeli civilian centers could be taken as a lesson by the Palestinians. Fourth, seeking to obtain such weapons has become a means to enhance national pride and the country's prestige. The desire to become a player taken seriously in the region and to increase the Palestinians' self-esteem could tempt Palestine to look toward the non-conventional option. Again, though, this would carry a significant danger of Israeli pre-emptive retaliation, as well as being the cause of significantly raised tensions.

Each one of the three courses of action would present Israel with a new set of strategic challenges not known since 1967. Israel could not sit by idly in the face of such a change in its strategic environment, and would be prone to take punitive action against Palestine. This makes Palestine a perfect candidate to become a casualty of the well-known 'security dilemma' in international relations: defensive measures one side undertakes to enhance its own security may be judged by the other side to have possible offensive purposes that endanger its security and hence require it to take measures of its own.

Any attempt by the Palestinians to enhance their security by adopting deterrence against Israel would ultimately leave Palestine less secure, economically damaged and diplomatically ostracized. Yet while such behavior would be highly self-defeating, history shows that the Palestinians are capable of taking action which contradicts their self-interest. Hence, these developments cannot be excluded.

IS PALESTINIAN MILITARIZATION INEVITABLE?

Assuming that an Israeli–Palestinian peace agreement includes a Palestinian pledge to accommodate the Israeli 'no army' red line, would Israel be able to enforce such a provision if the Palestinians continue to be determined – despite the agreement – to have their own army? If so, for how long? What mechanisms are needed for verification and monitoring of such an agreement? Who will inspect, and what will be the penalties, if violations occur?

History provides us with a few cases in which sovereign countries accepted, whether willingly or reluctantly, demands by their neighbors or patrons to limit their militaries to a certain size or to avoid using certain types of weapons. While in some cases such restrictions succeeded – as with Japan after the Second World War – they far more often led to negative, sometimes catastrophic, consequences. Germany after the First World War was almost completely demilitarized by the victorious allies. The Versailles Treaty, which went into effect on 10 January 1920, forbade conscription and limited the number of German troops to 100,000. The German General Staff was disbanded, as was the entire defense industry, and construction of aircraft, battleships heavier than 10,000 tons, submarines, tanks and heavy artillery was prohibited. To enforce compliance, the allies established a heavily staffed control commission, which was allowed to conduct on-site inspections throughout Germany.

But the German aspiration to restore its position as a leading European power could not be suppressed. It took Germany less than 15 years to destroy the disarmament regime, beginning with covert activities. In 1927, the control commission ceased to exist and evasions could proceed almost without disturbances. Twelve years later, when the Wehrmacht marched into Poland, Germany was Europe's strongest military power.[11]

Following the Second World War, another country, the Republic of Korea under Syngman Rhee, experienced the fallacy and dangers of the 'light army doctrine'. In June 1949, the last US occupation force left Korea, and responsibility for the defense of the Korean peninsula was left in the hands of the South Korean Army. As the Cold War intensified, the United States, South

Korea's chief patron, fearing unnecessary friction with the Chinese and Soviet Communists in Asia, saw great danger in allowing South Korea to become a regional military power. Rhee's army was, therefore, denied armor and heavy artillery, and was supplied with only the necessary means to combat the mounting internal guerrilla activity. The June 1950 invasion of North Korea into the south revealed how poorly prepared the South Korean army was to meet the country's security challenges. In four days, North Korean troops stormed the south and took its capital, Seoul, leading to the bloody Korean War.

Other examples reinforce this experience, including Iraq's violations of the Nuclear Non-Proliferation Treaty (NPT) and the gradual decline of anti-Iraq sanctions. The unwillingness of a country to abide by restrictions, plus international apathy or unwillingness to act toughly to enforce them, make imposed demilitarization a questionable tool.

In its relations with the PA, Israel has proved reluctant to act decisively against Palestinian violations of previously signed agreements. Even the government of Prime Minister Benjamin Netanyahu – which put the compliance issue at the top of its priority list in the 1998 Wye Plantation negotiations – was unable to make progress on this point. Israeli military officials have repeatedly expressed indignation at the weak response of Israel's civilian leadership to the ongoing violations. The most disturbing phenomenon, the military warned, as in the September 1996 and May 2000 riots and the intifada that began later that year, was when Palestinian policemen and Tanzim activists opened fire at IDF soldiers. Israel submitted a list of those holding weapons illegally and policemen suspected of misconduct, but the PA ignored Israel's demand to punish the violators.[12]

Security officials also gave the alert against the growing activity of Palestinian security forces in areas under Israeli security jurisdiction, such as parts of the West Bank and East Jerusalem. In this case, too, demands to discontinue the Palestinian security services' operations not coordinated with Israel went unheeded. Despite the PA's failure to comply with the agreements, Israel indicated that it was willing to move forward in the peace process. This lax attitude created a feeling among the Palestinian security officials that there was a wide gap between Israel's declared policies regarding the PA security forces and its actual willingness to enforce these policies.

The militaristic tendencies of the nascent state and its poor record of compliance with signed agreements leave little hope that Palestine will live up to its obligations in the long run. After all, why would a proud nation that so far has not failed to adopt any symbol of state sovereignty, from a parliament to a postal stamp, agree to accept such intervention in its domestic affairs? Why would a nation that invests so much of its resources in security, and which perceives itself to be under existential threats, accept ongoing, intrusive limitations on the principal instrument of defense? The answer is that the acquiescence is quite likely tactical. The Palestinians know that as long as their army is kept 'light', they can always present it as 'an improved police force'. After all, the line between an army and a lightly armed police force is often blurred. Once statehood is achieved, the Palestinians will be able to find ways to scuttle Israeli attempts to verify and enforce the demilitarization clauses of the agreement.

As a sovereign state, Palestine would enjoy a free exchange of goods with the rest of the world through Gaza's harbor and airport, allowing it to import a large variety of military articles, including heavy weapons. Smuggling is also possible, as was seen during the late 1990s with the use of tunnels in the Rafah section of Gaza's Egyptian border, arms transfers through the Jordanian–Israeli border, and arms sales by Israeli criminals. While many operations were thwarted by Israeli security forces, large amounts of firearms and explosives, including weapons stolen from IDF bases, found their way into the PA. With Palestine a state, Israel will be unable to prevent the import of light arms into the West Bank and the Gaza Strip. Monitoring the import of heavier weapons such as tanks, armored personnel carriers and artillery pieces – transported mainly by sea – could be discovered more easily.

One of the most difficult challenges Israel would face following Palestine's establishment would be to formulate a policy of sanctions and penalties to deal with future Palestinian breaches of the agreement on security-related matters. Intolerable breaches might include Palestinian deployment of anti-aircraft missiles in an attempt to disrupt Israel's air traffic, the acquisition of Weapons of Mass Destruction, an invitation or deployment of foreign forces in Palestine, support of terrorist groups, and the signing of bilateral or multilateral defense treaties with fellow Arab states. Such actions could prompt such counter-measures as economic sanctions, the termination of employment of Palestinian workers in Israel, an air and sea blockade, and the obstruction of free movement between Gaza and the West Bank.

STRATEGIC IMPLICATIONS OF MILITARIZED PALESTINE

The emergence of a Palestinian army in the West Bank and Gaza Strip could also change the nature of inter-Arab military alliances and the possibility of a wider regional confrontation between Arab armies and Israel. Palestinian control over the Jordan River valley would enable the Palestinian military to operate jointly with Iraqi, Jordanian or Syrian armies. Such a situation would enhance the possibility of a full-scale war between Israel and an Arab coalition.

Palestine's main contribution to the coalition effort would be the disruption of the IDF's mobilization system by creating chaos and confusion in Israel. Since the backbone of the IDF is its reserve units, the speed of their call-up and deployment carries strategic importance, especially in the event of a surprise attack. Israel's miniscule size, reliance on reserve forces, congested traffic and the IDF's use of a limited number of transportation routes (many of them through mountainous terrain) could be an Achilles heel easily exploited by the army of Palestine.

The emergence of a threat from the east would force the IDF to send armored reserve formations to the eastern border. These units would have to force their way through narrow corridors, possibly under the Palestinian army's direct fire. However, Palestinian success in disrupting IDF units from moving to the front in the case of a full-scale war would probably not have a decisive effect on the outcome. The IDF would apply enough air cover to allow reinforcements to reach the front line early enough to confront enemy forces crossing the Jordan River, even if their arrival were subject to delays and losses.

145

Another scenario, elaborated by Professor Yuval Steinitz, describes a Palestinian invasion into Israel's rear in the event of a comprehensive regional confrontation between Israel and its Arab neighbors. Steinitz asserted that the deployment of Palestinian forces in the immediate proximity of the Israeli rear is liable to transform them into a decisive factor in any Israeli war against an Arab coalition. Lightly armed Palestinian forces could disrupt the mobilization of Israeli reservists, harass from the rear IDF units deployed along the Jordan River valley, attack air force bases with shoulder-launched anti-aircraft missiles, attack settlements and create panic and havoc in Israeli population centers in the vicinity of the West Bank. Steinitz darkened the picture even more by suggesting that the Palestinian army is capable of launching a surprise attack against Israel. Teams of truck-mounted Palestinian soldiers could successfully infiltrate deep into Israel, attacking IDF headquarters, electronic media installations, public figures and government buildings.[13]

Though some of the elements of the Steinitz scenario may not seem very plausible, it cannot be totally dismissed. Attacks by Palestinian infantry are likely to fail, since they would face highly alert IDF units that would decimate them well before they reached their destination. But even a few successful penetrations into Israeli territory could cause significant operational as well as psychological damage.

A Palestinian army could have strategic relevance even in the case of limited Israeli–Palestinian military confrontation. Years of friction and cooperation with Israel have taught the Palestinians some important facts and lessons about the IDF's operational culture, including its weak and strong points. The Palestinians have also followed with great interest Israel's operations in Lebanon against Hizballah guerillas, especially regarding the Israeli public's high sensitivity to casualties. The unilateral withdrawal from south Lebanon in 2000 created the impression among Palestinians that Israel suffered from war fatigue, and that a well-trained, dedicated guerrilla group could drive Israel out of an occupied territory.

Attempting to emulate Hizballah's success, the Palestinians are apt to resort to use of force by means of guerrilla tactics that differ from the terrorism and popular uprising responses used so far. The mountainous territory of the West Bank and the densely populated refugee camps of the Gaza Strip would constitute typical, Lebanon-like, guerilla-friendly terrain. It could take place as sporadic attacks on IDF vehicles, planting of side-bombs and mines along Israeli routes of transportation, ambushing and attacking Jewish settlements and their residents, and sabotaging Israeli civilian and military installations. The 'Lebanonization' of the West Bank and Gaza Strip is one of the strategies the Palestinians are contemplating in the event of a major showdown with Israel.

The September 1996 riots following Israel's opening of the Hasmonean Tunnel in Jerusalem were a landmark in this regard. The three days of fighting were the first opportunity Arafat had to test his soldiers' combat performance. Despite the IDF's overwhelming superiority in manpower and weapons, the Palestinian police inflicted many casualties on the Israeli army. Among the IDF casualties were three senior officers, two colonels and a brigadier general. The PA also paid a heavy price in the riots: 69 killed, but only 12 of them were police officers. Four years later, the 2000 intifada saw the Palestinian army aided by the Tanzim and other paramilitary groups.

Consequently, while the Palestinian army is still very much in the process of formation, with many decisions about its structure and doctrine still to be answered, it is also very much in existence as an important institution.

NOTES

1. Gal Luft, *The Palestinian Security Services: Between Police and Army* (Washington, DC: Washington Institute for Near East Policy, 1998).
2. *Ha'aretz*, 12 July 2000.
3. Ze'ev Schiff, *Israeli Preconditions for Palestinian Statehood* (Washington, DC: Washington Institute for Near East Policy, 1999), pp. 43–4.
4. *New York Times*, 3 August 2000, p. A1.
5. *Ha'aretz*, 23 June 2000.
6. Defense expenditure as a share of GDP for 1996 of the PA was 6.4 per cent in comparison to Egypt – 4 per cent, Iran – 5.5 per cent, Lebanon – 3.7 per cent, Qatar – 4.3 per cent, Sudan – 2.2 per cent, Syria – 6.2 per cent, Tunisia – 1.8 per cent. Adapted from Shlomo Brom and Yiftah Shapir (eds), *The Middle East Military Balance 1999–2000* (Jaffee Center for Strategic Studies, London and Cambridge: The MIT

Press, 2000).

7. See Speaker of the Palestinian Legislative Council, Ahmed Qurie (Abu Ala), speaking at the Washington Institute for Near East Policy's Soref Symposium, in Washington, DC, 7 May 1998, www.washingtoninstitute.org/media/abuala.htm.
8. Khaled Abu Toameh, 'Uniform Culture', *Jerusalem Report*, 31 July 2000, p. 28.
9. *Defense News*, 13 July 1998, p. 20.
10. Yezid Sayigh, 'Redefining the Basics: Sovereignty and Security of the Palestinian State', *Journal of Palestine Studies*, Vol. 24, No. 4 (Summer 1995), p. 10.
11. See Barton Whaley, *Covert German Rearmament 1919–1939: Deception and Misperception* (Frederick, MD: University Publications, 1984).
12. Ze'ev Schiff, 'Anger in the IDF', *Ha'aretz*, 22 May 2000.
13. Yuval Steinitz, 'When the Palestinian Army Invades the Center of the Country', *Commentary*, December 1999.

8

The Jordanian Army: Between Domestic and External Challenges

ALEXANDER BLIGH

From the 1920s into the twenty-first century, the Jordanian Arab Army (JAA) – sometimes still referred to as the Arab Legion – has served the Hashemite dynasty in eastern Palestine, Transjordan, the Hashemite Kingdom and, since 1967, in the Jordanian Hashemite nation-state that emerged in the wake of the war of that year. Nevertheless, changing political circumstances contributed very little to the nature of strategic risks, real or potential, facing this state.

Domestic, regional and international constraints affect the definition of Jordanian national interests and, consequently, the main tasks of the army. While the armed forces are a central factor in Jordanian nationalism, the only function they can fulfill on their own is maintaining the incumbent regime against any domestic threat. The Jordanian army cannot guarantee the existence of Jordan on its own, and therefore the country, at times of crisis, always requires coalitions with other regional forces.

THE CONSTRAINTS

The JAA was first created as a police force on the East Bank in 1921.[1] Its main task at that time, as today, was to protect the Hashemite rule over that territory. In spite of its involvement in the 1948 and 1967 wars – obviously external threats – the army has continued throughout this period to serve primarily as the regime's defender and it is mostly structured to be able to respond rapidly to domestic challenges. The main improvement in the second third of the twentieth century came in the context of the terrorist presence on Jordanian territory in the late 1960s, during which time the first commando battalion was established, and the first police brigade (as differentiated from local police forces).

With a population composed of a majority of Palestinians, be it 51 or 70 per cent of the total, the regime has always been on the defense in domestic terms. Palestinian participation in the Jordanian economy is significant, but their service in the armed forces is problematic at best. They are always suspected of not being fully loyal to the regime, even though their economic involvement and history of not joining with the PLO (Palestine Liberation Organization) during the 1970–71 civil war speak favorably of them in Jordanian terms. Moreover, many do identify themselves today as Palestinian Jordanians, meaning that their main focus of national identity and solidarity is Jordanian. Yet, traditional mistrust still dictates the policy of limiting the promotion of Palestinian officers in the Jordanian army: Palestinians cannot rise in combat units above the rank of major or lieutenant-colonel at most, whereas in supporting units they can reach the rank of general.

From a political standpoint, the outlook for relations between Jordanians and Palestinians seems positive. This is the result of the fact that one of the major elements of King Husayn's legacy is the existence of Jordanian nationalism as a uniting force. That ideology, analyzed by this author elsewhere,[2] is composed of several ingredients, one of them – attributes of sovereignty – referring to the Jordanian armed forces as a source of solidarity for Jordanians and legitimacy for the Hashemite rule.

References to the Jordanian army were made frequently in Husayn's public appearances. They were not made as often as references to Jerusalem, but both are used along similar lines: providing two pillars of sovereignty in the form of national symbols: one spiritual, one material. If Jerusalem is a source of inspiration and a reason for *jihad*,[3] then the armed forces are the Jordanian connection with the past, the carrier of *jihad* and the unchanged solid foundation Jordan is built on. The armed forces are, in a sense, Jordan itself, since the kingdom began with the

Arab revolt against Ottoman rule of 1915 and so did the armed forces.[4]

Identifying the armed forces with Jordan, Arabism and Islam was a recurrent motif in Husayn's speeches. On many occasions he spoke of the army being the spearhead of Jordan and its defenses, connecting all the elements of Jordanian nationalism.[5] But the king included in this category the claim that Jordan's armed forces also served the entire Arab nation, saying their prime directive is the defense of Arab sovereignty, Arab pride and Arab civilization.[6] All these expressions tie in very clearly in the king's speeches with the concept of Israel as an enemy, since this is the army that protects for the Arab nation the longest border with Israel. These references to Israel disappeared with the 1994 peace treaty, but the army continues to be depicted by the incumbent king as a symbol of nationalism and sovereignty.

Above its claimed ideological role, however, the army is first and foremost a weapon to head off domestic criticism or challenge. For example, during the deep economic crisis of 1989, Husayn explained the problem as the result of military procurement needs.[7] This connection immediately rendered impertinent any criticism regarding corruption and mismanagement, since that would seem to be an attack on the armed forces.

While that particular economic analysis was not accurate, it is quite true that the capabilities of the Jordanian army have been shaped by the severe financial constraints facing the country. Since the 1980s, Jordan has not implemented any significant military modernization program and has also suffered from an acute problem of obtaining spare parts.[8] Moreover, Jordan's siding with Iraq during the 1991 war caused a break in the channeling of funds already earmarked for Jordan by the United States and the Gulf Arab monarchies. All efforts since then to improve the Jordanian economy have not resulted in any significant upturn.

Throughout the 1990s, Jordan had a high rate of unemployment – about one-fifth of its work force – and foreign debt reached almost $8 billion. In early 1999,[9] international lenders rescheduled the kingdom's debt payments. Later that year, the International Monetary Fund complimented Jordan on its achievements, including a rise in foreign exchange reserves to $1.180 billion. Yet Jordan still faced serious external factors. The ongoing international embargo on Iraq, formerly Jordan's largest trading partner, hurt Jordan despite efforts to circumvent those sanctions. The eruption of violence in the West Bank in late 2000 reduced trade with the Palestinians, which already stood at disappointing levels from a Jordanian perspective. A severe regional drought damaged agriculture.

Jordan's basic strategic problem arises from its geopolitical situation. It is surrounded by countries that are all militarily stronger or richer than itself. Each of these states has some friction or problem with the kingdom. Syria and Iraq have ambitions to dominate Jordan. Saudi Arabia has a historical grudge in regard to past Hashemite domination over the western part of that country, and a more recent conflict arising from Jordan's 1991 support for Iraq. Israel is a historic enemy, whose dispute with the Palestinians threatens Jordan in different ways whether it flares into violence or is resolved with an agreement. The Palestinians are led by the same people who tried to overthrow King Husayn in 1970. As one observer wrote in 1989, 'Jordan will never again rule the West Bank, but the Palestinians may eventually rule Jordan.'[10] This concern is perhaps the main interest guiding Jordanian strategists to this day.

Iraq and Syria are perhaps Jordan's two most frightening neighbors. Since the Iraqi republican revolution in 1958, which deposed the Hashemite Iraqi dynasty, Jordan–Iraq relations have varied periodically from open hostility to virtual alliance. Periodically, Jordan preferred cooperation with Iraq as a better alternative to dependence on Syria.

This Iraqi orientation for Jordan was especially visible during the 1980–88 Iran–Iraq War and the 1990–91 Kuwait crisis. On both occasions, Jordan and Syria backed opposite sides in these conflicts. If Syria constituted a risk to Jordan, Syria's two-decade-long alliance with Iran made this threat even more serious. Damascus views Jordan – like Lebanon, Israel, the West Bank and Gaza Strip – as a proper part of 'Greater Syria'.

Yet if Syria has pushed Jordan toward Iraq, Israel and the American factor pulled Amman away from Baghdad during the 1990s. While Jordan once distanced itself from Israel from fear of

Iraq's reaction, the Iraqi defeat in the 1991 war helped lead to the Oslo accords and Israel–Jordan peace treaty. The United States quickly forgave Jordan – far more quickly than did Saudi Arabia and Kuwait – for its pro-Iraq policy in 1991.[11] By moving toward Israel and the United States, and even going so far as to accept high-ranking Iraqi defectors in 1995, Jordan risked confrontation with Iraq. The United States provided Jordan with an important ally that could defend it against both Iraq and Syria.

Still, in case of war between Iraq and Israel, Jordan might be caught in the middle and face a serious strategic challenge that would not be easy to solve. Thus, the Iraqi massing of forces on its western borders during the October 2000 Palestinian intifada posed as much of a threat to Jordan as to Israel. Even after a decade of international sanctions, Iraq's army remained far more powerful than that of its Jordanian counterpart.

If Iraq is currently only a potential enemy, Syria already has a proven track record of open confrontation with Jordan. Syria's planned 1970 invasion of Jordan was stopped due to an Israeli warning that it would intervene militarily.[12] In 1980, Syria, then the Soviet Union's closest Middle East ally, massed troops and threatened Jordan with a new invasion. Again, a parallel Israeli concentration of troops along the Syrian–Jordanian–Israeli border removed the danger. Tensions have recurred sporadically. As with Iraq, Jordan has periodically sought good relations with Syria in order to reduce frictions.

Similar shifts over time have marked Jordan's posture toward Israel. While Israel helped guarantee Jordan's sovereignty against Syrian and Iraqi threats, Jordan publicly viewed Israel as its main threat and enemy for many decades. Several months after Israel secretly intervened to stave off a Syrian invasion, King Husayn made a speech, in June 1981, declaring that the main problem in the Middle East is 'Israel's seizure of the entire territory of Palestine, expulsion of its people and occupation of other parts of our Arab land adjoining Palestine'.[13] Part of Jordan's strategic dilemma is how to steer a course that takes advantage of Israel's need to preserve the kingdom against more radical forces, without antagonizing other Arab states to the point that it hurts Jordanian interests. In this equation, Jordanian governments must take into account such additional factors as the United States – which wants Jordan to be friendly with Israel – and domestic Palestinian and Islamist movements that demand a strong anti-Israel stance.

Despite its public rhetoric, one of the Jordanian regime's main concerns is that the creation of a Palestinian state might lend help to a longer term Palestinian takeover of Jordan itself. The Oslo peace process revived this fear, beginning in 1993. Jordan expected that the western side of the Jordan valley would be left in Israeli hands, thus leaving a barrier between the Palestinian territories and Jordan. Israel's conditional offer to turn parts of the valley over to a Palestinian state in 2000 encouraged Jordan to rethink its strategic view.

JORDAN'S MILITARY POSTURE

The Hashemite Kingdom is not known to have an attack plan against any of its neighbors. Jordan's investment priorities in the 1990s, for example, focused on anti-aircraft and anti-tank equipment in order to fend off any attack. However, Jordan does have offensive plans on the tactical level. Such plans are to be implemented in case of a defensive war and mainly revolve around special operations, a specialty of the JAA for many years, particularly since 1996 and the establishment of the Special Operations Command for that purpose.

The overall defensive doctrine of the Jordanian forces reflects a synthesis of British and American principles, modified to suit Jordanian needs and capabilities. A key premise is that Jordan will only have to fight on one front and that in a military confrontation with Israel the kingdom will not fight alone. After the signing of the 1994 peace agreement with Israel the chances of such a confrontation are slim. Still, Jordan could expect that an Israel–Syria or Israel–Iraq confrontation could drag in Jordan and result in military operations and confrontations on its territory. This could also happen if two warring parties fought an aerial war over the heads of Jordanians.

Even though Jordan has never had any offensive posture, it did modify its defensive doctrine as a result of two crises: the 1967 war and the 1970 crisis that came close to bringing about a Syrian invasion. These events occurred some 30 years ago, but Jordan has not had other challenges that supplanted these lessons, which thus remain valid. A key element in this planning is that tanks would carry the burden of battle. The infantry, which has been made much more mobile and is still being improved, would carry out commando raids in front of the tanks and mopping-up operations behind them.

Since the implementation of reorganization programs in 1977, the Jordanian army has consisted of four divisions: two armored, and two mechanized. Their deployment has not changed for many years either: the 5th Royal Armored Division is deployed between the Iraqi border to Ramtha on the Syrian border, the 12th Royal Mechanized division is deployed from Ramtha through Umm Qays to the Zarqa River and is designed to respond to challenges both from Israel and Syria, and the 4th Royal Mechanized Division is usually deployed from Zarqa River, north of as-Salt to the Dead Sea, in order to protect Jordan on its Israeli wing. The 3rd Royal Armored Division functions as the Jordanian strategic reserve and is deployed between Zarqa, to the north-east of Amman, and Qatraneh in the south on the way to Saudi Arabia.

This deployment of forces indicates that most of the Jordanian tanks are concentrated in the Amman–Zarqa–Mafraq area, so that they are about the same distance from all major potential theatres of operation. In addition to these forces, some others underline the basic function of the JAA – protection of the regime. One brigade of Royal Guards is deployed in Amman; its troops have been picked from Beduin tribes known for their long-standing loyalty to the Hashemite family.

Last but not least on this list of units making up the backbone of the Jordanian army is the Special Operations Command, the brainchild of King Abdallah. While serving as a senior officer in 1996 he collected from all branches of the army special operations units, led by two special forces battalions (71 and 101), and two paratroop battalions (81 and 91). Attached to them are several other special operations units, equipped with advanced equipment to make them as mobile as possible. This is the command that is supposed to stop any attempt by foreign hostile forces to move into the kingdom. In other words, its main task is to buy time for the regime until an ally comes to the rescue. Equally important is the ability of the force to supplement the Royal Guards in Amman, if and when they require such help against any domestic unrest.

Aware that its forces have lacked real combat experience for 30 years, Jordan embarked in 1975 on a policy of sending its troops on international missions. In the mid-1970s, paratroop battalion 91 was sent to Oman, where it helped fight against an internal radical insurgency. More recently, Jordanian forces participated in several UN missions, mainly in the Balkans. Infantry and artillery units joined with other forces on these missions, contributing much-needed military experience while adding to Jordan's image as a peace-loving nation and trustworthy member of the international community.

The Jordanian armed forces' deployment and defensive doctrine has been a guiding light to the kingdom for many years. Three out of the four divisions are deployed along the borders ostensibly to counter any attack on Jordan. The task of the 12th Royal Mechanized division, however, is somewhat different. It is supposed to delay any Israeli advance into Syria through the Umm Qays area – a traditional route for armies invading the Damascus area from the south. Still, Israel has never been an enemy of Jordan in Hashemite eyes, and this particular responsibility is a sort of lip service to the Arab cause.

Comparing Jordan to its immediate neighbors strongly suggests that it stands no chance of resisting their standing armies. Its position gets even worse when their reserves are added. Only Saudi Arabia, which has never considered military confrontation despite its differences with Jordan, could be said to be weaker among the neighboring states. In general, then, Jordan has no ability to initiate or stand on its own in any military confrontation. Nevertheless, it can contribute to any coalition. Deploying one division along the border with Syria, another along the border with Iraq, and the rest along the border with Israel indicates a strategy of trying to hold back any invading forces until a coalition can be forged to save the regime. The regime counts on strong loyalty and good training among its ground forces and is strengthening its air umbrella, planning to have 70 to 80 F-16 fighters by about 2007.[14]

TABLE 8.1:
COMPARING MAIN MILITARY STATISTICS [15]

	Jordan	Syria	Saudi Arabia	Iraq	Israel
Active Armed Forces	103,880	316,000	126,500	429,000	172,500
Reserves	35,000	396,000		650,000	425,000
Corps		(3)		(7)	(3)
Divisions	4	12		23	8
Independent Brigades (infantry, artillery, etc.)	3	12	9	13	4
Main Battle Tanks	1,246	4,850	1,055	2,200	3,900
Self-Propelled Artillery	412	450	200	150	855
			417	310	446
Combat Aircraft	106	589			133
Attack Helicopters	16	87			

The other task of the relatively small JAA is to keep the regime in power by blocking any domestic challenge. In an indirect way, this would include the capacity to block forces that sought to attack Israel from Jordanian soil. It is important to note that the Jordanian army lacks a large reserve system, a compulsory draft, or a plan to call up major elements in the population. Owing to the fact that Jordanian Palestinians are not considered completely loyal and might use arms to attack Israel on their own Jordan built a standing volunteer army, mainly based on Beduin from traditionally loyal tribes. While this arrangement has worked to the regime's interest, some anti-regime demonstrations by Beduin in the south during the late 1980s did raise questions about that strategy.

Given the quantitative inferiority of the Jordanian army compared to all its neighbors, with the exception of Saudi Arabia, it is clear why Jordan cannot defend itself from a major attack from any of its neighbors. This strategic situation dictates key elements of Jordan's foreign policy. It must at all times ally itself with Iraq or Syria (assuming they are at odds with each other), count on Saudi neutrality, and try to ensure that Israel would not be motivated to attack Jordan. The United States also provides some protection against Iraqi or Syrian ambitions. Such a posture minimizes the danger to Jordan, though it does not rule out the possibility that it might be dragged into an unwanted war by a Syrian or Iraqi confrontation with Israel.

An additional unknown element in this situation is the Arab–Israeli factor, and especially the Israeli–Palestinian relationship in the future. A regional Arab–Israeli showdown would put Jordan in a difficult position. An Israel–Palestinian peace would be welcome, especially if it minimized the militarization of any emerging Palestinian state and any Jordanian-Palestinian common border. On the other hand, Palestinian–Israeli violence or the emergence of a Palestinian state unilaterally, which included the Jordan valley, could bring some type of future confrontation between Jordan and a Palestinian entity.

These considerations attest to the fact that Jordan is always in need of a strategic ally, stronger and more reliable than its regional allies. In the Jordanian analysis, the United States should be the force behind this alliance. But the United States itself need not necessarily dispatch troops in time of need. A long list of historical crises taught Jordan that the moral commitment of the United States to Jordan's survival usually stops short of any direct tangible moves. The most that Jordan can expect from the United States is an airlift in case of need.

Israeli–Jordanian–Turkish cooperation is definitely to the liking of the United States. Indeed, this alliance, though it has never been put to the test of a real crisis, has already helped Jordan by forcing Syria to retreat on several issues. In this context, Israel and Jordan held joint consultations on military cooperation in early 1996 and the two countries, despite their attempts to downplay their military relations, conducted several operations chasing terrorists infiltrating into Israel and returning to Jordan. In fall 1998 the commander of Jordanian military intelligence, General Bakhiti, visited Israel, perhaps to continue negotiations on the consolidation of the Israeli–Jordanian–Turkish trilateral alliance. About the same time, Jordan also participated in the Bright Star exercise held with the United States and Egypt on Egyptian soil.

Considering the worsening demographic balance in Jordan

between Trans-Jordanians and Palestinians and the prospects for a Palestinian state, which might induce irredentist sentiments among East Bank Palestinians, Jordan cannot afford to extend its army beyond its current size. Any enlargement would necessitate enlisting more Palestinians and weakening the current strong position of the East Bank Beduin.

Actually, with the economic constraints taken into account, it makes more sense for Jordan to downsize the army to about two-thirds of its current size, while maintaining its domestic function and ability to delay the progress of an advancing hostile army until help arrives. That means cutting back from four divisions to two divisions – a change to be compared with the revision from five divisions to four in the 1970s for similar reasons. It also means improving the quality of troops and equipment as far as mobile units are concerned.

The other side of that change would be modernizing the remaining units by supplying them with more improved material. Thus, in late 2000 Jordan took delivery of 44 Challenger 1 main battle tanks out of 288 scheduled eventually to be supplied by the United Kingdom.[16] Challenger is a development of the Centurion/ Chieftain line, which had been in use in the JAA for many years as its main battle tank. It took part in Operation Desert Storm, where the Iraqi forces failed to take a single vehicle out of combat, while Challenger destroyed roughly 300 Iraqi tanks.[17]

CONCLUSION

Jordan has for many years been subject to a potential threat by one or more of its neighbors, which at times has turned into open confrontation. In spite of the enormous degree of risk of war, Jordan could not put together a suitable army. The country's small size and relatively small population did not allow it to build a large standing army, and even a reserve army could not be put together, since the majority of the East Bank population is Palestinian and traditionally has been suspected by the regime of disloyalty. Under these conditions, Jordan, since its independence, has had to depend on a system of revolving coalitions.

At any given moment in its history, Jordan has been in a coalition with one of its neighbors against a potential attack by another neighbor. Those coalitions, at most times, were backed by the United States. Given the size of the army, the alliance system, and the nature of Jordanian procurement over the years, the Jordanian army's main utility has been as a tool in maintaining the incumbent regime. When it comes to real external battle it would always operate as part of a larger coalition.

Jordan is incapable of defending itself from an external enemy. Its defense is based on the presence of Arab expeditionary forces, if Israel is the enemy, and Israeli support if it faces an Arab enemy. Since the 1970 crisis, the United States is practically responsible for the kingdom's existence, usually by using diplomatic means. At times, the Israeli military served as a major deterrence force. In terms of domestic stability, the Jordanian army has reached its optimal capacity. It is loyal and fully capable of protecting the regime.

NOTES

1. On the history of the Jordanian armed forces, see P. J. Vatikiotis, *Politics and the Military in Jordan: A Study of the Arab Legion, 1921–1957* (London: Frank Cass, 1967).
2. Alexander Bligh, *The Political Legacy of King Hussein: 'Smaller Jordan' as a Nation-State* (Brighton: Sussex Academic Press, 2001), Chapter 4.
3. Speech of 1 November 1969 before Parliament, official text of his proposal: *al-Majmu'ah al-Kamilah li-Khutab Jalalat al-Malik al-Husayn bin Talal al-mu'azzam* (Arabic) [The full collection of HM King Husayn bin Talal's speeches] (Amman: 1985?), Vol. 3, 139; PRO/ FCO17/806/ NEJ1/4/[2 November 1969], from Amman.
4. 7 June 1967, *al-Majmu'ah*, Vol. 2, 597 (7 June 1967), Vol. 3, 254 (3 April 1971), 364 (15 March 1972); *Amman Home Service in Arabic*, 15 September 1971, 4:00 p.m. and 5:00 p.m. GMT, BBC Monitoring, Summary of World Broadcasts, ME/3789/A/5; 1 September 1980 *Der Spiegel* interview, *FBIS*, 8 September 1980; Husayn's interview to Jordanian press published in all Jordanian newspapers on 13 June 1989.
5. *al-Majmu'ah*, Vol. 3, 254.
6. Speech before the 28th class of graduates of the General Staff College, as broadcast by *Amman Radio*, 16 December 1987; Address to the nation, Amman Television Service, *FBIS*, 27 April 1989.
7. Address to the nation, Amman Television Service, *FBIS*, 27 April 1989.
8. *Janes's Sentinel Country Focus – Jordan*, 2 October 2000, www.janes.com/regional _news/africa_middle_east/sentinel/country_focus/jords110.shtml.
9. Following economic data based on Frederik Sladden, '1999: A Pivotal Year for Jordan's Economy', *US–Arab Tradeline*, 19 November 1999; *The Star On-line*, 11 February 1999.
10. Ze'ev Schiff, *Security For Peace: Israel's Minimal Security Requirements in Negotiations with the Palestinians* (Washington, DC: Washington Institute for Near East Policy, 1989), p. 66.

11. See George Bush, *All the Best, George Bush: My Life in Letters and Other Writings* (New York: Scribner, 1999), p. 538.
12. Henry Kissinger, *White House Years* (Boston, MA/Toronto: Little, Brown, 1979), pp. 594–631.
13. Husayn speech at Kremlin, 27 May 1981, *FBIS*, 2 June 1981.
14. *Jane's Foreign Report*, 24 August 2000.
15. International Institute for Strategic Studies, *The Military Balance 2000–2001* (Oxford: Oxford University Press, 2000), pp. 141, 143–4, 152–4.
16. *Janes's Sentinel Country Focus – Jordan*, 2 October 2000.
17. Federation of American Scientists, Military Analysis Network, www.fas.org/man/dod101/sys/land/row/challenger1.htm.

9

The Israel Defense Force: Continuity and Change

STUART A. COHEN

One of the criticisms most frequently leveled against today's Israel Defense Force (IDF) is that of conservatism. Specifically, the present force is said to lean too heavily on the laurels of its past martial successes and to lack the qualities of adaptability and inventiveness that were considered its hallmarks in an earlier era. As a result, it has been argued, the IDF has failed to keep pace with the radical nature of current shifts in Israel's strategic environment and is still committed to fighting the last war – perhaps even the last but one.[1]

This chapter subjects such charges to more detailed scrutiny. To that end, it first surveys evidence that ostensibly supports the contention that the IDF of the twenty-first century is little more than a pale imitation of its predecessor. Thereafter, in greater detail, it will go on to itemize those areas in which, beneath the surface of continuity, significant transformation of both structure and tone can nevertheless be observed. In the final analysis, I shall argue that the forces of innovation, some for better, others not, outweigh those of inertia. Although the IDF does indeed display several signs of continuity with its parentage, in many respects it is in the process of becoming a radically new force.

The evidence for continuity in Israeli military practice and thought is easily observed.

One obvious sign can be found in the country's continued commitment to remaining a 'people's' (i.e. mass) army. Most other armies in the Western and democratic modern world have dropped the draft.[2] But Israeli legislation nominally continues to impose two to three years of conscription on all (Jewish) 18-year-olds (female as well as male). It also requires all servicemen to be available after discharge for mandatory reserve duty until middle age.

The service patterns presently followed by all those troops seem equally familiar. A simple count of heads reveals that the IDF of the year 2000, much like its predecessors in previous decades, is principally a ground force. As such, it is still built to fight what some Israeli analysts have termed classic 'wars of territory' rather than up-to-date 'wars of fire'.[3]

Indeed, in terms of outward structure, very little seems to have changed since 1973 or even 1967. The ordnance, of course, has been regularly and considerably upgraded and modernized. But now, as then, the IDF's combat strength remains concentrated in large formations of tanks and motorized infantry, which are supported by what is principally a tactical air force and mobile field artillery. Even though the IDF deploys increasing numbers of missiles, both offensive and defensive, it still lacks an independent 'missile command'. Likewise, Israel's navy – although incomparably stronger than was the case even just a few years ago – remains very much the junior of the country's three services.

Finally, there are apparent continuities in Israeli military doctrines. This, admittedly, is somewhat more nebulous territory, principally because the Israeli 'style' in matters of strategic conceptualization has always been brazenly unsystematic. Its National Security Council (itself a fledgling body that still lacks any real influence) has yet to formulate a written version of an integrated national security doctrine. Similarly, neither has the IDF itself ever published anything like a comprehensive and 'official' manual of force missions, let alone subjected them to regular and systematic review. Most of the fundamental notions which have dominated the discourse of Israeli strategy for almost half a century have more often been treated as axioms to be revered, than as propositions which deserve periodic critical examination.

It has always been taken for granted, for instance, that Israel's preferred military posture is one of deterrence, primarily conventional, but in the last resort of a nuclear variety too.[4] Should deterrence fail, it has similarly been assumed the IDF would wish to fight an offensive (and if possible pre-emptive) 'short war', characterized by the deployment of conventional forces in intensive battles of maneuver, preferably on enemy territory.[5]

Those assumptions still hold. Hence, to read whatever expositions of current official Israeli security thinking is to gain a rather monotonous impression of entrenched strategic diagnosis and repetitive military prognosis. Much like their predecessors, the latest versions too stress the need for Israel to adopt a basic posture of deterrence. Likewise, they also emphasize that – should deterrence fail – Israel must strike swiftly and forcefully, and aim at the decisive destruction of Arab forces, conventional and irregular alike, in place.[6]

Striking and significant though all such signs of continuity are, they must not be allowed to mask the evidence indicating substantial – and in some cases transformatory – changes under way in the IDF. Such changes are clearest in four specific areas: the force's composition, structure, posture and its relationship with its societal and civil environment.

COMPOSITION

Indications of a shift to a form of 'professionalism' in the IDF have been apparent since around 1990.[7] Like the vast majority of their political masters, most members of the General Staff loudly proclaim the need to remain faithful to the notion of the IDF as a 'people's army', which embodies the ideal of military service as a rite of passage toward full citizenship and an all-encompassing enunciation of national identity.[8] In practice, however, they have themselves taken several of the steps that presage the gradual demise of universal conscription, not least by generating a movement toward what Moskos has termed a far more 'occupational' mode of selective enlistment. This tendency is apparent at every one of the IDF's three 'tiers' of human resource: conscripts, reservists and professionals.

Amongst conscripts, differentials between terms and conditions of service (always inherent in any military system) in the

1990s became steadily more pronounced.[9] The quantity of 18-year-olds altogether excused from service has increased, owing mainly to the steep rise in the number of ultra-Orthodox youth receiving deferments on the grounds that 'the [study of the] *Torah* is their profession'.[10] So, too, has the number of those enlisted who receive discharges long before their official terms are due to expire.

By 1995, the resultant inequalities had become so stark that the IDF began to insist on the need to supply some form of 'compensation' to those youngsters who do nevertheless complete their full terms of duty, especially when they serve in combat units. One solution was to provide them with better amenities (soldiers' clubs, etc.). Another was the institution of some form of pecuniary reward. Since 1997, front-line troops receive double the pocket money given to those who serve in rear units. Moreover, legislation passed in 1996 and updated in June 2000 specifically instituted a 'sliding-scale' of post-service financial benefits, linking the amount of the discharge grant to the number of months of active duty performed.[11]

A similar process has taken place with respect to the reserves. In this case, too, the motivating factor has been the need to repair some of the most blatant inequalities produced by the system itself. Thanks to drastic cuts in summonses to duty, reduced by over 50 per cent since 1993, reserve service – once a ubiquitous feature of many an Israeli's private life – has now become the exception rather than the norm. A study carried out by the Knesset (Israel's parliament) member Ra'anan Cohen revealed that in 1995 only one-third of the male Jews eligible for annual reserve duty were called upon. Moreover, of that number, about half served for ten days or less. Only one in ten of those summoned (2.3 per cent of the nominal complement) performed stints of 33 days or more.[12]

The following year, the head of IDF Human Resources Division, General Gideon Sheffer, admitted that only 25 per cent of listed reservists aged 21–51 actually performed any service at all, and that 90 per cent of those who do so were under 39 years of age.[13] The IDF had long advocated the need to provide some form of financial compensation to the minority who thus carried the burden of national service, and had at various times suggested providing them with tax breaks. In June 1999, the Knesset at long last accepted the IDF's reasoning, providing a cash reward to all citizens performing over 21 days of reserve duty per year.[14]

But it is with respect to the professional component that the new ethos of materialism has become most pronounced. Long gone (if they ever truly existed) are the days when talented conscripts on the eve of discharge could be expected to 'sign on' for extended terms of professional service simply in response to the call of national necessity. Gone, too, however, are the days when the IDF was itself prepared to offer tenure (with the promise of retirement on full pension at the age of 45) to virtually anyone who expressed a wish to enlist as a military professional. Matters are now much more complex. Marketplace pressures (of which the most compelling is the demand for talented personnel in Israel's booming high-tech industries) are clearly compelling the IDF to offer more attractive incentives to those whom it wishes to contract for professional service, especially in technology-based combat support units.[15] On the other hand, budgetary pressures – the most pressing of which is the rising proportion of expenses on military personnel as a percentage of the overall IDF budget – are compelling the force to become far more selective in its own employment policies.[16]

The result has been the adoption of an explicitly dualistic policy. On the one hand, successive chiefs of staff have considerably increased the various incentives being offered to personnel whose employment and retention are deemed 'essential' to the maintenance of the IDF's qualitative combat edge. Salary increases granted to this category have been maintained and fiercely defended by senior staff.[17]

Moreover, other forms of incentives have been added. Over the past few years, the IDF has opened several fast tracks for the promotion of young officers, who are also being offered an increasingly attractive package of educational, housing and other benefits.[18] At the same time, however, the IDF has clearly made it plain that these benefits are fiercely competitive, and by no means automatic. Altogether, the IDF now draws a clear distinction between what it terms 'initial professionals' (*keva rishoni*) – i.e., personnel accepted into service for probationary periods of two to three years – and 'pure professionals' (*keva tahor*). Only persons in the latter category are now entitled to receive the full range of traditional benefits (the most important of which is a full pension and, in many cases, a comparatively late retirement age); others are being discharged.[19] The first to go have been 'non-essential' servicemen, many of whose medical, construction and food services are being progressively out-sourced to civilian contractors. Chief of Staff General Ehud Barak dismissed 5,000 professionals (7 per cent of complement) during his term of office (1991–94); within his first year of office, beginning in July 1998, General Shaul Mofaz reduced their number by another 3,000.

STRUCTURE

Budgetary constraints must certainly be deemed responsible for many of the changes in the IDF composition outlined above. Although the precise costs of Israel's defense establishment to her national economy are impossible to audit with any accuracy,[20] the overall picture is nevertheless clear. Spurred in part by public and political demands for tangible peace dividends, the Treasury mandated successive cuts in the overall military budget, as measured in real terms. As a result, the proportion of Israel's GNP devoted to defense needs between 1985 and 2000 was slashed by over a half, from roughly 22 per cent to 10 per cent. During the same period, outlays on social services were increased from 14 per cent to 21 per cent.

Pressure to accelerate the pace of cutbacks in manpower, at all levels, has further been generated by several other factors. One is the massive waves of immigration from the former Soviet Union and from Ethiopia, which have created what the IDF admits to be a 'surplus' of recruits and exposed the existence of large pockets of 'hidden unemployment' in some military units. Another is the revision in the methods of computation of charges for reserve duty, once debited to social security, which are now deducted directly from the IDF's own budget.

Economic statistics, however, tell only part of the story. Probably an even more compelling spur to structural change has been the need to adapt Israel's entire military framework to shifts in the nature of her military commitments. In this context, two developments warrant particular attention.

One is the changing nature of the technological environment within which Israel's large-scale wars of the future (should they erupt) can be expected to take place. Israeli military planners have always been receptive to the notion that they need to maintain a qualitative edge over potential enemies, in order to compensate for the IDF's inherent numerical inferiority.[21] In recent years, they have displayed even more eagerness to exploit the opportunities provided by the various battlefield 'force multipliers' now available, many of which are produced in Israel's own military industries.

At the same time, however, they have also become increasingly sensitive to the requirements imposed by the introduction and assimilation of new high-tech fighting platforms and of the communications and intelligence networks which lie at the heart of what has been described as the 'Revolution in Military Affairs' (RMA).[22] Not only does the RMA mandate higher standards of proficiency and training – in order to produce the sort of 'technological warriors' who can make best use of the equipment and software at their disposal – it also requires an entirely new structure of command frameworks, which can ensure that the battle platforms and their command, control and surveillance systems are put to most efficient use.[23]

To this must be added, secondly, the pressures towards organizational restructuring generated by underlying shifts in Israel's entire strategic environment. The superstructure of the IDF's order of battle was crafted and created at a time when the principal military challenge to Israel's existence was deemed to emanate from the threat of a cross-border invasion by neighboring conventional armies, most of which possessed virtual freedom of access to the Soviet arsenal. In the terms of Israel's strategic jargon, 'basic security', i.e., Israel's very survival, fundamentally depended on the IDF's ability to deter – and if necessary to repel – massive ground attacks on Israel's perimeter, such as seemed imminent in 1956 and 1967 and took place in 1973.[24]

The collapse of the Soviet Union, together with other convulsions in the Middle East, has turned that order of priorities on its head.[25] For one thing, the immediate threat of a massive cross-border invasion has perceptibly abated. After all, Israel now has peace treaties with Egypt and Jordan and a relationship with Turkey that is clearly designed to deter Syria.

These improvements are offset, however, by a simultaneous upgrading in the status of aspects of military commitment formerly considered of only secondary importance. Israel's need to invest far more resources (including military resources) in the maintenance of what was once termed 'current security' missions – notably, the 'personal security' of citizens – was made painfully apparent during the 1990s, by both the intensity of terror attacks during the intifada and the disruption to life in Israel's northern towns by katyusha volleys launched from southern Lebanon. Even starker was the exposure of the country's vulnerability to long-range missile attacks, launched by Iraq – a non-neighboring state – during the second Gulf War of 1991.

By the last third of the 1980s (and hence, in fact, some time before the intifada had run its course and Iraqi Scud missiles were fired at Israel) this combination of twin pressures had given rise to a call to create what was popularly termed 'a smaller and smarter' IDF. Indeed, the possible implications of that phrase were fully thrashed out as early as 1987 by a subcommittee of the Knesset's Foreign Affairs and Security Committee (the Meridor Committee), which produced a specific checklist of Israel's future requirements with respect to technology, operations and structure.[26] Both General Dan Shomron (Chief of Staff 1988–91, who first minted and mobilized the 'smaller and smarter' slogan), and Ehud Barak (who waxed especially eloquent on the need to prepare the IDF for 'the future battlefield') enthusiastically endorsed these recommendations.

Hence, even though their implementation was delayed, as much by the operational distractions of the intifada and the Lebanon campaign as by organizational inertia, there was rarely any doubt that they would eventually bear fruit. An analysis of what is known of the latest IDF multi-year plans, collectively known as *Tzahal 2000*, indicates that they are now becoming reality.

Superficially, the concerns of *Tzahal 2000* seem limited to the sort of administrative detail that can make military analysts yawn with disdain. Certainly, its subject matter possesses little of the appeal conventionally enjoyed by the more ostensibly glamorous spheres of high military strategy. Nevertheless, it would be wrong to belittle its implications. Beneath the surface of its ostensibly dry content lie a series of reforms which, in the long run, promise to revolutionize the IDF's entire superstructure. Indeed, and as Gal Luft has pointed out,[27] if Israel is experiencing a 'revolution in military affairs' it is in the sphere of overall structural reforms that the evidence for that development is best found.

Three clusters of such reforms warrant particular attention. The first, and undoubtedly most fundamental, focuses on what might be best termed the force's ethos. At all levels, commanders and their troops are being encouraged to stress the virtues of professional expertise, as opposed to amateur zeal. More specifically, they are being made aware of the potential for victory promised by mastery over the information systems, which radically change not only what armies can do but also military perceptions of what might be doable. Much of the credit for this new atmosphere goes to Ehud Barak, whose enthusiasm (some say obsession) with the application of technological innovations to administrative staff work became something of a byword during his term of office as chief of staff. Virtually single-handedly, Barak bullied the IDF into adopting new management techniques[28] and into introducing computerized systems of accountancy and surveillance at all levels of command.

Under his aegis, especially, the IDF's computer unit (*MAMRAM*) and highly specialized intelligence unit (*TALPIOT*) attained additional respect, not least by receiving precedence in the recruitment and training of suitably qualified conscripts.[29] This development reached a new height in 1999 with an overhaul of the IDF's entire logistic structure. The old Quartermaster's Branch (AGA – *Agaf Afsanaut*) then became the Technology and Logistics Branch (ATAL – *Agaf le-technologiah ve-logistikah*), and with the new name came new authority. *ATAL* was given an explicit mandate to coordinate the activities of most combat-support frameworks (ordnance, munitions and medicine) and a mandate to establish its own high-tech unit (*Yachtal*) in order to centralize matters relating to munitions development and acquisition.[30] Moreover, plans exist to create the new post of 'information coordinating officer' (*katzin nihul yeda*) within each of the regional commands.

A second area of reform encapsulated in *Tzahal 2000* relates to ordnance acquisitions. Not unexpectedly, details are particularly difficult to come by. Nevertheless, the information that has been released leaves no doubt that a similarly fundamental shift in direction is underway. Indeed, it is in this area that the new balance between continuity and change might be most marked. True, the IDF continues its traditional policy of upgrading the staples of its ground, air and naval arsenals. But far more obtrusive – and significant – are its investments in the relatively new areas dictated by the changing nature of its operational commitments. Within this latter category comes, most obviously, the production of the Arrow (*Chetz*) missile defense system, whose development was authorized by the then Minister of Defense, Yitzhak Rabin, as early as 1988 (again, some time before the Scud attacks) and which was declared to be operational in March 2000.

Equally worthy of note, however, are the investments in satellite surveillance systems, Unmanned Aerial Vehicles (UAVs), precision-guided weapons, sensors (again, many are home-produced) and, most interestingly as an indication of their increasing prominence on IDF thinking, what are termed 'non-lethal weapons'. In 1999, General Dr Yitzhak ben Yisrael (who has gained a reputation as the IDF's in-house expert) specifically singled out these latter areas – rather than a new generation of fighter planes, tanks and missile boats – as those on which Israel must concentrate for the IDF to retain its qualitative edge.[31]

In order to ensure that IDF command structures will be capable of taking full advantage of such advances, *Tzahal 2000* also encompasses, finally, a far-reaching reorganization of the IDF's hierarchy. Command frameworks that were in many cases untouched for almost half a century are now being entirely recast, and structures once approached as a legacy to be cherished and preserved are now being considered as needing constant revision. The result has been a degree of organizational turbulence probably unparalleled in IDF history. This process, too, has a genealogy that stretches back into the 1980s. One early sign of change was the establishment of a Ground Forces Command in 1983. Another was the decision, taken as early as 1989, to replace the old and very inadequate civil defense framework (HAGA – staffed mainly by persons considered too old or otherwise unfit for regular military duties) with a much more powerful Rear Command (*Pikud Oref*).

These, however, were mere preludes, and it was only towards the end of the 1990s that the process of organizational change really gathered pace. In November 1997, the IDF announced the implementation of 'Spring Youth' (*Aviv Ne'urim*), a program designed to 'flatten' the military structure by granting greater managerial and budgetary autonomy to middle-range commands.[32] In July 1998, the IDF's Planning branch (AGAT) was incorporated into the General Staff branch, thus facilitating a greater degree of synthesis between short-range needs and medium-range preparations.[33] But the most important development occurred early in 1999, when a three-day General Staff seminar, chaired by Mofaz, finally authorized the establishment of the Ground Arms Command (MAZI, *Mifkedet Zero'ot Ha-Yabashah*).[34]

In this case, too, far more is involved than a mere reshuffling of existing structures and alteration of nomenclature. The new framework endows the IDF's land forces with the status of an independent arm. As such, not only does it place them on a par with the air force and navy. More substantively, it also promises to provide them with the organizational superstructure required if they are to be prepared to confront the multi-level and combined-arms nature of the future battlefield. MAZI's staff (headed by a general) is gradually assuming responsibility for the recruitment, training and build-up of all ground forces (infantry, armor, engineers, artillery and field intelligence – the latter an entirely new unit). As such, MAZI is becoming equipped to coordinate needs and priorities with respect to manpower placement and training, as well as weapons' procurement and development, and thereby greatly rationalize the utilization of resources.

The establishment of MAZI can already be counted as a success. For one thing, the transition to the new structure of recruitment and training (initially applied to just two infantry brigades and the armored corps) has been far smoother than expected.[35] What is more, and notwithstanding the distractions contingent upon the latter stages of Israel's embarrassing involvement in southern Lebanon, MAZI has already enabled the IDF to thin out command and logistic functions. Once the Lebanon imbroglio was hopefully a matter of history, Mofaz felt confident in proceeding to the next stage of his program, constructing divisional frameworks which can incorporate all the IDF's infantry brigades and ensure a more parsimonious and rational allocation of logistic and adjunct services.

FORCE MENUS

Whether or not the IDF General Staff has also formulated a coherent new set of doctrines for using the power at its disposal must remain a matter of conjecture. Certainly, its current senior command has not been able to do so by dint of practical trial and error. Almost three decades have passed since the IDF was last engaged in large-scale combat, a fact which makes the present General Staff less experienced in the exercise of senior command over sizable formations than any of its predecessors since 1948.[36] Worse still, there seems to have been no sustained attempt to substitute coherent theory for practice. Despite all the talk of the need to reformulate Israel's national security doctrine, and notwithstanding the fact that in 1996 the Minister of Defense, Yitzhak Mordechai, did establish various task forces for that purpose, no end-product appears to be in sight. Indeed, as far as is known, the task forces themselves have been disbanded.

Presumably, the IDF (and more specifically AGAT) continues to draft contingency plans with respect to future operational postures. But that exercise is, of itself, no guarantee that whatever recommendations are tabled have ever been fully debated in the General Staff, let alone approved by that forum.[37] As has always been the case, Israeli force doctrines still owe less to an organized process of reasoned analysis than to the random predilections of individual generals and ministers of defense (especially when the latter also happen to be prime minister). Indeed, and as Israel's

State Comptroller remarked as recently as his annual report of September 2000, the IDF has itself yet to formulate a coherent manual of force missions – even though it was explicitly mandated to do so by the Agranat Commission into the Yom Kippur War, a body that presented its findings over a quarter of a century ago.

All that said, various new straws in the wind can nevertheless be identified, suggesting that in this sphere, as in the others already itemized, the pressures for change in the IDF's traditional force menus have been more compelling than might initially seem to be the case. True, faith in an overall strategy of deterrence, notwithstanding the palpable erosion of its effectiveness, remains pronounced.[38] As in the past, senior figures in the Israeli defense establishment, civilians as well as soldiers, continue to warn potential foes of the IDF's ability to inflict destruction on their peoples and armies. In this context, they regularly reiterate their commitment to a policy of nuclear 'ambiguity'.[39] But once attention shifts from the declarative umbrella of general intent to the more specific details of operational and military implementation, matters appear far less familiar. For one thing, the IDF appears to be reversing its time-honored preference for maneuverability over firepower. Moreover, its once almost instinctive predilection for 'high-tempo' offensive battles which might force the enemy to a 'decision',[40] has been replaced by a more sober assessment that the IDF must prepare for more static campaigns of attrition and defense.

Significantly, such changes in posture are not limited to any particular level of potential conflict. They have begun to influence choices of force menus and of force missions with respect to both 'low'- and 'high'-intensity combat contingencies.

Within the first category, for which a better term is perhaps 'small wars', come such scenarios as a renewal of the fighting against Hizballah units in southern Lebanon and an armed confrontation with Palestinian forces of the type that began with a renewed intifada in September 2000.[41] The most widely touted prospects of 'high-intensity conflict' are another round of warfare against Syria and/or the need to protect Israel's rear against surface-to-surface missiles (some of which, it is now widely assumed, will carry unconventional as well as conventional payloads) launched from deep within Iraq or Iran.[42]

Necessarily, the nature and composition of forces to be used in each of these contingencies will vary considerably (a consideration that accounts for both the kaleidoscopic variety of the IDF's arsenal and, even more, for the recent proliferation in the number of its 'special' forces).[43] Nevertheless, the nature of the operations in all cases promises to reveal traces of a similar underlying impulse. Israel's wars of the future – unlike most of those which it was accustomed to fighting in the past – are likely to be protracted and hence not all amenable to the sort of 'in and out' measures for which the IDF once principally trained. Far from lending themselves to mobile battles of envelopment and of 'deep penetration', they will demand, from all ranks, high standards of field intelligence and surveillance, patience and defensive ability.

As the IDF only belatedly learned, those were precisely the qualities required during the unexpectedly protracted Lebanon wars and the intifada.[44] They will once again be in demand should Israel ever find herself having to conduct another large-scale ground and air campaign against an immediate neighbor (although Syria remains the most likely candidate, Egypt also occasionally turns up in intelligence assessments).[45] A battlefield saturated with thick covers of precision-guided missiles, it has long been argued,[46] is unlikely to permit the IDF to repeat its own armored campaigns of 1967 and 1973, still less to imitate the sort of ground maneuvers carried out by the US-led coalition forces against Iraq in 1991. Given the havoc which missiles aimed at Israel's rear are now likely to wreak on reserve mobilization schedules, neither can the IDF depend on being able to repeat its success of 1973 and respond to a ground attack by amassing the forces required for an immediate counter-offensive.[47] Instead, the IDF will here too have to adopt an essentially defensive posture. Rather than seek to gain theater superiority by deploying ground forces, it will have to rely more than ever in the past on the 'stand-off' potential inherent in its artillery and air firepower.[48]

The more the specter of another missile attack assumes realistic proportions, the more pronounced such emphases become. This is most apparent from the chronology of Israel's investments in the production of the Arrow anti-missile missile system and in the development of a home-grown satellite capability. Both programs commenced some time before the 1991 Scud attacks, but both were greatly accelerated by that experience. Ever since, Israeli thought with regard to the best military response to a renewed bout of ballistic warfare seems to be dominated by the strategic defense program generically code-named 'Wall' (*Homah*),[49] itself supplemented by massive investments in the development of an independent satellite surveillance capacity to be provided by Ofek-4.[50]

Supplementary options do possibly exist. The air force, for instance, has a reputation for a pre-emptive ability to strike at targets deep within enemy territory which goes back to the attack on PLO headquarters in Tunis in October 1985 (a distance of some 2,000 kilometers), to the Osiraq raid against Iraq's nuclear reactor in 1981, and to Operation Moked (the strike against Arab air fields on the morning of 6 June 1967). Indeed, its long reach was extended with the procurement, in September 1999, of 50 advanced F-16I's, with the option for buying 60 more.

In an interesting departure from previous norms, the IDF appears also to have begun to exploit the potential inherent in Israel's situation as a maritime state, and to explore the possible exploitation of the navy's growing strength in order to acquire a second layer of strategic strike capabilities.[51] Nevertheless, all such abilities to inflict 'offensive' damage in the style of the 'classic' IDF now seem to be considered secondary preferences. Where the threat of missile attacks is concerned, most military thinking in Israel seems to be predicated on the argument that deterrence, and security, now depend upon a proven ability to thwart an attacker. Hence, the best possession of an 'active defense' capability has virtually attained the status of an article of faith.[52]

THE NEW DOMESTIC ENVIRONMENT

The shift in IDF postures prompted by the changing nature of its military environment is further reinforced by even more dramatic transformations in the force's domestic status. Throughout the first quarter century of its history, the IDF basked in a climate of virtually totemistic domestic esteem. This public support constituted an essential ingredient of what has been called Israel's 'civil religion'.[53] Military service was broadly recognized to be the primary expression of citizen fulfillment. Under those circumstances, the IDF had no cause to fear that civilian agencies (whether governmental or non-governmental) might exert a restrictive influence on its behavior by intruding into professional spheres of military activity.

The principle of military subordination to political direction was, of course, widely touted and deeply ingrained. Moreover, public interest in all aspects of military behavior was high – and, indeed, deliberately cultivated – by the official orchestration of an entire panoply of activities.[54] But within those confines, the IDF enjoyed a degree of corporate autonomy that extended to the very limits of democratic acceptability. Other spheres of government – education, social welfare, international alignment, immigration and religious legislation – were publicly scrutinized with a degree of intensity that was sometimes inquisitorial. Military affairs, however, were protected by a cocoon of reverence that invariably precluded any form of public inspection whatsoever. By the same token, generals (in and out of uniform) were invested with a quasi-mythological stature and thus all but placed beyond the reach of conventional public accountability.

It has long been apparent that those conditions no longer apply.[55] Ever since the IDF first swayed on its pedestal of infallibility during the Yom Kippur War of 1973, the traditional intimacy of Israel society's 'partnership' with its army has come under increasing strain. True, military influence on all spheres of public life remains uncommonly high, as is illustrated by the number of retired generals who continue to effect a lateral transfer into politics or local government. True, too, 'motivation to service' – especially as measured by the proportion of conscripts volunteering for combat units – remains remarkably high.[56] But in other respects, overall Israeli public attitudes towards the IDF and its commanders have begun to reveal several of the characteristics of 'post-military' societies elsewhere in the Western world. Specifically, popular belief in the efficacy of the use of force has declined; so too, by similar proportions, has domestic confidence in the IDF's ability to provide Israel with security.[57]

More striking still has been the extent of public readiness to cast off the previous bounds of self-imposed restraint and subject the military and its operations to an increasing degree of domestic scrutiny.

Of all the many expressions of this latter development, three deserve particular notice.

First, and undoubtedly the most obtrusive, is the change in media coverage of the IDF. As Yoram Peri has noted, gone are the days when the press was prepared to take the announcements of the IDF spokesman at face value and even to exercise a degree of self-censorship on matters thought to affect 'national security'. Altogether more sulphurous and intrusive in style, the electronic and printed media of today in Israel have turned sensationalist exposés of alleged military mismanagement, ineptitude and corruption into a norm.[58]

Second, the IDF's relations with the civilian judicial system have followed a similar trajectory. Considerably modifying its previous readiness to bend or even suspend laws in the name of 'state security', Israel's Supreme Court now insists that IDF practice conform to civilian judicial norms. Thus, contrary to its own former practice, the Court has during the past decade evinced a growing willingness – even eagerness – to pass judgment on sensitive spheres of military conduct. As a result, several areas of intra-military activity hitherto considered the IDF's exclusive preserves have been opened up to civilian appeal. Supreme Court rulings have set new standards with respect to the limits of the authority of the Military Censor and the levels of moral conduct which IDF troops are legally bound to maintain. They have also laid down guidelines for gender integration within the ranks and specified the behavior that might disqualify promotion to senior command.[59]

Third, families of non-professional servicemen and women have likewise abandoned their once-characteristic deference to military authority. Now often organized into ad hoc associations of parents and wives, they increasingly insist that the IDF acknowledge their right to a hearing on matters affecting the welfare of their loved ones. Their demands are not limited to calls for improvements in conditions of conscript and reserve service.

Frequently, they now encompass calls for adequate representation on the military tribunals established in order to investigate deaths and injuries resulting from accidents, exercises and engagements and the right of families to personalize the epitaphs on military graves.[60] In extreme cases (such as that of the 'Four Mothers' who long campaigned for the IDF to withdraw from southern Lebanon), the arc of involvement is stretched to include the very substance of operational policy.

To attribute such phenomena to nothing more than war-weariness is, it seems, to mistake their origins and thrust.[61] In fact, they cannot be dissociated from the deeper transformations in values which, in some accounts, are said to be generating a shift towards a post-modern attitude towards military institutions and personnel throughout the Western world.[62] They are certainly fuelled, too, by the breaking of many of the bounds of restraint that once ensured a high degree of public deference in Israel towards public authority in any form.[63] Whichever the case, there can be little doubt that in Israel, as elsewhere, a serious gap has opened up between what are generically termed civilian and military cultures.[64]

That, certainly, is the feeling among senior officers. Admittedly, not all react to the new phase of societal–military relations in Israel with the near-hysteria once voiced by Chief of Staff Lipkin-Shahak.[65] But even those who are more moderate acknowledge the need to address the issue. Indeed, most now wryly concede the irony in the fact that, whereas their strategic environment has probably never been more favorable (especially now that Israel is allied in all but name with Turkey), the domestic constraints on the IDF's operational freedom of action have probably never been more severe. Given that contrast, it is hardly surprising that the retention of the IDF's position at the very core of Israel's national consciousness has become a primary military mission.[66]

The IDF's reactions to its new domestic status have generally been defensive. Contrary to the views of some of its critics, the force does not seek to recover the ground thus lost by confrontational exchanges with the societal pressures that now undermine its public authority. Instead, it is adopting a more cautious and realistic policy of accommodation with them. In practical terms, this policy translates into a concerted effort to court the IDF's domestic critics and to defuse potential military–societal conflicts long before they become operational.

Evidence for this new course turns up at virtually every point of contact between the IDF and Israeli society at large. The signs are not limited just to the IDF's adoption of a noticeably more deferential attitude toward the press and the civilian judicial system. They can also be seen in the introduction of a more user-friendly system of conscription assignments, that takes into account the wishes of the individual new recruit, and – even more so – in the allocation of a larger portion of commanders' time to contact with his or her parents. Amongst the many other steps that the IDF has taken in an attempt to bring itself into line with public expectations, particular mention might be made of its publication of an Ethical Code,[67] its new-found emphasis on gender integration and the efforts being made to reduce the incidence of sexual harassment.

In itself, the new atmosphere generated by such measures obviously has much to recommend it. But several senior IDF officers have also begun to note its possible adverse trade-offs. Specifically, they have expressed fears that societal intrusions into military affairs might impede operational effectiveness. Public insistence that the IDF reduce the number of deaths and injuries in the Lebanon in 1999–2000,[68] for instance, generated fears that an erosion in casualty tolerance might reduce effectiveness, most notably by injecting an unprecedented degree of caution into command decisions and actions. By the end of 1997, some senior officers were openly expressing concern that fear of an igno-minious 'trial by the press', possibly followed by formal legal charges, were seriously prejudicing the propensity of junior officers to take risks.[69] Hayyim Heffer, the poet whose writings did much to sustain the fighting image of the Palmach (one of Israel's pre-State militias) during the 1940s, had a few months earlier been still more explicit. 'The IDF', he warned, 'will not be the same IDF if in the wake of every accident or mistake officers become so afraid of parents that they jeopardize the main thing: initiative; the willingness to take risks; comradeship; and ingenuity.'[70]

It remains to be seen whether or not this version of what

Edward Luttwak terms *mammisimo* might also mandate what he considers to be its corollary: the adoption of an 'unheroic' form of warfare, characterized by the pre-eminence of casualty avoidance over all other military considerations.[71] What have already become apparent, however, are indications of changes in the relations between the IDF's High Command and its political masters. Here, too, a more defensive military posture seems to be becoming the norm. Even though the profile of ex-servicemen of senior rank at all levels of Israeli political life and government remains (in comparison to the situation in other democratic societies) extraordinarily high, the corporate influence of those still in uniform at the apex of the decision-making process is very much in regression. Not one of Israel's most significant recent departures in foreign and security affairs has owed anything at all to institutional military planning or even prodding. On the contrary, they were undertaken by politicians who – precisely because they were also retired generals – were able to exploit their previous military backgrounds in order to overcome explicit (and in some cases outspoken) military advice.

Thus, the IDF played no part whatsoever in the process that led to the publication of the Oslo accords in September 1993, about which Barak and Lipkin-Shahak (once apprised of their content) initially expressed considerable skepticism.[72] Similarly, the decision to withdraw IDF troops from southern Lebanon in June 2000 was entirely that of the political elite, and was taken despite Mofaz's repeated public warnings of its undesirability from a strictly military point of view. Equally significant is the manner whereby in September 2000 Barak appointed the retiring Deputy Chief of Staff, General Uzi Dayan, to head the National Security Council, despite Mofaz's objections to the fact that Dayan was still in uniform.[73]

This departure from the previous collusive pattern of Israeli civil–military relations[74] lends itself to at least two interpretations. One is that Israel's new domestic ambience (compounded by the IDF's own comparatively poor recent record of operational achievement) has generated a crisis of self-confidence in the High Command, which, in turn, has led to a form of institutional paralysis. More charitable is an alternative point of view, which regards the new balance of civil–military relations in Israel as yet another expression of the IDF's growing trend towards 'professionalization', a trend which is also apparent in other areas of military behavior.[75] Whichever the case, relations between Israel's civil and military elites has certainly entered a new phase, and one which is radically different from the country's previous experience.

CONCLUSIONS

Disentangling the ingredients of continuity from those of change in the current IDF discloses much evidence that the Force has reached a critical stage in its history. Clearly, attachment to the retention of time-honored patterns of Israel's military organization and modus operandi (an attachment which is as much cultural as empirical) remains powerful, within both the military and political hierarchies. Equally apparent, however, is the momentum generated by the perceived need to adapt the force's traditional structures, composition and order of battle to the dictates of rapid transformations in its overall strategic, technological and societal environments. The inherent contradictions between these two clusters of pressures now clamor for resolution.

NOTES

1. This point is made with particular acerbity in Martin Van Creveld, *The Sword and the Olive: A Critical History of the Israeli Defense Force* (New York: Public Affairs, 1998), especially pp. 249–355. For a milder view, see Eliot A. Cohen, Michael J. Eisenstadt and Andrew J. Bacevich, *Knives, Tanks and Missiles: Israel's Security Revolution* (Washington, DC: Washington Institute for Near East Policy, 1998).
2. James Burk, 'The Decline of Armed Forces and Compulsory Military Service', *Defense Analysis*, 8 (1992), pp. 45–59 and Karl W. Haltiner, 'The Definite End of the Mass Army in Western Europe', *Armed Forces & Society*, 25 (1998), pp. 7–36.
3. See Yitzchak Ben Israel, 'Technology and Decision – Thoughts on the IDF in the Wake of Kosovo', *Ma'archot* (Hebrew; IDF journal), 371 (July 2000), p. 40. The statistics published annually by the International Institute for Strategic Studies (IISS) support that contention. They show that throughout the 1990s the percentage of IDF army personnel (principally infantry and armor) as a proportion of the total complement remained consistent at some 70 per cent. *The Military Balance* (London: IISS, annually).
4. Avner Yaniv, 'Deterrence and Defense in Israeli Strategy' (Hebrew), *Medinah, Mimshal ve-Yahasim Beinle'umiyim*, 24 (1985), pp. 27–62, and the same author's *Deterrence*

without the Bomb: The Politics of Israel's Strategy (Lexington, MA: Lexington Books, 1987).

5. Dan Horowitz, 'The Israeli Concept of National Security', in Avner Yaniv (ed.), *National Security and Democracy in Israel* (Boulder, CO: Lynne Rienner, 1993), and Michael I. Handel, *Israel's Political-Military Doctrine*, Occasional Papers in International Affairs, No. 30 (Cambridge, MA: Harvard University Center for International Affairs, July 1973). The linkage between deterrence and a war-winning capacity has also been central to Israeli security thinking. In the words of one its architects: 'It should always be remembered that our security doctrine has always asserted that the Israel Defense Forces must maintain a deterrent force, and if this fails and war breaks out, they must win it. We have never placed the capacity to deter as against the capacity to fight, but have rather regarded deterrence and the strength to win as two sides of the same coin.' Israel Tal, 'Israel's Security in the Eighties', *Jerusalem Quarterly*, 17 (Fall 1980), pp. 13–18. The author is a former Deputy Chief of the General Staff and thereafter acted as senior adviser to successive ministers of defense.

6. Tal, again, provides a prominent example; see his *National Security: The Few against the Many* (Hebrew) (Tel Aviv: Dvir Publications, 1996). Echoes of precisely the same approach can be found in the style and content of Israeli warnings about the punishment that the IDF would inflict on Lebanon should Hizballah forces violate the cease-fire attained by the withdrawal of 2000.

7. Stuart A. Cohen 'The IDF: From a "People's Army" to a "Professional Military"', *Armed Forces & Society*, 21/2 (Winter 1995), pp. 237–54.

8. For a recent reiteration: Levi Morav, 'A Platter of Silver' (Hebrew), *Ba-Machaneh* (IDF weekly), 21 July 2000, pp. 15–17.

9. Stuart A. Cohen, 'Military Service in Israel: No Longer a Cohesive Force', *Jewish Journal of Sociology*, 39 (1999), pp. 5–23.

10. A committee established by the government in May 1998 and chaired by Judge Tal of the Supreme Court found that some 30,000 deferments of service were now granted on these grounds each year. After lengthy deliberations, the committee finally recommended that ultra-orthodox (*haredi*) students decide at the age of 24 whether they wish to continue their studies or perform a short stint of military or civil service, which would enable them to join the labor market (*Ha'aretz*, 5 April, 2000, A1). It is generally agreed that, even if implemented, these recommendations would have only marginal numerical effect.

11. *Ha'aretz*, 18 July 2000, A4.

12. For full details, see report in *Yedi'ot Aharonot*, 23 August 1996, pp. 11–13.

13. *Hatzofeh*, 3 December 1996. Since 1995 the age ceiling for reserve duty has been steadily lowered from 54 to 45.

14. *Ha'aretz*, 19 July 1999. The former Deputy Chief of Staff, General Uzi Dayan, has publicly stated that these benefits have to be further supplemented by an additional package of compensations. See interview in *Shiryon* (Hebrew journal of the IDF armored corps), 8 (May 2000), pp. 12–15.

15. On IDF awareness of this need, see *Ha'aretz*, 16 August 2000, A1, and the report of Mofaz's speech to members of the Military Industries' Forum, ibid., 12 September 2000, A6.

16. It has been calculated that between 1990 and 1996 the proportion of the IDF budget devoted to salaries and post-service benefits rose from 39 per cent to 48 per cent. Over the same period, the proportion allotted to equipment acquisitions declined from 56 per cent to 39 per cent. See Ya'akov Lifshitz, *The Economics of Security: General Theory and the Israeli Case* (Hebrew) (Jerusalem: Jerusalem Institute for the Study of Israel, 2000), p. 261.

17. On one now notorious occasion the current Chief of Staff, Mofaz, announced that he would rather shut down tank motors than cut professional service salaries, *Ha'aretz*, 30 June 1999.

18. Cohen, 'The IDF'. More recent incentives include studies towards a degree in the military academy opened in July 1999 and the promise of speedy promotion. The air force has made particularly strenuous efforts to offer prospective pilots a contract package which – although lengthier than those of the past – is also more attractive. See report in Ha'aretz, 25 July 2000, A5.

19. Amnon Barzilai in Ha'aretz, 28 April 1999, A3. On Mofaz's determination to maintain this momentum see his 'The IDF in the Year 2000: A Different Army' (Hebrew), Ma'archot, 363 (March 1999), pp. 2–9.

20. All attempts to pin down the elusive statistics, including those made by a committee set up for that purpose under the auspices of the Bank of Israel in 1984, have failed. The difficulties stem from both the secrecy that still surrounds individual items in the defense budget and – perhaps even more so – from the extent to which 'pure' defense outlays (such as reserve duty) are incorporated in ostensibly 'civilian' costs. See Lifshitz (2000), and Yehezkel Dror, 'The Politics of the Defense Budget – Comparing Western Europe and Israel', in Zvi Lanir (ed.), Security and the Israeli Economy in the 1980s (Hebrew) (Tel Aviv: Jaffee Center for Strategic Studies, 1985), pp. 204–48. For the situation during the first decades of Israeli statehood, see Yitzchak Greenberg, Calculus and Power: The Defense Budget between War and War (Hebrew) (Tel Aviv: Ministry of Defense Publications, 1997).

21. Zvi Ofer and Avi Kober (eds), Quality and Quantity in Military Buildup (Hebrew) (Tel Aviv: Ministry of Defense Publications, 1985).

22. For which the Hebrew acronym is MASHAK – mahapeichah bisdei ha-krav.

23. For a recent analysis of the needs, see General Udi Adam, 'To Be an Officer – a Profession' (Hebrew), Shiryon, 6, October 1999, pp. 47–9. The author is head of man-power resources in the Ground Forces Command (Mifkedet Zero'ot Ha-Yabashah, MAZI).

24. The link between the challenges to Israel's security and the IDF's response is analyzed in Van Creveld, The Sword and the Olive, pp. 103–245.

25. Stuart A. Cohen, 'Israel's Changing Military Commitments, 1981–1991', Journal of Strategic Studies, 15 (September 1992), pp. 330–50.

26. For a revealing insight, see remarks by Knesset member Dan Meridor, who chaired the committee, in 'The Political-Strategic Challenge to Israel' (Hebrew) (paper delivered on 7 May 1991), Dapei Elazar, 14 (Tel Aviv: Jaffee Center for Strategic Studies, 1992), pp. 111–27.

27. Gal Luft, 'Israel's Impending Revolution in Military Affairs', Peacewatch, No. 199 (Washington, DC: Washington Institute, 4 March 1999). See also interview with General Shlomo Yannai (CO, IOF planning branch), 'The IDF is Undergoing a Military Revolution', Shiryon, 6 (October 1999), pp. 8–11.

28. See, for example, his interview in Yedi'ot Aharonot, weekend supplement, 23 March 1993.

29. Alex Fishman, 'The Computer will Win the War', Yedi'ot Aharonot, 4 December 1995. Not incidentally, this development creates a vast number of new opportunities for women in the force. See Dafna N. Izraeli, 'Gendering Military Service in the Israel Defense Force', Israel Social Science Research, 12/1 (1997), pp. 129–63.

30. Especially noteworthy is the high proportion (over 50 per cent) of engineers and systems analysts in the staff of this unit, which is deliberately attempting to attract high-tech personnel who might previously have preferred service in intelligence or the air force. Amnon Barzilai in Ha'aretz, 9 August 2000, A7.

31. Yitzchak Ben-Israel, 'The Law of Relativity in the Construction of Forces – Part 1' (Hebrew), Ma'archot, 353 (August 1997), pp. 33–42 and Part 2, idem., 354 (November 1997), pp. 33–43.

32. Ma'archot, by far the most authoritative of all IDF publications, devoted its entire issue no. 358 (published in April 1998) to an analysis and description of Aviv Ne'urim ('Spring Youth'), including an 'Introduction' by then Deputy Chief of Staff Shaul Mofaz and articles by other senior officers.

33. Ze'ev Schiff, 'A Quiet Re-organization in the General Staff', *Ha'aretz*, 9 July 1998, B1.

34. Within the IDF grapevine, credit for the establishment of MAZI remains a point of contention. One school of thought attributes this initiative (and others) primarily to General Matan Vilnai, who after serving as Deputy Chief of the IDF General Staff throughout most of Lipkin-Shahak's tenure as Chief of Staff (1994–98) was, virtually at the last minute, deprived of supreme command by the appointment of Mofaz. Certainly, Vilnai undertook much of the preparatory staff work required to get MAZI on the IDF agenda. Nevertheless, Mofaz's own contribution cannot be belittled. It was he who convened and chaired the three-day General Staff seminar in January 1999 which ultimately authorized the reform, and used his authority to overcome organizational opposition within the IDF to the measures necessary for its implementation.

35. Alex Fishman, 'The IDF's New Army', *Yedi'ot Aharonot*, weekend supplement, 25 August 2000.

36. This feature of their professional biographies is not negated by the fact that several have commanded large-scale field formations, since they have done so only in 'low intensity' situations, during the intifada and the Lebanon campaigns – when most of the actual fighting was conducted at the brigade level. Hence, unlike even their Egyptian and Syrian counterparts, members of the present IDF General Staff have had no first-hand experience of the most senior level of command under the conditions of battle that appertained during the 1991 Gulf War.

37. As is pointed out by General (ret.) Aviezer Ya'ari, 'We Need a New Security Doctrine' (Hebrew), *Ma'archot*, 357 (March 1998), pp. 68–9.

38. Tal, *National Security*, and General (ret.) Ilan Biran, 'Our Secret Weapon – Deterrence', *Shiryon*, 6 (October 1999), pp. 42–3. The author was director general of the ministry of defense. On the erosion in Israel's deterrence posture, see Efraim Inbar and Shmuel Sandler, 'Israel's Deterrence Strategy Revisited', *Security Studies*, 3 (Winter 1993/94), pp. 330–58.

39. On the origins of this policy, see Avner Cohen, *Israel and the Bomb* (New York: Columbia University Press, 1998).

40. Avi Kober, *Decision: Decision in Israel's War* (Hebrew) (Tel Aviv: Ministry of Defense Publications, 1996). See also Stuart A. Cohen and Efraim Inbar, 'A Taxonomy of Israel's Use of Force', *Comparative Strategy*, 10/2 (April 1991), pp. 121–38.

41. As the events of October 2000 clearly showed, the IDF had taken to heart the lessons of the confrontations which earlier occurred with PA forces (especially, the 'tunnel' incident of September 1996 and 'the Land Day' shootings of March 2000). Indeed, urban-warfare exercises have for some time constituted a regular part of infantry training, a fact which – together with other precautions – is thought to account for the relatively low incidence of IDF casualties.

42. For IDF intelligence assessments regarding chemical and/or biological attacks, see Amos Harel, 'Preparations for Chemistry and Biology', *Ha'aretz*, 20 July 1999, B4.

43. Stuart A. Cohen, 'Towards a New Profile of the (New) Israeli Soldier', in Efraim Karsh (ed.), *From Rabin to Netanyahu: Israel's Troubled Agenda* (London: Frank Cass, 1997), pp. 77–114.

44. Efraim Inbar, 'Israel's Small War: the Military Reaction to the Intifada', *Armed Forces & Society*, 18 (Fall 1991), pp. 29–50. and Stuart A. Cohen, 'How did the Intifadah Affect the IDF?', *Conflict Quarterly*, 14 (1994), pp. 7–22.

45. See, for example, interview with General Mosheh Ivri Sukenik (CO MAZI) in *Shiryon*, 7 (January 2000), p. 11.

46. Ariel Levite, *Offense and Defense in Israeli Military Doctrine*, JCSS Study, No. 12 (Boulder, CO: Westview Press, 1989) and S. Naveh, 'The Cult of Offensive Pre-emption: Future Challenges for Israeli Operational Thought', in E. Karsh (ed.), *Between War and Peace: Dilemmas of Israeli Security* (London: Frank Cass, 1996), pp. 168–87.

47. See Mofaz's statement to this effect, reported in *Ha'aretz*, 13 January 1999, A4; and Ron Ben Yishai, 'Israel No Longer Relies Solely on Reservists', *Yedi'ot Aharonot*, 13 January 1999, p. 11.
48. IDF tactics in the latter stages of its south Lebanon campaign are in this respect particularly instructive. Contrary to past practice, by the late 1990s the IDF had become noticeably reluctant to commit more than a fraction of its infantry forces in that theater to offensive ground operations. Most personnel attached to the four infantry brigades which rotated duty in the area were deployed in a defensive – or, at most, reactive – mode. They manned a string of heavily protected outposts in and along the 'security zone' beyond Israel's northern border. There, their principal mission was to deny the enemy any gain (particularly, any publicity gain) that could result from the conquest of a fortification held by either the IDF or the South Lebanese army, which Israel armed and financed. The only ground troops regularly engaged in 'deep penetration' raids of the traditional kind were the members of the elite units (*sayarot*) especially trained for that purpose. Heavier attacks on the *Hizballah*'s infrastructure and concentrations were almost entirely entrusted to long-range artillery units and to attack aircraft, UAV's and helicopters. For a critical assessment of this policy, see Colonel (ret.) Shemuel Gordon, 'The Vulture and the Snake: Counter-guerrilla Air Warfare: The War in Southern Lebanon', *BESA Security and Policy Studies*, No. 39 (July 1998). On the extent to which fear of casualties also influenced this posture, see the discussion later in this chapter.
49. Marvin Feuerwerger, *The Arrow Next Time? Israel's Missile Defense for the 1990s* (Washington, DC: Washington Institute for Near East Policy, 1991) and Gerald M. Steinberg, 'The Iraqi Chemical Threat during the 2nd Gulf War: Israeli Perceptions and Reactions', in Jean Paul Zanders (ed.), *The 2nd Gulf War and the CBW Threat: Proceedings of the 3rd Annual Conference on Chemical Warfare* (Brussels, 1995), pp. 53–72.
50. Investment in this program accelerated subsequent to the failure of a test in January 1998, after which the then defense minister, Yitzhak Mordechai, announced that the satellite was to be adopted as a military project under the direction of MAFAT, the ministry of defense's administration for the development of battle platforms.
51. Now that the Israel navy has taken possession of the last of the three German-built Dolphin class submarines, each capable of delivering missiles, and of the first batch of Sa'ar 5 missile boats, the IDF seems ready to capitalize on the strategic depth which Israel's maritime location allows. See Ze'ev Schiff, 'Overture to a New Strategy', *Ha'aretz*, 31 May 2000, B1. On the earlier picture, see Efraim Inbar, 'The Israeli Navy', *Naval War College Review*, 43 (Winter 1990), pp. 100–12.
52. Angelo M. Codevilla, 'Missiles, Defense and Israel', *Nativ* (Hebrew), 11 (September 1998), pp. 52–72. For the earlier debate, see Reuven Pedahtzur, *The Arrow System and the Active Defense Against Ballistic Missiles: Challenges and Queries* (Hebrew), JCSS memorandum, No. 42 (Tel Aviv: Jaffee Center for Strategic Studies, October 1993) and Aharon Levran, *Israeli Strategy after Desert Storm: Lessons of the Second Gulf War* (London: Frank Cass, 1997).
53. Charles S. Liebman and Eliezer Don-Yehiyah, *Civil Religion in Israel: Traditional Religion and Political Culture in the Jewish State* (Berkeley: University of California Press, 1983).
54. Uri Ben-Eliezer, *The Making of Israeli Militarism* (Bloomington: Indiana University Press, 1998).
55. Moshe Lissak and Dan Horowitz, *Trouble in Utopia: The Overburdened Polity of Israel* (Albany, NY: SUNY Press, 1989), pp. 36–239.
56. The conventional measure of 'motivation' is the percentage of male conscripts who request placement in combat units. According to the IDF Spokesman's office (private communication), the figures show a steady rise from 68.2 per cent in March 1996 to 77.7 per cent in August 1999.
57. Asher Arian, *Israeli Public Opinion on National Security* (Tel Aviv: Jaffee Center for Strategic Studies, 1999).

58. Yoram Peri, 'The Media and the Military: From Collusion to Collision', in Stuart A. Cohen (ed.), *Democratic Societies and their Armed Forces: Israel in Comparative Context* (London, Frank Cass, 2000), pp. 184–214.

59. See, for example, Supreme Court rulings in (1) the case brought by a female soldier who claimed eligibility to apply for the pilot's training course in November 1994 (*Miller vs The Defense Minister*, no. 4541/94) and (2) the injunction against the promotion of a senior officer in April 1999 on the grounds of his previous record of sexual harassment (*Anon. vs The Chief of Staff*, no. 1284/99), both in www.court.gov.il. In general, Amnon Straschnov, *Justice Under Fire* (Hebrew) (Tel Aviv: Yedi'ot Aharonot, 1994). The author was the Military Judge Advocate, 1986–1991.

60. Michal Shavit-Fredkin, 'Parental Involvement and Interference in the IDF', unpublished MA thesis (Hebrew), Dept of Sociology, Tel Aviv University, 1996. For more recent evidence, see Ronen Bergen, 'The Specter of Bereaved Parents', *Ha'aretz*, 8 July 1999, B3.

61. Which is not to deny that some degree of 'war weariness' does certainly exist. See Gad Barzilai and Efraim Inbar, 'The Use of Force: Israeli Public Opinion on Military Options', *Armed Forces & Society*, 23/1 (Fall 1996), pp. 49–80.

62. Charles Moskos, 'Towards a Postmodern Military?', in Stuart A. Cohen (ed.), *Democratic Societies*, pp. 3–26.

63. Sam Lehman-Wilzig, *WILDFIRE: Grassroots Revolts in Israel in the Post-Socialist Era* (Albany: SUNY Press, 1992).

64. Don M. Snider, 'An Uninformed Debate on Military Culture'; Williamson Murray, 'Does Military Culture Matter?'; and John Hillen, 'Must US Military Culture Reform?', *Orbis*, 43/1 (Winter 1999), pp. 11–58.

65. Most notably in October 1996, during his eulogy on the first anniversary of Yitzchak Rabin's assassination:

> The ties binding the IDF and civilian society – which once constituted the very soul of the army, part of its uniqueness and a source of its strength – have now become burdensome ... How far we are, O captain, from the days when a military uniform was a source of pride and self-respect. During the past year, as a result of a process which commenced long ago but which has gained momentum, [we have seen] soldiers and officers, conscripts, professionals and reservists, walking around in our midst with an almost apologetic look on their faces ... Definitions alter, values are replaced, and as if subject to the whims of computerized graphics, the Israeli changes his demeanor and society revises its form. Non-service in Tzahal [the IDF] no longer constitutes a stigma, and voluntarism, the act of giving out of a wish to contribute, no longer receives the respect it deserves .... (official IDF transcript)

See also report of Shahak's lecture at Tel Aviv University, *Ha'aretz*, 15 July 1997, A3.

66. For example, interviews with General Uzi Dayan (Deputy Chief of Staff), *Ha'aretz*, 3 February 1999, A5, and with General Shlomo Yannai, *Shiryon*, 6 (October 1999), pp. 8–9. Both echo Mofaz's speech to members of the Military Industries' Forum, *Ha'aretz*, 12 September 2000, A6.

67. For the text, see Asa Kasher, *Military Ethics* (Hebrew) (Tel Aviv: Ministry of Defense, 1996), pp. 232–7.

68. According to the IDF Spokesman, personnel losses in southern Lebanon averaged 26 deaths and 88 wounded in each of the years 1993–97. The numbers dropped to 12 deaths and 56 wounded in 1999, when a more 'defensive' posture was adopted.

69. '[As a result of the changed social climate] we are witnessing the emergence of a new genre of IDF officer – one whose main purpose is to avoid making mistakes. This results in a situation in which many do nothing at all.' Colonel Nitzan Nuriel (deputy commander of the Gaza division) interviewed in *Ba-Machaneh*, 19 December 1997, p. 14.

70. *Yedi'ot Aharonot*, 25 April 1997, p. 25.
71. See Edward N. Luttwak, 'Where Are the Great Powers? At home with the Kids', *Foreign Affairs*, 73/4 (July/August 1994), pp. 23–38, and 'Towards Post-Heroic Warfare', *Foreign Affairs*, 74/3 (May/June 1995), pp. 109–12. For a partial critique of Luttwak's thesis, see James Burk, 'Public Support for Peacekeeping in Lebanon and Somalia: Assessing the Casualties Hypothesis', *Political Science Quarterly*, 114/1 (Spring 1999), pp. 53–78. Compare Dan Reiter and A. C. Stam, 'Democracy and Battlefield Military Effectiveness', *Journal of Conflict Resolution*, 42 (June 1998), pp. 259–77 and A. C. Stam, *Win, Lose or Draw: Domestic Politics and the Crucible of War* (Ann Arbor: University of Michigan Press, 1996).
72. Lipkin-Shahak interview, *Jerusalem Post*, 1 September 1993.
73. Mofaz created a minor storm when publicly voicing his objections to both the substance and the manner of Dayan's appointment. The fact that Barak had, without Mofaz's knowledge, cleared the appointment with the Attorney General did nothing to assuage his anger.
74. Which – especially after Ben-Gurion's departure from office and the Six Days' War – had usually been marked by considerable (and sometimes decisive) military influence on all matters of security-related decision making. See Yehuda Ben-Meir, *Civil–Military Relations in Israel* (New York: Columbia University Press, 1995).
75. Stuart A. Cohen, 'Israel and Her Army: Towards a Posture of Military Role Contraction?', *Journal of Political and Military Sociology*, 22 (1993), pp. 3–18. On the effect of military 'professionalization' on the balance of civil–military relations, the 'classic' formulation remains; Samuel P. Huntington, *The Soldier and the State: The Theory and Practice of Civil–Military Relations* (New York: Vintage, 1957). Compare, however, the critique in Bengt Abrahamsson, *Military Professionalization and Political Power* (Beverly Hills, CA: Sage, 1972) and Eliot Cohen, *Citizens and Soldiers: The Dilemmas of Military Service* (Ithaca: Cornell University Press, 1985). For an Israeli perspective, see Colonel Yair, 'Professionalism and Military Ethics' (Hebrew), *Ma'archot*, 337 (August 1994), pp. 2–9, and Yehudah Wagman, 'Service in the IDF: Not a "National Mission" but a "Profession"' (Hebrew), *Ma'archot*, 363 (January 1999), pp. 8–15.

10

The Military and Politics: A Turkish Dilemma

UMIT CIZRE SAKALLIOGLU

The armed forces have always regarded themselves as the guardian of the Turkish republic's democracy and stability. This world-view intensified during the late 1990s and in following years. Changes in civil–military relations in Turkey were connected with the armed forces' redefinition of internal security threats in the post-Cold War era, and with the growing importance of political Islam and the Kurdish question in the military hierarchy's calculations. At the same time, an additional factor – Turkey's application for membership in the European Union (EU) – affected the military's role in Turkish politics.

On four occasions during the 1960s, 1970s and 1980s, the military intervened in some fashion to reshape Turkish politics, always returning control, however, to civilians after a short interval. The fifth intervention, on 28 February 1997, marked a qualitative change in the situation, when the military-dominated National Security Council[1] (*Milli Guvenlik Kurulu*, MGK) brought down a constitutionally elected coalition government headed by Prime Minister Necmettin Erbakan, leader of the pro-Islamic Welfare Party (RP).

Like its counterparts elsewhere, the Turkish military's mission is to maintain the republic's security, officially defined as 'The protection and maintenance of the state's constitutional order, national presence, integrity, all political, social, cultural and economic interests on an international level, and contractual law against any kind of internal and foreign threat'.[2] What is striking about this definition is the broad and complex character attributed to security. It includes not only the traditional national defense against external threats, but also guaranteeing the constitution. Moreover, security in the Turkish sense involves securing non-military objectives pertaining to economic, social, cultural and political goals.

Turkish constitutions have not openly proclaimed any guardianship role for the military. But developments and some provisions of Act No. 2945, on the National Security Council and the National Security Council General Secretariat, have acted together to assign significant and broad political powers to the MGK, placing it on par with the executive branch.[3] Other laws, too, enshrine this national security concept in legislation on anti-terrorism, public order, the media, political parties and rules on the internal regulation of the armed forces. Article 35 of the Military Internal Service Code assigns the military the task of safeguarding Turkish territory and the republic as defined by the constitution. This Article has been invoked on each occasion when the military intervened into politics. Governance through 'emergency rule', as the basic instrument of managing the Kurdish problem, has played a large role in enhancing the political parameters of the military. The military bureaucracy's autonomous intelligence and surveillance functions, and jurisdiction over crimes against internal security and terrorism, also reaffirm its position in Turkish politics and are reflected in its autonomy from parliamentary oversight in its budget and internal affairs.

In the ministry of defense's White Papers for 1998 and 2000, in the section entitled 'Principles of National Security Policy', the substance and sources of threats to internal security which fall within the responsibility of the military are clarified in no uncertain terms. These are threats to 'Turkey's unitary state quality' and to 'the principle of secularism guaranteed in Articles No. 2 and 4 of the Constitution'.[4] The last issue of secularism is characterized as 'of great significance in terms of our internal security'.[5] Clearly, these definitions indicate that the Turkish General Staff is more weighty than its counterparts in other Western democracies. As the German scholar Heinz Kramer writes, it is 'not only a professional military organization but a core element of Turkey's political system'.[6] The *de facto* and *de jure* positions it enjoys in the political system place it in a situation 'ideal for following a political agenda of its own',[7] which is sure to be carried out even in the face of strong civilian resistance.

One fundamental and durable feature of Turkey's multi-party parliamentary democracy since 1950 is the role and influence of the military in politics. In the 1990s, however, the post-Cold War situation, the Kurdish issue and the growth of Islamic political factors made for some change and increase in the military's role. At the same time, the EU's demands for democratic norms as a precondition for Turkish membership became an important issue in this process.

THE TURKISH MILITARY'S STRUCTURAL AND STRATEGIC PROFILE: AN OPEN MYSTERY?

The Turkish military's strategic objectives, force sizes and structures, armaments provisions and modernization programs are chiefly guided by a security-conscious approach. During the Cold War, the Turkish military's primary role was to fulfill its responsibilities as a NATO member and to halt Communist expansion. With no more risk of war between Western and Communist blocs, the military leadership shifted its priority toward building a strong military machine to deter and defend emerging regional threats and domestic subversive groups challenging Turkey's unitary state and secular character.[8] The post-Cold War era brought considerable instability and uncertainty to several areas on Turkey's borders, including the Middle East, the Balkans, the Caucasus and central Asia. Justifying the unprecedented scale of the military's modernization program, Yalcin Burcak, then Under-Secretary of Defense Industries, said in 1999, 'These weapons are indispensable. In Europe, they've dropped their budgets ... But [this situation] doesn't apply to the Turkish army. For us, the dissolution of the Warsaw Pact brought uncertainties, not stability.'[9]

The perception that Turkey occupies a unique strategic position is frequently stated by military and civilian leaders, in order to emphasize the country's military and political value to the

West and to justify a large armed force with a big budget. Turkey was said to have a vital 'geo-strategic position', as 'a bridge', with 'a key position', as 'a gate opening to Eurasia', and 'being centrally located' in the Balkans, the Caucasus, Eurasia and the Middle East – to cite some of the main terms used.[10] Turkey was portrayed as 'A pillar of stability and balance directly in the middle of a region full of risks and challenges such as ultra-nationalism, religious fundamentalism, the proliferation of weapons of mass destruction, terrorism and ethnic conflicts which emerged following the Cold War period and intensified in the Balkans, the Caucasus and the Middle East.'[11]

Many foreign observers agreed that Turkey faces genuine security risks on its borders, and its 'comparative advantage lies in its ability to influence trans-regional risks and opportunities'.[12] In short, Turkey's leaders argued that the country had moved from being a secondary member of NATO to a country of primary importance (from a 'flank country' to a 'front country'),[13] a view first expressed by US Assistant Secretary of State Richard Holbrooke in March 1995.[14]

Based on ministry of defense (MOD) reports, its share of the government budget shows a slight decline from 10.5 per cent in 1997 to 9.4 per cent in 1998, then to 9.2 per cent in 1999 and to 8.8 per cent in 2000. The share of the MOD budget in GNP, however, is more stable, averaging around 2.2 per cent between 1994 and 1998.[15] However, the budget is not the only source of allocation for military expenditure in Turkey. The true profile of the armed forces is understated in open sources, since there are extra-budgetary funds not disclosed in official documents and the armed forces are a growing part of national expenditures in Turkey.[16]

In the late 1990s, the Turkish armed forces began a huge modernization program involving new helicopters, tanks and other equipment. Some foreign analysts have warned that profligate military spending could pose a threat to Turkey's economy, especially the efforts to reduce inflation.[17] Turkey's is the second largest standing army in NATO after the United States'. All these factors, according to Morton Abramowitz, 'have made Turkey the most powerful state in the area'.[18] The responsibility for defending national security, and the internal and external challenges that have emerged, also inspired the armed forces to play a bigger role in political and foreign policy issues. Consequently, Turkey's posture toward the Middle East, Cyprus, the Caucasus, Balkans and Caspian regions, as well as its relations with Greece, the EU, the United States and Israel, are all dominated by a military perspective.

ROOTS OF THE MILITARY'S POLITICAL AUTONOMY

There are many factors that explain the guardianship role of the Turkish armed forces as embedded in the law, political rhetoric and practices of the Turkish republic. The republic's history and the culture of army and society legitimize the military institution's primacy in what might be called a 'protected democracy'. In turn, the military's guardian role has shaped a political culture, mythologizing and rationalizing a 'benign' political role for the armed forces in national politics.

The military's autonomy has historically taken the form of maintaining a privileged position, vis-à-vis non-military groups, initiating or vetoing political proposals, and remaining beyond governmental democratic control.[19] Its institutional autonomy is also manifested by governments' limited control over military education, appointments and promotions, military budgets, arms production and procurement.[20] The army's recruitment policies, which favor the sons of military personnel and civil servants, helped to perpetuate its social distance from society. The aloofness from mainstream society is also observable in the totally isolated situation of the working, living, shopping and entertainment quarters of the officer corps.[21]

The most critical source for the political autonomy of the Turkish army is its defence of the official ideology of Kemalism,[22] named after the republic's founder, Mustafa Kemal Ataturk. This holds especially true for the doctrine of secularism. Kemalism has also been associated with upholding of a particular modern lifestyle as well as a specific view of politics and democracy.

It is clear that the formal separation of the military institution from politics in the young republic[23] was not intended to establish civilian supremacy along the lines of west European and North American models. The military was to be denied a direct political role so that it would not seize power permanently.[24] Officers were deprived of the right to vote and the number of retired officers in parliament declined. But the armed forces were to be the guardians of the republic, viewing themselves as a proper participant in politics during periods of crisis or emergency.[25]

Thus, the military refrained from directly wielding legislative and executive power, considering such behavior as endangering its professional cohesion. The army therefore could view political interventions as a necessary defensive maneuver to protect itself. This was true of the army intervention of 1980 and the MGK ultimatum of 1971, seen by the officers as a response to their being drawn somewhat unwillingly into partisan politics by having to enforce government decisions to impose martial law in many provinces.[26]

The most crucial feature of the Turkish military's political autonomy, distinguishing it from Third World armies, has been its acceptance of the legitimacy of both democracy and civilian rule. In the past, it adopted a refined concept of autonomy, by which it controlled politicians without usurping the basis of civilian supremacy. The late Ernest Gellner spoke of this paradox when he identified Turkey as a country in which the tradition of constitutionally elected government is both interrupted and deeply rooted.[27] The military's acceptance of the civilian regime's legitimacy and staying power has required it to use unobtrusive mechanisms to disguise its political weight. One significant method used by the military to achieve this end has been to restructure the political process after each coup in such a way as to equip itself with more 'constitutional' powers.

For example, after the 1980 coup, the 1982 constitution narrowed the bases of political participation, strengthened state institutions and enhanced the MGK's role. While extensively restricting individual rights and freedoms, the constitution entrenched the military's vetoing power in the political system to such an extent that it made crude military intervention into politics redundant. But the 1980s was also the period in which the military seemed to withdraw from the political arena, although the civilian governments gave it a free reign in its combat against the Kurdish nationalist insurgency.

'FEBRUARY 28 PROCESS': WHAT CHANGED AND WHY?

In contrast to its past thinking and action, the military trespassed more on the civilian realm after the February 1997 intervention. The basis for this type of behavior was a concern over the rising power of Islamic political forces. After the 1995 election, the military brokered a coalition government between two center-right parties to keep the Islamic party from entering the government.[28] That attempt failed, and the Islamic RP became the leading partner of a coalition government on 28 June 1996. At that point, senior commanders began making public statements or issuing formal declarations stressing their guardianship role over secularism, and criticizing civilian government initiatives on various key issues.

At the same time, in combating Islamic activism and Kurdish nationalism, the armed forces became more actively involved in politics. They made and broke governments, became directly involved in political intrigues, issued public demands and warnings to civilians, structured new bills through their own research units and departments, launched campaigns to inform the public on the threat of political Islam acting as cover for reactionary intentions, and continually impinged on the daily operations of elected governments.

Also in contrast to the past, the armed forces seemed to question the logic and institutions of representative democracy and the principle of majority rule more and more. Multi-party democracy and the electoral process are now perceived as being used by Islamic activists in seeking to subvert the secular ideology of the republic. It is clear that the military has adopted a more critical and confrontational stance against politicians and existing political channels. Civilians are accused of creating 'an authority vacuum', which subsequently disqualifies them from leading the fight against Islamic reactionism. As bulwark of the nation's fundamental principles, the armed forces see themselves as the proper leadership in the fight against reactionary forces.

The New National Security Discourse

On 29 April 1997, the Turkish General Staff announced a radical change in their basic doctrine (National Military Defence Concept). Henceforth, priority would be given to combating internal threats from Islamic activism and Kurdish separatism, rather than safeguarding against interstate wars and external threats. This new document replaced the one formulated on 18 November 1992, which singled out Kurdish terrorist acts as the primary security threat to the state. Both documents were prepared by the secretariat of the MGK and became governmental policy. The parliament was not fully informed about this new decision. During its meeting on 31 October 1997, the MGK announced that 'reactionary Islamic movements' were a greater threat to the state than the terrorist acts of Kurdish separatism. The defeat inflicted on the PKK by the capture, arrest, trial and conviction of its leader, Abdullah Ocalan, reinforced this shift.

To cope with the perceived magnitude of the threat, new organizational devices were created. A new unit called the Western Study Group (WSG, *Bati Calisma Grubu*) was instituted within General Staff headquarters to collect information about the political orientations of civil society groups, mayors, governors, government employees, political party cadres and media personalities. Moreover, by a governmental decree published in the official gazette on 9 January 1997, a new organ called the 'Prime Ministerial Crisis Management Center' (*Basbakanlik Kriz Yonetim Merkezi*) was formed within the MGK secretariat to observe and report on 'crises' caused by Islamic reactionism and formulate responses to them. As the center was placed within the MGK but called 'Prime Ministerial', it had an ambiguous structural and functional position. It bypassed parliamentary control of its activities and was seemingly responsible to the prime minister but was, in reality, answerable only to the MGK.

Why Is 'Islamic Reactionism' Considered the Foremost National Security Threat?

The army views the rise of Islamic sentiments and political parties in Turkey as a security threat, though arguably these forces peaked in the mid-1990s and declined somewhat thereafter. Unlike

Kurdish subversion, the Islamic threat is regarded as being potentially present in all parts of the country and all sectors of society. As one general put it, 'The reactionary sector has been continuing its activities towards broadening its power of appeal in the society through 19 newspapers, 110 journals, 51 radio and 20 television [channels] … They have 2,500 associations, 500 foundations, over 1,000 business corporations, 1,200 student dormitories, over 800 private schools and courses …. The figure of those attending officially registered Koran courses is 1,685,000 and this figure doubles every five years.'[29] Since the aims and activities of Islamic activists supersede the tactics, methods and techniques of a conventional war, it becomes impossible to draw the line between politics and war.

To root out any threat within the armed forces, there were unprecedented purges of those suspected of Islamic activism. Purges took place in April and December 1996, and in May, August and December 1997. During 1998, 61 officers and 101 non-commissioned officers were expelled.[30] The figure was 43 in 2000.[31]

What makes political Islam's activities so subversive to this line of thinking is their 'identity' dimension, challenging the most basic principle of the republic: construction of a Western identity for Turkey. Secularism, understood as the separation of politics from religious considerations, has been seen as the fundamental instrument in achieving that end. From the military's perspective, political Islam is not just 'aiming … at breaking the Turkish Republic's institutions, but at an internal insurgency'[32] capturing the hearts, spirits and values of the body politic to impose its own hegemonic political order.

Islamic reactionism is also seen as reinforcing Kurdish unrest, since it tries to Islamicize the Kurds and sometimes to cooperate with the PKK.[33] The movement cooperates with and seeks the backing of other states, like Iran, Libya, Iraq, Sudan and Saudi Arabia. It is the perceived magnitude of the threat as apocalyptic that makes it possible for the military, as ultimate guardian of the republic, to set the standards for measuring and judging the Islamic threat as a life or death question, governing the survival of the existing regime.

Political Islam is believed to challenge the existing order

through politicizing religious cultural symbols, such as the wearing of headscarves by women and beards by men. Indeed, in the war against Islamic reactionism, both sides heavily resort to a symbolic use of politics: while in office, the RP's leaders made symbolic promises of building a mosque in Taksim, one of the prominent sites of tourist attraction in Istanbul. The party leader, Necmettin Erbakan, invited the heads of religious brotherhoods in their religious attire to the prime minister's official residence. Secular modern sectors, in turn, adopted the wearing of Ataturk badges, singing the national anthem, holding patriotic marches and visiting the Ataturk mausoleum.[34] These symbolic acts reflected a struggle over the national identity.

The moralization of national security turns the struggle against Islamic reactionism into a total war in which official forces of 'good' confront the 'evil' forces of Islam in an all-or-nothing situation. The Turkish military must remain in a permanent state of alert as the last hope of the regime. Negotiation, reconciliation, moderation or neutralism are regarded irreconcilable with the military's reading of the conflict.

The Kurdish Internal Threat: New Realities, Old Insecurities
The fight against the PKK has also enhanced the armed forces' political role as the instrument for preserving a unitary state. This long war was fought in the predominantly Kurdish region of south-eastern Turkey, resulting in the loss of around 30,000 lives and costing $6 to $9 billion every year.

The armed forces advocated a two-stage strategy for the conflict with the PKK. First, the enemy's capacity to wage war would have to be destroyed. Next, after military victory was won, the civilian authorities would have to ensure the social and economic modernization of the region to eradicate the bases of Kurdish discontent. The war also spilled beyond Turkish territory. Syria, Iran and the autonomous Kurdish area in northern Iraq provided help to the rebels. Turkish troops made frequent incursions into northern Iraq to destroy the bases of the PKK. In addition, the Kurdish question became a European political issue, affecting Turkey's interests there.

Together with the Cyprus question, the Kurdish conflict

provided the main justification for maintaining a high military budget and major modernization programs. The Kurdish war also provided the rationale for abandoning plans for an all-volunteer force by the year 2000, and brought reversal of an earlier decision to cut conscription from 18 to 15 months as a first step toward reducing the armed forces' reliance on the draft, in keeping with Western trends.[35]

In handling both the Kurdish and the Islamic issues, the armed forces focused on socioeconomic factors in political dissent.[36] In a January 1998 speech, Chief of Staff General Ismail Karadayi suggested the armed forces might do a better job than civilians in solving problems ranging from environmental issues to discrimination. He stated, 'A general should sometimes act like a diplomat and a diplomat should have a good background of military matters. But they should all be economists.'[37]

The PKK suffered an extremely serious defeat after the capture and trial of its leader and his call to end the rebellion. On 9 February 2000, the remaining leadership of the PKK announced that they had given up their war and would press their cause within the framework of peace and democracy.[38] But fighting continued with those PKK militants who did not heed Ocalan's call to lay down their arms, both in Turkey and in northern Iraq. The government demanded that PKK forces surrender unconditionally. At the same time, Ocalan's death sentence was not implemented, lest this damage Turkey's chances of being accepted as a candidate for EU membership at the approaching Helsinki summit. Former President Suleiman Demirel expressed the military hierarchy's view when he remarked, 'The decision by the terrorist organization to retreat from Turkey and abandon armed struggle does not alter the potential threat of terrorism.'[39]

TURKISH MILITARY: A STABILIZING FACTOR OR A DILEMMA FOR THE REGIME?

Clearly, the armed forces' political power is an important factor affecting Turkey's full admission into the EU, which has demanded a reduced role for the military and more guarantees for human rights and civil liberties. Nor is this role in keeping with the professional standards of Western military organizations. The acceptance of Turkey as a candidate state for EU membership at the December 1999 Helsinki summit did, however, raise hopes for creating an externally induced motivation for the Turkish system to meet the EU's standards. In short, EU pressure seemed the only visible factor that might lead to a smaller role for the military in Turkish politics.

After gaining candidate country status in Helsinki, Turkey was called upon to fulfill the criteria for full membership that were set at the 1993 European Council meeting in Copenhagen. One key point in these criteria was the need to achieve stability of the institutions guaranteeing complete freedom of expression, human rights, respect and protection for minorities and an efficient market economy. As long as the government – pressured by the military – refuses to meet these demands, Turkey's bid for membership will not succeed. The military high command defends the thesis that such compromises can be too high a price, endangering the state's ability to survive the threats it faces.

Nevertheless, the EU situation has given rise to a debate in Turkey, for the first time openly challenging the military's guardianship role as a major problem and the source of all other shortcomings in democracy. The politically privileged position of the armed forces creates a paradox for the democratic credentials of the Turkish regime, seeking membership in a bloc where the civilian control of the armed forces is a cardinal principle. While the West was somewhat more tolerant of deficiencies in the democracy of its allies during the Cold War, as one observer notes, 'The dominant role [of] the military in Turkey ... has proved perhaps more worrying at a time when NATO has been trying to give lessons in political-military relations to the countries of central-Eastern Europe.'[40]

In this context, there is an interesting contradiction in Turkey's dominant ideology. The legitimizing ethos of the republic was not just independence, territorial unity and secularism. The ultimate goal is also to establish a Western-like identity that would make possible integration into the Western world on an equal basis. If the military's power within Turkish society, and limits on rights that it favors, inhibits that integration, then these policies also go against the Ataturkist program. Should the generals, as Ben Lombardi suggests, 'consider a paradox – the possibility of international isolation fomented by Western states as a consequence of seeking to save Ataturk's Republic?'[41]

The point here is that this issue is not today's paradox. The republic's modernizing discourse was not necessarily committed to all dimensions of modernity and not really interested in political liberalism. Instead, it was connected in the military's eyes with building a homogenous nation-state, economic prosperity and military strength. It can be argued, then, that today's tension with the West regarding the military's role is largely derived from the regime's ideological and institutional underpinnings and its incomplete understanding of democracy.

The Turkish military does not give any signs of willingness to relinquish its guardianship role.[42] Instead, it has formulated a counter-argument that the armed forces' secularism, and battle to maintain that value, is proof of its allegiance to the Western world, democracy and societal peace.[43] It may well be that the military hierarchy does not believe it has ever moved away from the goal of Europeanization, which was part of the republic's *raison d'être*. The hierarchy still feels itself engaged in ensuring the survival of the Kemalist republic, a mission which should take priority over the other goals. This being said, it would also be correct to say that to survive as the chief interlocuter in politics, the military has a vested interest in maintaining a strategy of tension against the threats to the republic, which it alone has the power to define.

To be fair to the military, it is true that the armed forces are assured of a disproportionately powerful position by virtue of the weakness of Turkey's politics. Parties are dominated by leaders who disregard internal democracy. Their atrophy makes it impossible for them to adapt to the changing needs of Turkey and its people. They are unable to distinguish themselves from one another, nor can they legitimize themselves on the basis of ideas and policies. New leadership and initiatives cannot emerge, because the old configuration blocks them. As a result, it is not unnatural for most to think that 'the role and influence of the military in politics remain unchanged because the civilian politicians seem unable to provide long-term political stability and guidance'.[44]

But there is something amiss in this argument, too. What if the military's position of never being far from the seat of power has played a major role in diminishing the civilian forces' potential to control their political environment sufficiently so as to correct the asymmetry in civil–military relations and manage the key political problems effectively? It can be argued that, to some extent, behind the weakness and lack of confidence of Turkey's civilian politics lies the special custodial position of the military, which is inter-woven into the nation's social fabric and historical memory. The political class looks over its shoulder for fear of offending the military.[45] Simultaneously, issues considered political, social, economic or cultural in normal democracies are turned into security issues. The exercise of normal freedoms is criminalized in the name of internal security. Under such conditions, the space within which the political class can act politically to resolve the problems is so restricted that this causes further ineffectiveness and decay of that group as well as lack of popular support and trust.

Contrary to the dwindling popular faith in civilian politics, confidence in the military is very high. But the military plays a key role in maintaining this situation through compulsory military service. The rituals and symbols of Kemalist teaching in the classroom is the next most effective channel for socializing the public into the military's perspectives. In the 1990s, new strategies became available as the military increased its knowledge of politics, foreign policy, and the use of the media to promote its views. The Turkish media took up a staunchly nationalist position under the impact of the Kurdish war, and to some extent the Islamic political factor as well, which made it a vehicle for mobilizing support of the military and promoting its concepts.[46]

The military is still the single most important political force in Turkey, and the extent of civilian control over it remains extremely weak. This, however, does not mean Turkey is a military dictatorship. Despite its weak foundations and instability, Turkey's multiparty experience has translated real-life diversity, pluralism and dynamism into politics. The capacity of the civilian system of governments to cope with challenges and crises is amazingly strong. In Turkey, the military enjoys great influence and the ability to dominate in some crisis situations and specific issues. But it falls far short of ruling or controlling the country as a whole.

NOTES

1. The MGK was created in 1961. Reflecting the more liberal outlook of the post-coup Constitution of 1961, the MGK essentially embodied the principle of the bureaucracy's primacy over the popularly elected General Assembly. As a result, the number of its civilian members exceeded those of the senior commanders. With the 1973 constitutional amendments, in the aftermath of the 1971 intervention by memorandum, the primary function of the MGK extended to making policy recommendations to the government. Finally, according to Article 118 of the post-coup Constitution of 1982, its position was enhanced to one of submitting to the Council of Ministers 'its views on taking decisions and ensuring necessary co-ordination with regard to the formulation, establishment and implementation of the national security policy'. The Council of Ministers is then required to give 'priority consideration' to the decisions of the MGK. The wording of the article does not, however, absolve the Council of Ministers – four members of which are represented in the MGK in addition to the five higher-echelon armed forces commanders, the president and the prime minister – of the function of deliberating on these policy recommendations before and after they are discussed in the MGK. Indeed, Article 117 authorises the Council of Ministers as the organ responsible for formulating national security issues and for the preparation of the armed forces for the defence of the country. In practice, however, the Council of Ministers carries out the MGK's recommendations. The politically superior position of the MGK to the civilian organs of the government is a serious problem for Turkish–EU relations.
2. *White Paper – Defence 1998*, p. 12; *Beyaz Kitap 2000* (*White Paper – Defense 2000*), p. 2, Part 3. White Papers are published by the ministry of defense (MOD) every two years. The pages of reference to the last White Paper (2000) are from its web format in Turkish (the English version not being available on the web, www.msb.mil.tr/genpp/beyaz_kitap.htm.
3. Act No. 2945 assigns three important functions to the MGK's secretariat, which enable the MGK to function like the Council of Ministers. First, the secretary (a general) of the MGK has the authority to prepare the agenda of the meetings. Next, he is authorized to follow up and check the implementation of the decisions reached in the MGK meetings on behalf of the president, prime minister and the MGK. Finally, the secretary can present his suggestions on domestic and foreign policy to the Council of Ministers directly. See Gencer Özcan, 'Doksanlarda Turkiyenin Ulusal Guvenlik ve Dis Politikasinda Askeri Yapinin Artan Etkisi', in S. Kut and G. Özcan (eds), *En Uzun Onyil* (Istanbul: Buke Yayinlari, 2000), pp. 70–4.
4. *White Paper – Defence 1998*, p. 14, and *Beyaz Kitap 2000*, p. 3.
5. Ibid. Secularism from the state perspective is understood as the disestablishment of Islam as the public religion and separation of politics from religion. To the extent that the state praxis does not itself conform to this simplistic definition is a matter of debate in Turkey. See Umit Cizre Sakallioglu, 'Parameters and Strategies of Islam–State Interaction in Republican Turkey', *International Journal of Middle Eastern Studies*, 28 (1996), pp. 231–51.
6. Heinz Kramer, *A Changing Turkey* (Washington, DC: Brookings Institution Press, 2000), p. 30.
7. Ibid.

8. See *Cumhurbaskani Suleyman Demirel'in TBMM'nin 20. Donem 4. Yasama Yilinin Acilisinda Yaptiklari Konusma* (Ankara: Basbakanlik Basimevi, 1998), p. 44. See also *White Paper – Defence 1998*, p. 17.
9. The official was quoted after orders were placed for a $1–$2 billion fleet of 145 military helicopters, a $4–$7 billion order for 1,000 tanks and a probable purchase of long-range missile systems from outside. See *Wall Street Journal*, 14 October 1999.
10. All these terms are quoted on one page in *White Paper – Defence 1998*, p. 6.
11. Ibid.
12. Ian O. Lesser, 'In Search of a Post-Cold War Role', *Private View* (Autumn 1997), p. 94.
13. Ibid.
14. Morton Abramowitz, 'The Complexities of American Policymaking on Turkey', in Morton Abramowitz (ed.), *Turkey's Transformation and American Policy* (New York: Century Foundation Press, 2000), p. 159.
15. *White Paper – Defence 1998*.
16. SIPRI (Stockholm International Peace Research Institute), *Military Expenditure Report 2000*, http://projects.sipri.se/milex/mex_trends.htlm, p. 1.
17. 'Turkey Promises IMF To Trim Military Spending', *Turkish Daily News*, 23 December 2000.
18. Abramowitz, 'Complexities of American Policymaking, p. 158.
19. Umit Cizre Sakallioglu, 'The Anatomy of the Turkish Military's Political Autonomy', *Comparative Politics*, Vol. 29, No. 2 (1997), p. 153.
20. Ibid., pp. 152–62.
21. James Brown, 'The Military and Society: The Turkish Case', *Middle Eastern Studies*, 25 (3) (1989), p. 399.
22. The official Republican ideology gradually became known by this name in a series of general congresses of the secular–bureaucratic state party, the Republican People's Party (*Cumhuriyet Halk Partisi* – CHP), beginning in 1927 and culminating in 1935, as a project of politically constructing a modern Turkish nation-state on secular and Western precepts.
23. In 1924, the ministry of Shari'a and of the chief of general staff were simultaneously abolished and turned over to governmental departments on the grounds that 'for religion and the military to be interested in politics leads to various undesirable results'. Quoted from Mustafa Kemal Ataturk, in Mahmut Gologlu, *Devrimler Ve Tepkileri*, 1924–1930 (Ankara: Basvur Matbaasi, 1972), p. 9.
24. This is the view shared by the majority of writers on the Turkish military. Examples are Daniel Lerner and Richard O. Robinson, 'Swords and Ploughshares, the Turkish Army as a Modernising Force', *World Politics*, 13 (1960–61), Dankwart A. Rustow, 'The Army and the Founding of the Turkish Republic', *World Politics*, 4 (July 1959), and William Hale, 'Transition to Civilian Governments in Turkey: The Military Perspective', in Metin Heper and Ahmet Evin (eds), *Democracy and Military in Turkey in the 1980s* (Berlin: De Gruyter, 1988).
25. George Harris, 'The Role of the Military in Turkey in the 1980s: Guardians or Decision Makers', in Heper and Evin, *Democracy and Military in Turkey*, p. 181, and Jacob Landau, 'Turkey, Democratic Framework and Military Control', in J. Chelskowski and Robert Pranger (eds), *Ideology and Power in the Middle East* (Durham, NC/London: Duke University Press, 1988), p. 314.
26. Ben Lombardi, 'Turkey, the Return of the Reluctant Generals?', *Political Science Quarterly*, Vol. 112, No. 2 (1997), p. 210.
27. Ernest Gellner, *Encounters with Nationalism* (Oxford: Blackwell Publishers, 1994), p. 151.
28. In the 1995 elections, the RP received the largest share (21.3 per cent) of the total votes.
29. From the briefing to journalists by General Fevzi Turkeri, 11 June 1997. Quoted in

Muzaffer Sahin, *MGK, 28 Subat Oncesi ve Sonrasi* (Ankara: Ufuk Kitabevi, 1998), p. 119.

30. 'Ordudan Rekor Ihrac' (Record-Breaking Expulsions from the Army), *Milliyet*, 17 June 1998.
31. 'YAS'ta 43 Ihrac' (43 Expulsions in the Supreme Military Board), *Milliyet*, 2 August 2000.
32. Ibid., p. 119.
33. Sahin, *MGK*, p. 116.
34. Other particularly symbolic acts were the official celebration of the 75th anniversary of the republic in October 1998, and an incident the following year after the unsolved assassination of a prominent Kemalist academic/journalist (Ahmet Taner Kislali). Both were turned into symbolic spectacles demonstrating the military's clout against Islam. In Kislali's funeral procession, the generals and the Ankara garrison turned out in full uniform, and were applauded by the crowds while the government officials were jeered at and their speeches heckled. During the 75th year celebrations, for the first time since the military coup of 1960, the War School cadets marched in their uniforms in the streets as a show of force against the existing government, and uniformed officers took to the streets to march with thousands of civilians as part of their determination to safeguard the secular character of the regime.
35. Interview with the then Defence Minister, Ismet Sezgin, *Jane's Defence Weekly*, 28 (17 December), 1997.
36. 'Irticaya Yaptirim Yok' (There Are No Enforcements Against Islamic Reactionism), *Milliyet*, 4 June 1998.
37. 'Ekonomist Asker' (Officers as Economists), *Milliyet*, 1 January 1998.
38. Stephen Kinzer, 'Kurdish Rebels Tell Turkey They Are Ending Their War', *New York Times*, 10 February 2000.
39. 'Pline Kurdish Rebels Surrender to Turkey', *Reuters*, 1 October 1999.
40. John Roper, 'The West and Turkey: Varying Roles, Common interests', *International Spectator*, 34 (January–March 1999), p. 99.
41. Lombardi, 'Turkey, the Return of the Reluctant Generals?', p. 211.
42. Soon after Turkey was given candidate status at the Helsinki summit in 1999, the High Command issued open statements rejecting the ideas pertaining to the establishment of civilian control over the armed forces in order to adjust civil–military relations in conformity with Western norms. One such rejection was of the idea of making the chief of general staff answerable to the ministry of defense. For example, General Cumhur Asparuk, then secretary general of the MGK, said in February 2000 that subordination of the general staff to the MOD could lead to dangerous 'politicization of the military'. See Leyla Boulton, 'Kurds Arrest Dents Turkey's EU Hopes', *Financial Times*, 2 February 2000. Another example is the denial of press reports on the issue of the armed forces considering granting the allegedly pro-Islamic expelled officers the right to appeal to civilian courts. See 'Domestic News Summary', *Turkish Daily News*, 24 January 2000. For a representative statement of the hierarchy on the necessity of accepting the accession requirements on conditions, see 'AB Zorunlu Ama ...' (EU is a Must But ...), *Milliyet*, 10 October 2000.
43. Sahin, *MGK*, p. 77.
44. Kramer, *A Changing Turkey*, p. 25.
45. On the double discourse of Turkey's political class towards the military, see Umit Cizre Sakallioglu, *AP_Ordu Iliskileri: Bir Ikilemin Anatomisi* (The Relations between the Justice Party and the Military: The Anatomy of a Dilemma) (Ankara: Iletisim Yayinlari, 1993).
46. Upholding Turkey's secularism has always involved an ethnicized element in terms of Turkifying Arab Islam.

11

Saddam Husayn, the Ba'th Regime and the Iraqi Officer Corps

AMATZIA BARAM

President Saddam Husayn al-Majid al-Nasiri al-Tikriti was born on 28 April 1937 in the same provincial town of Tikrit where, almost precisely 800 years earlier, Salah al-Din (Saladin) al-Ayyubi, the legendary Muslim warrior and victor over the Crusaders, was born. If Saddam's contemporary personality cult is any indication, this fact played an important role in his self-image and career. Portraying himself as the last major link in a chain of great warriors ending with Salah al-Din has become probably the single most prominent feature of his propaganda campaign since he became the president of Iraq in July 1979.[1]

Contrary to a tradition that had started in his home town in the late 1920s, however, Saddam has never served in the armed forces. In the Iraq of his youth, and especially in Tikrit and among his tribe, al-Bu Nasir, becoming an army officer was by far the most important symbol of social status and the most prestigious socio-economic upward mobility route. It is reported by some that Saddam attempted to enter the Military Academy, but failed the entrance exams. Whether or not this is true, if he had applied at all Saddam's chances of being accepted by the school were extremely low. By 1958, when he threw himself totally into his clandestine party's activity, he had not yet graduated from high school. In 1959, he fled Iraq after his attempt on the life of the dictator Abd al-Karim Qasim failed. Furthermore, even when still enrolled in al-Karkh High School, one of the less regarded of Baghdad, he spent most of his time in political activity. In those days the Military Academy was known for its solid academic standards, and while family, tribal and regional connections could (and did) help, this was so only up to a point.

During his formative years as a youth, Saddam was fascinated by the stories of his uncle (himself a retired army officer) about the war against the British in 1941.[2] In school, he was taught about the glory that was ancient Babylon, as well as about the great Arab battles and conquests under the Prophet Muhammad and the caliphs who followed. As is evident from his artistic initiatives as well as his fascination with military uniforms and insignia, Saddam Husayn never abandoned these childhood images. During the eight years of war with Iran he was rarely seen in anything but his specially designed uniform, and he ordered the nation's overwhelmingly civilian leadership to wear uniforms in all their public appearances. He also designed for his government ministers and Revolutionary Command Council (RCC) and Regional Leadership of the ruling party (RL) members special golden insignia. His monument to mark his costly victory over Iran combines two sets of gigantic, 40-meter long shining steel swords held by replicas of his own hands above a military parade ground.

Nevertheless, the stain on his reputation of having never served in the armed forces has had tremendous influence on the way that Saddam Husayn treated the Iraqi officers corps. It has also played an important role in the attitude of Iraqi army officers toward Saddam Husayn since he became a leading politician. Like Saddam, most of the highest echelon of Ba'thi leaders when the party gained power in 1968 were civilians, but all of them had some intellectual aura and party veteran status. Saddam, who had hardly graduated from high school and had joined the party as late as 1957, had no such feathers in his cap.

When the party came to power in 1968 it carried with it a phobia against army officers for two reasons. In the first place, in November 1963, the President, General 'Abd al-Salam 'Arif and some army officers – including the Ba'thi prime minister, General Ahmad Hasan al-Bakr, and a few civilian Ba'this – ousted the rest of the civilian party leadership from power. A few months after, even those party civilians and officers who had collaborated with General 'Arif and his officers were ousted, and were later imprisoned. This trauma has never left Saddam and his colleagues.

The second reason was the threatening presence of a large number of officers sympathetic to Egypt's Gamal 'Abd al-Nasir in the Iraqi armed forces. Despite his defeat in the June 1967 war, that Egyptian ruler was still the most prestigious Arab leader and relations between him and the Iraqi Ba'th party were extremely strained. When that party came to power on 17 July 1968 by its own military coup, Saddam and his civilian colleagues were adamant that they would never allow another military takeover. Finally, Saddam's own lack of service in the armed forces gave him an incentive to undermine any idea that serving army officers should be at the helm, as had so often happened in Iraqi history.

The first step in emasculating the army officer corps came immediately following Saddam's takeover. On 30 July Saddam led a coup within a coup: he and a few civilian party activists arrested and banished two non-Ba'thi senior officers who had helped the party to power only some two weeks earlier. These two had betrayed the trust of President 'Arif, to whom they had had been very close, and the party could not trust such people even though it had no hesitations in using them. Yet, as will be shown below, the party's mistrust and the ensuing purge did not limit itself to non-Ba'thi officers.

The second phase started immediately afterward. Between two and three thousand army officers, whom the new regime considered politically unreliable (mostly supporters of Egypt's Gamal 'Abd al-Nasir), were retired. This was the work of one of Saddam's closest supporters, Captain (ret.) Taha Yasin Ramadan (currently Iraq's vice-president).[3] The next step in the same direction was to flood the RCC, the highest decision-making institution, with civilian party activists. In November 1969 the RCC, which had consisted of five army generals, was expanded to 15 members, all the new ones being civilians.

Saddam Husayn himself, who since the first day of the new Ba'th rule was made the czar of domestic security, may have also already been appointed by President Bakr as deputy secretary-general of the Iraqi party. Now he was made, in addition, vice-president and deputy chairman of the RCC.[4] This turned him into the regime's number two man, placing him above decorated, well-known and highly respected army generals like Deputy Commander-in-Chief, Deputy Prime Minister and Minister of Defense, Hardan 'Abd al-Ghafar al-Tikriti, Deputy Prime Minister and Minister of the Interior Salih Mahdi 'Ammash and Chief of Staff Hammad Shihab.

President Ahmad Hasan al-Bakr's decision to elevate his young, civilian, poorly educated relative to this powerful position was made under the influence of Bakr's childhood friend and tribesman, Khayr Allah Talfah, Saddam's maternal uncle. Saddam spent much of his childhood in Khayr Allah's home, and the two were very close. As Khayr Allah explained to the president, the party's debacle in 1963 proved that the danger to the regime's survival required making his nephew the government's number two man by nominating him chief of security, deputy secretary-general of the party, vice-president and deputy chairman of the RCC.[5]

It may also be assumed that Bakr was fully aware that the reliability of army officers was even weaker than party cama-raderie. The repeated military coups in Iraq between 1936 and 1941, and even more so between 1958 and 1968, provided suffi-cient evidence. In addition to his inclination to rely on tribal – rather than on political – solidarity, Bakr apparently also con-sidered Saddam a safe choice precisely because he was a civilian and was not well known in Iraq. Bakr could view Saddam as totally dependent on him and lacking the connections or prestige that came with being a high-ranking officer. Moreover, within the party Saddam was only considered a muscle man, not a true leader. In that highly hierarchical organization, he had relatively little prestige, except for the record of his unsuccessful assassination attempt against General Qasim in 1959.

In exchange for his consent to dilute the army officers' component of the RCC, President Bakr received other advan-tages. For example, in a new constitution introduced in mid-1970 it was stipulated that the president 'may appoint himself' prime minister and that he can appoint and dismiss cabinet ministers, apparently at will.[6] Bakr also supported some of Saddam's initi-atives to reduce the army's political power and remove generals whom he saw as potential rivals. In 1970, Saddam ousted from the RCC two formidable generals who had held highly sensitive positions: Interior Minister General Salih Mahdi 'Ammash and Defense Minister Hardan 'Abd al-Ghaffar al-Tikriti. The latter was soon assassinated in his exile in Kuwait.

Using such methods, however, Saddam outmaneuvered Bakr himself. By mid-1973 he was already the strong man in Baghdad. In June of that year he crushed a coup hatched by his own head of general security, Nazim Kazzar. He took advantage of the ensuing confusion to remove several of his personal rivals in the party, such as 'Abd al-Khaliq al-Samarra'i.

The party could not, of course, control Iraq without the army, let alone defend it against a hostile Iran that challenged Iraq's control over the Shatt al-Arab waterway. But the party could manipulate the army officer corps to obey it docilely through patriotic indoctrination ('the enemy is in our gates') and intimidation. After the Ba'th takeover, Saddam saturated with his fellow tribesmen the presidential bodyguard units and the party internal security organs, the most important of which was Jihaz Hanin (the Apparatus of Yearnings), later to be called al-Mukhabarat al-'Amma (General Intelligence).

Other recruits were drawn from friendly tribes, at first from the Tikrit area, then from other Sunni Arab areas of Iraq. These were provincial young men with relatively little education, mostly from a low socioeconomic background. For such young men to be brought to the capital and given power and lavish perks was a sufficient reason for loyalty, even devotion, to Saddam. More senior security operators were devoted party members who would do anything to prevent a repeat of the 1963 coup. Some of them were Shi'ites. When the army officers were preparing to fight an external enemy and spending much of their time in the field or in the barracks, Saddam consolidated control in Baghdad. The officers were fully aware that any sign of disobedience, let alone rebellion, was very likely to lead to harsh retaliation against their families.

Saddam also brought the officer corps under control from within, using a tightly controlled security system. Every senior officer, down to the level of battalion commander, was accompanied at all times by a political officer who had the power to veto all instructions and orders. The army also introduced a crash officers' course for party activists. After a few months they graduated as second lieutenants and then were promoted at breakneck speed. During the Iraq–Iran War these party activists-turned-officers reached the ranks of major and lieutenant-colonel. This did not improve the fighting ability of the Iraqi army, but it greatly enhanced regime security.

WHO GETS TO BE GENERAL?

In 1976, Saddam persuaded President Bakr, who by then was totally dependent on him, to promote him in one day from a civilian with no military record whatsoever to the rank of a four-star general (*fariq awwal*).[7] The promotion ceremony took place on the day before Army Day, so he could wear his new uniform at the military parade on the most important day of the Iraqi army. It is also significant that, while two years earlier he had received from President Bakr the highest medal in the land, the Order of the Twin Rivers (*Wisam al-Rafidayn*) of the *civilian* type, he was now awarded the same medal of the *military* type. This signaled to all that, from January 1976, Saddam Husayn was no longer a civilian but, rather, a military man.[8] In his speeches he began to use distinctive military jargon, speaking of trenches and offensives.[9]

The practice of promoting people who served him well to the highest military ranks, regardless of their military background, gathered momentum after he became president. He began by immediately promoting himself to field marshal (*muhib*). Then, during the Iraq–Iran War, he promoted a number of his chief bodyguards to generals. Each was nicknamed 'Chief Companion' (*murafiq aqdam*) and all of them, people like Sabah Mirza, Rukan Abd Ghafur Sulayman Razuqi and Abd Ihmid Hmud were relatives.

Particularly humiliating for career officers was the promotion of three people lacking any military background to the rank of four-star general. All three had graduated from al-Bakr Staff

Academy, but had never served in the armed forces. Among them was the RCC's deputy chairman, 'Izzat Ibrahim al-Duri, who was also made deputy commander-in-chief of the armed forces in April 1991, in the wake of the Gulf War and the Shi'a intifada. His only qualification was his total loyalty to Saddam and his brutality during the suppression of the 1991 Shi'a revolt.

The promotion of Saddam's second cousin, Husayn Kamil, made more sense – at least he had some military background. Husayn Kamil was born in 1958.[10] When he turned 18 he joined the Military Academy, graduated as second lieutenant in 1979, and was appointed to the Palace Guard (al-Himaya or Himayat al-Ra'is).[11] In the early 1980s Saddam started paying attention to him. According to Saddam Husayn, he prepared the Republican Guard for the defense of Baghdad's outskirts against a probable Iranian offensive in mid-1982, by picking out officers from the whole army and beginning to turn the Guard into an Army Group (*faylaq*).[12] This description is exaggerated: in 1982 Kamil was a junior officer with little experience. The man really behind the very successful expansion of the RG was Major-General Husayn Rashid, a Kurdish tank officer from Tikrit, but Husayn Kamil was certainly very helpful.

In 1983 Saddam offered him his elder daughter, Gharad, in marriage and in early 1989, less than a decade after he graduated from military academy, he was already a major-general. Soon afterward he became minister of industry and military industries.[13] In April 1991 he was awarded the ultimate honor, when he was sworn in as minister of defense[14] and soon afterwards was promoted to lieutenant general.[15] On 6 November 1991, apparently as a result of a successful maneuver by Saddam's son, 'Udayy, Husayn Kamil received a most humiliating presidential kick downstairs. This demonstrated to all that even the president's most popular and successful 'general' was at his mercy.

Soon afterward, however, he was again in the saddle as director of the huge Military Industrialization Organization. Giving lavish praise to Husayn Kamil in a speech to his government ministers, Saddam urged them to introduce into their ministries the same 'spirit and capabilities' which Kamil had instilled into his organization.[16] In September 1993 Kamil was made minister of industry and minerals.[17] In late 1993 or early 1994 he was also promoted to a staff four-star general of the army.[18] Occasionally, Saddam would refer to Kamil as 'Ibn Shab'adh', meaning the son of the Sumerian queen who Iraqi archaeologists believe excelled in technological and scientific inventions. This did not prevent Kamil from defecting to Jordan, following another brush with 'Udayy. If the insecure career of a man who was Saddam's cousin, son-in-law and a favorite 'general' was so perilous, one can imagine the sense of terror and tight-rope walking that fills the souls of regular generals.

The disdain with which officers of the Iraqi army related to these promotions and nominations was reflected in an interview given outside Iraq by the expatriate ex-chief of staff (1987–90), General Nizar 'Abd al-karim Faysal al-Khazraji. Khazraji described 'Ali Hasan al-Majid, Saddam's favorite paternal cousin and one of the leader's overnight 'generals', as:

> Illiterate ... arrogant and violent. He suffers from diabetes and is always shouting at the soldiers and officers. Finan-cially he is corrupt. They call him 'the Thief of Baghdad' ... He was an assistant corporal in the air force. The best military position he deservedly occupied was that of a driver of a fuel tanker, which supplies fuel to aircraft. Now he is a staff [four-star] general.[19]

Indeed, in November 1991 'Ali Hasan al-Majid replaced Husayn Kamil as minister of defense and was promoted from reserve corporal to general of the army.

STRATEGIC DECISION-MAKING: RESPECTING THE OFFICERS AND HEEDING THEIR ADVICE

After he became president, Saddam's decision-making skills seemed to deteriorate fast. As vice-president, all his major deci-sions, political and economic as well as military-related, were balanced and well calculated, if sometimes somewhat risky. He undermined Kurdish rebels, neutralized Iranian intervention in

Iraq's internal affairs, made an alliance with the Soviet Union, and gained full control over Iraq's oil.

In 1970 he signed an Autonomy Accord with the Kurdish rebels, ending their war with the central government which had been backed by Iran, Israel and the United States. This accord let him build up Iraq's armed forces, a project for which he gained massive Soviet support through a 1972 alliance agreement. Next, he strengthened his financial base by nationalizing the property of the Western-controlled Iraqi Petroleum Company. His agreement with the Soviet Union shielded him against any Western military and economic reprisal, and the decision brought big profits when oil prices rose sharply from 1973. Finally, in 1975, Saddam conceded to Iranian territorial demands and gave up Iraq's sovereignty on the eastern (Iranian) bank of the Shatt al-Arab waterway. This was a humiliating decision, but it let him crush the Kurds without Iranian interference.

Had he kept a cool head in the same manner between 1980 and 1990, Saddam would have become a nuclear power, the strongest state in the Persian Gulf, and in a position to dictate world oil prices. But he did not keep a cool head, and some of his major miscalculations involved the military sphere. The lack of advice – or at least candid counsel – from professional officers probably helped ensure such mistakes occurred.

For example, the decision to go to war against Iran was made without any consultation at all with the military command. There were signs of preparations for that war soon after Saddam became president in July 1979 (mainly through an intensified strategic intelligence-gathering and upgrading of the regular armed forces).[20] Yet, the actual decision to invade Iran was made in April 1980 by Saddam alone, at Lake Tharthar, one of his favorite holiday resorts, and was sent to his officers without any military input. The trigger was an attempt on the life of Tariq 'Aziz, Saddam's (Christian) closest associate, initiated in April by the Da'wa Islamic Party, a Shi'a group supporting Iran's Islamist revolution. 'Aziz was only wounded, but Saddam saw in it an Iranian attempt to humiliate him. Saddam arrived at the scene and swore: 'By God! I will make them pay for this!' After spending three days at Lake Tharthar alone with his cooks, bodyguards and servants, having only swam, slept and eaten his meals in total isolation, he returned to Baghdad and ordered his officers to prepare for war.[21]

In view of the preference for loyalty over performance among the officer corps, it is hardly surprising that the Iraqi army's performance during the war's first phases was dismal. This was the result not only of bad military leadership but also of lack of confidence between the political leadership and field officers. Until the debacle when Iraq lost the Faw Peninsula and suffered other defeats in early 1986, army officers were extremely limited in their scope for military decisions. The presidential palace (apparently, Saddam in person) intervened in numerous field decisions and thus greatly hampered military initiative. In fact, operational control was in the hands of ignorant civilians and in the palace in Baghdad, rather than in those of the professionals and close to the battlefield.

The civilian leadership, mainly Saddam himself, insisted on a very tight control of every military move and denied the officers any independence in their decisions. When an officer gave a retreat order without his permission, or when a unit surrendered, the responsible parties were summarily executed.[22] During the first half of 1982, when the Iraqi forces were pushed from the conquered Iranian cities of Abadan and Khorramshahr back into Iraqi territory, professional officers were placed in a no-win situation. If, in order to save the unit, they ordered retreat without first clearing it with headquarters (which then had to clear it with Saddam), they were executed, demoted or dismissed. If, on the other hand, they waited for authorization, it was often too late to retreat, in which case they paid with their lives or their jobs for losing their troops.

The most devastating such event occurred in what was called by the Iraqi troops 'The Exterminating Pocket' (al-jib al-muhlik), near Muhammara, where tens of thousands of Iraqi soldiers became prisoners of war. Three army divisions were encircled, and then surrendered. The divisional commanders and, possibly, the army group commander as well were summarily executed by one of Saddam's chief bodyguards (and maternal relative), Sabah Mirza.[23] This did not help the Iraqi army much, but was a useful way for Saddam to demonstrate to his hostile officers that he was the boss. There was also very little air-to-ground support, due to fears that air force pilots might turn around and strafe the presidential palace rather than the Iranian enemy.

Toward the end of the Iraq–Iran War, Saddam gathered self-confidence again and lesser – albeit still humiliating – punishments were given to generals, but with great publicity. For example, in a high-profile public announcement the commander of the 19th Armored Division, General Majid Mahmud Husayn, was retired and demoted for 'his failure in command and hesitation in battle', a horrible humiliation for any officer.[24] The commander of the 7th Infantry Division, too, was dismissed and humiliated in public during the battles of the south.[25] Major General Sa'id 'Abd al-Hadi Muhammad Salih 'Asaf, commander of the 39th Division, too, was dismissed in a humiliating way in 1988. 'Freezing' generals at their ranks for long periods because they 'made private visits' to each other's offices to chat was yet another means by which the president disciplined his top officers and ensured that he kept tight control.[26]

The result of the president's monopoly on decision-making was passivity, a lack of offensive initiatives and poor military performance. The loss of Faw became a turning point. At an extraordinary party congress in July 1986, the military managed to convince Saddam to let them win the war for him. He transferred operational control to his maternal cousin, Minister of Defense General (a legitimate one for a change) 'Adnan Khayr Allah Talfah. This proved to be a relative success.[27] At the end of the war Saddam took back all his power from Talfah, who died in May 1989 in a mysterious helicopter crash. While many suspected that Saddam had his cousin assassinated, this may not be true. There was a strong sandstorm near Mosul, from where Talfah insisted on flying his helicopter back to Baghdad.

Still, when the war ended Iraq's president reverted to his old habit of not consulting with his army officers over military affairs, or ignoring their advice when it conflicted with his wishes. Certainly, Saddam had learned that a war against Iran was a mistake, as he himself explained to eager officers who wanted to continue the successful offensive of spring–summer 1988 deep into Iran again. As he described it,

All the Iraqi armed forces commanders without exception were very upset when Iran accepted [a ceasefire] … They wanted to take revenge … However, we [read: I] stopped them … We stopped the Iraqi armies and pushed them back to their positions, leaving to Iran its territory and giving it a chance to reconsider its stands.[28]

There is no reason to doubt this account, or at least its spirit. Saddam's decision was a sound one. The trouble was that, by denying his army officers the revenge they sought, Saddam was trapped in a quest for some other victory. This time, however, he needed to be sure the war was easily winnable.

In the spring of 1990 he discussed with the officers how to deter Israel from an attack on Iraq's 'industrial' (meaning nuclear) installations. There was general consensus that a non-conventional deterrence was needed. Saddam thus reported proudly that the threat 'to burn half of Israel' (implying the use of chemical weapons in response to a conventional Israeli attack) was worked out in a lengthy meeting with his senior army officers.[29]

But the decision to invade Kuwait was taken in near isolation. It was made by Saddam in brief consultation with only three people – two of them his cousins – who had no real military experience. On 30 June 1990, Saddam assembled the whole senior leadership, about 20 people, and a decision was made that Kuwait was behaving in an unacceptable manner and must be punished. There was no clear decision about what to do, but the intention was to occupy a part of Kuwait, possibly the oil field of south Rumayla, the small island of Warba, and at least a part of the larger Bubyan island.

In mid-July, Saddam met secretly with his cousins, Husayn Kamil and 'Ali Hasan al-Majid. The only professional military man present was the fourth participant, General Iyad Khalifa al-Rawi, commander of the Republican Guard. Saddam disclosed to them that he had decided to occupy the whole of Kuwait, and they immediately agreed. The rest of the military was not informed. Apparently, the General Staff and the minister of defense learned of the decision only from public radio broadcasts. Even two days before the invasion happened, as few as 10 people – most of them

RG officers – knew about the decision. As civilian or military officials were informed, they followed a practice known as 'Pink (optimistic) Information', assuring Saddam that his decision was the right one and that all was going to be just fine. Saddam's decision not to withdraw from Kuwait before 15 January 1991, when the Allied ultimatum expired, was also apparently taken in isolation.[30]

There was at least one more occasion when Saddam did consult some of his generals but, again, when their professional advice was not to his liking he simply ignored it, to his detriment. In 1994, when Iraq's leadership realized that the embargo was continuing and that even a timetable for its lifting was not in sight, the hardliners (and the hardline inclination in Saddam's own personality) gradually won the day. In July 1994, senior army and air force officers, both in active service and in retirement, were sounded on a military option. They were asked what were the chances of 'a second threat to Kuwait' (a new attack and occupation), and 'the possibility of a second blow to Iraq' (an Allied retaliation). At least ex-chief of staff, four-star General Nizar al-Khazraji, as well as Lieutenant-General Hamid Sha'ban – a member of Saddam's tribe, former commander of the Iraqi air force and, at the time, Saddam's military adviser – as well as the secretary of the General Command, a serving officer, all agreed that Iraq should refrain from further military threats 'because the Allies would strike and destroy everything that we had built'. Saddam's personal secretary and chief bodyguard, 'Abd [Hamid] Hmud, who recorded the discussion in order to give a record to Saddam, represented the president.[31]

But Saddam ignored the advice of his professional officers. In early October 1994 he ordered his Republican Guard to march on Kuwait again or, at least, to move toward the Kuwaiti border in a threatening fashion. The reason for the order was, apparently, that he was humiliated by the UN Security Council's decision not to lift the embargo, even though he had accepted its Resolution 715 on long-term ongoing monitoring of his arsenal, and he may have feared the reaction of his power base. Also, having been promised by the French that this step would bring about the lifting of the embargo, he was certainly angry and felt betrayed. However, when threatened with a decisive US response he withdrew.

It would seem that Saddam wanted to consult his generals only in the hope they would endorse his project. Apparently, since he was unsure this would be their conclusion, he preferred not to meet them in the flesh. Eventually, having to withdraw his troops under Allied threat was most humiliating, far more so than the retention of the embargo.

THE MILITARY GENIUS: TEACHING THE OFFICER CORPS

Following the Iraq–Iran War, Saddam took advantage of every opportunity to demonstrate to his officer corps his deep understanding of military affairs as well as their own shortcomings. On numerous occasions, he made them admit his strategic ingenuity and their own inferiority. For example, the man who had never commanded a platoon would meet with his senior army officers to teach them how to conduct modern warfare.[32] They paid him the utmost deference as a great military leader. Thus, following the liberation of the Faw Peninsula in April 1988, the president was given all the credit for 'supervising and managing' the whole battle, at the expense of commander of the RG, General Iyad Khalifa al-Rawi and commander of the 7th Army, Mahir 'Abd Rashid.[33] A few months later Staff Major General Hasan Mustafa wrote, in a study of Iraq's military preparations to liberate the Faw, that the plan prepared by himself and his colleagues (at the General Staff) was 'ordinary'. By comparison, Saddam's plan was 'ingenious … excellent, exemplary and unique and much greater than [our] plan' in achieving both the tactical goal (the liberation of the Faw Peninsula) and the strategic one (ending the eight-year-long war in victory).[34]

In contrast, when Saddam's relative, General Mahir 'Abd Rashid, whose daughter was already married to Qusayy, the president's second son, and whom many Iraqis called 'Rommel of the Arabs', forgot to mention Saddam's role in the liberation of the Faw Peninsula, he was sacked and placed under house arrest.[35] An additional reason for the dismissal was the fact that Mahir did not wait for the RG and sent his army group into the Faw first, hoping to score a victory on his own. Instead, his troops were bogged down, and eventually it was, indeed, the RG that won the battle. Mahir's attempt to snatch the victory from Saddam's private army did not result in his death, thanks only to his special status – his membership in the tribe, his daughter's marriage to Qusayy and his popularity in the army.

Meanwhile, throughout the 1980s, the Iraqi media portrayed the president as a great warrior equal to, and sometimes greater than, Sargon the Akkadian, Hammurabi the Babylonian, Ashubanipal, the great Assyrian warrior-king, Nebucadnezzer the Chaldean, the early Islamic war heroes al-Muthnna Bnu al-Haritha, al-Qa'qa', Khalid Bnu al-Walid, Tariq Bnu Ziyad, and the Iraqi-Kurd from Tikrit, Salah al-Din (Saladin) al-Ayyubi.[36]

Following the disastrous 1996 defeat at the Faw Peninsula, the Iraqi leader badly needed his professional officers. A few days after the most humiliating defeat in Iraqi history, the press showed Field Marshal Saddam Husayn surrounded by his General Staff, and all of them laughing uncontrollably.[37] This was during the very days when Iraq was launching a spasmodic, mad, counter-offensive to regain the lost peninsula, which cost 53,000 of its best troops, including hundreds of Saddam's personal bodyguards, who were thrown into the battle to save the troops' morale. The senior army officers were not fooled. In fact, they were stunned. Thus, as described above, in an extraordinary party congress in July, they collectively forced Saddam to relinquish many of his military authorities and allow them much more freedom of action.

THE OFFICER CORPS' RESPONSE

The fact that the Iraq–Iran War ended in a draw, despite the overwhelming Iraqi advantage in equipment and some advantage in terms of the number of men under arms, was a major embarrassment for Saddam. This can be gauged from his largely inflated descriptions of the proportions of the Iraqi victory over Iran in his annual Victory Day speeches starting 8 August 1988. The more he congratulated his army officers and himself for their decisive victory, and the more medal and Victory Sword award ceremonies, the starker the contrast between these descriptions and reality.

Indeed, at the end of the Gulf War Saddam made sure that his army officers received medals for questionable achievements and substantial economic rewards, in the hope that this would keep them out of mischief. He also, however, kept his army officers under unprecedented internal security surveillance. Every complaint they uttered was reported immediately to the president. This applied also to retired officers, because of their close ties with serving officers.

Most prominent was the case of General (Ret.) Dr Raji al-Tikriti, ex-commander of the army's medical corps. During a visit to Jordan in 1993, he was foolish enough to crack a joke on Saddam in the company of Jordanian and Iraqi friends. As soon as he returned to Baghdad he was arrested. After an encounter with the president, he was tortured and killed.[38] Less serious offenses have been treated differently, but with no less presidential attention. For example, officers who complained about lack of ammunition or shortage of engine hours necessary to train their tank crews were summoned to the president and told that their lives depended on never repeating such criticism. The sole decision maker in terms of military policy in Iraq, they were told, was Saddam, and any complaint against the system was a complaint against him. They could make such a mistake only once.[39]

Saddam himself indicated a few times after 1988 that there were problems in the army. These indications started as soon as the Iraq–Iran War ended and continued after the Gulf War. Thus, for example, as early as February 1989, only some seven months after the Iran–Iraq war ended, Saddam darkly warned his army officers that they did not understand their society as did army officers in the West and thus that 'devils may play in the dark' and 'big surprises may result here'.[40] This warning was based on real concerns. A few months later a large group of Jubburi officers did, indeed, try to topple the regime (see below). After the Gulf War, by way of a joke, Saddam suggested to his senior officers in a social meeting to hatch, together with him, a coup against himself in order to please the West.[41]

More seriously, Saddam often warned officers against 'spreading rumors'.[42] Saddam also called upon officers not to 'lie' to their soldiers that Iraq was not ready for the Gulf War.[43] His paternal cousin, 'Ali Hasan al-Majid, warned officers against 'treason' in collaboration with Iraq's enemies.[44] Saddam even felt the need to explain to his army officers the great binding power of the Islamic oath of allegiance to the Khalifah-Caliph (al-Bay'a) and, nowadays, to the supreme leader.[45] At the same time the RCC issued the Republican Decree, according to which any military man whose disloyalty to the 'Revolution and its principles' is exposed would be retired and demoted.[46]

These often-repeated warnings were not without reason. In the dozen years since the Iraq–Iran War ended in 1988, there have been at least three cases when senior and middle-level officers prepared coups against Saddam. Officers from the army and the RG, all hailing from the Jubbur tribe, planned the first one for the 6 January 1990 military parade on Army Day. Saddam's security had already penetrated the group. The parade was cancelled at the last moment and all culprits were arrested, tortured and executed.

Another coup was exposed in the summer and fall of 1993. It involved mainly army officers, some of them from Tikrit, as well as some members of the Mukhlis clan, the most prominent family of Tikrit under the monarchy. The exposure was made easier this time due to the fact that information was leaked from members of the Iraqi opposition in Britain. The third coup, apparently orchestrated by the CIA, was exposed in summer 1996, involving mainly RG and SRG officers. This time, again, an Amman-based opposition group, the National Accord (al-wifaq al-watani) was reported to have been involved.

In all three cases hundreds of officers were arrested, and many scores were executed. In addition, in-between these incidents, many officers were executed or imprisoned as a result of suspicions, or because they did not report cases when colleagues-turned-agents-provocateurs asked them to join a plot against Saddam. The most famous case is that of air force General Mazlum al-Dulaymi in 1995. He was tortured and killed. When his mutilated body was brought to his family in Ramadi, this started a spontaneous revolt by al-Bu Nimr of the Dulaym, west of the capital.[47]

All these purges created more fear, but also more hate, within the armed forces. This presented Saddam with a serious problem: the army's loyalty to his person was continually in question. All the existing evidence indicates that the army officer corps (as opposed to that of the RG) is performing repression duties in the Shi'a south only very reluctantly. While not completely unaffected, despite over 30 years of coercive Ba'thization and Saddamization, the army officer corps still seems to have retained some of its original independent spirit.

THE REPUBLICAN GUARD

The RG officers have, naturally, been more privileged. All the same, however, in all known coups between 1990 and 1996 RG and army officers alike were involved. It would seem that Saddam's dwindling economic resources, and the widespread sense that the embargo will never end as long as he was in power, may explain the resentment even in the RG. According to some reports in the mid-1990s, the rate of desertion in the army was very high, up to 30 per cent, and perks, even for the RG, were reduced.

Nevertheless, the RG is an exception in this strange relationship with a leader who has never served in the armed forces, but who promoted himself to the rank of field marshal and constantly made momentous decisions about war and peace. It was established as an army corps following the 1986 defeat at Faw. The two men behind it were General Husayn Rashid Ibrahim (a capable Kurdish tank officer from Tikrit) and Husayn Kamil, Saddam's second cousin and son-in-law. This unit was made up of officers and men who were recruited from many army units for their ability and loyalty alike, with a high percentage of university students and graduates. It also consisted of a high percentage of Sunni Arab soldiers and Sunni Arab tribal officers. It received the best training and equipment, in addition to salaries and gifts, and enjoyed relatively easy access to the president. This secured the RG's loyalty to the regime and its leader.

Furthermore, the RG has been under the command of the presidential palace rather than the army's chief of staff. It may be seen as Saddam's private army. During the last stage of the Iraq–Iran War it fought well, was the most successful unit and acquired the most experience in the battles that started in April 1988 with the liberation of the Faw, and ended with deep penetrations into Iran's Khozestan region in July–August of that year. In the Gulf

War it again fought better than any other unit and did not flee the fighting arena as other units did. The RG was Saddam's only hope when massive Shi'a and Kurdish revolt erupted in March 1991, at the end of the war and, indeed, it suppressed the revolts in rivers of blood.

In August–September 1996, the RG again proved its loyalty and relative efficacy when it was ordered into Kurdish-held Irbil. It devastated the forces of Jalal Talabani and the Iraqi National Congress and put an end to a US intelligence operation in Kurdistan. Finally, in October 2000, the RG Hammurabi Armored Division moved into the western desert toward the Syrian border, on Saddam's orders, to prepare for war with Israel in support of the Palestinian uprising. This was clearly a mere political show of force, but it also demonstrated that, when Saddam needs a military unit to demonstrate for him he can and does rely on the RG. Even though a few RG officers were involved in two coup attempts in 1993 and 1996, there were no reliable reports of any such involvement later on. In short, while his relations with the regular army officer corps are often rocky and always complex, those with the RG officer corps are reasonably healthy.

By the year 2000 there was evidence that the surge of oil prices, and thus the revenue from smuggled oil, had enabled Saddam to pamper the officers of the RG again and to provide them with new spare parts and ammunition. The regular army, however, is still in a bad shape and can hardly be considered a fighting force. Its officers seem to be demoralized and extremely unhappy, and their attitude toward the leader is likely to be negative. Yet they are powerless to do anything about it as long as the RG is still loyal to Saddam: usually, the RG is stationed between the regular army units and the capital city. Marching on Baghdad is therefore rendered completely hopeless.

CONCLUSION

How does the tension between Saddam and his army officers affect Iraqi politics? An important reason (though, clearly, not the only one) for Saddam's intransigence regarding his Weapons of Mass

Destruction seems to be that he believes his officer corps blames him for undermining Iraq's military prowess. Owing to his mistaken decisions in 1990–91, Iraq lost much of its conventional forces. Worse still, as a result of UN Resolution 687, Iraq has, since April 1991, been losing its edge in terms of non-conventional weapons over Iran and its chance of fast achieving strategic parity with Israel. Army officers are charged with responsibility for national security, and Saddam seriously damaged Iraq's national security in both realms.

It is not clear to this writer to what extent the strategic non-conventional weapons are dear to the hearts of senior army officers. It may be that many of them are unenthusiastic: after all, these missiles' warheads have always been kept strictly in the hands of the Special Security Organization (SSO, *Jihaz al-Amn al-Khass*), a security force most of whose members hail from Saddam's tribe, al-Bu Nasir. This force is an extension of Saddam's person and has only the president's interests at heart, not those of the Iraqi nation-state. Very senior Iraqi army officers told UN officials that the orders Saddam gave the SSO in the Gulf War, in case Baghdad were besieged and they lost contact with him, were blood-curdling. Officers are aware, then, that their leader was ready to sacrifice the capital's population in that event.[48]

Further, once he is in possession of nuclear weapons, Saddam would need only his tribal missile units to win a war. The proud Iraqi officer corps would be reduced to an auxiliary body, servicing and guarding Saddam's missile force. It is also not clear to what extent the army's officer corps identifies with Saddam's grand design of turning Iraq into the hegemonic power in the Gulf and the Arab world, but for those who do endorse it, enforcement of Resolution 687 threatens to terminate Iraq's hope for such a quest for Arab leadership.

The tension between a president, who never served in the armed forces but insisted on promoting himself to field marshal, and his officers, is bound to affect the leader's political decisions under the best of circumstances. In Iraq, where, until the early 1970s, the military was deeply involved in politics, this is doubly so. Saddam's need to demonstrate to his professional officers his strategic ingenuity, even infallibility (he has always defined both

225

the Iraq–Iran and Gulf Wars as huge victories), will probably continue to prick the sides of his ambition for as long as he is in power.

Would things be different under a different authoritarian leadership, for example, of a career army general or a military junta? The answer is probably a qualified yes. A popular army or air force general enjoying the respect of his peers would be under far less pressure than is Saddam Husayn to prove his military and strategic omniscience and omnipotence.

Judging by at least five historical precedents in Iraq, this seems to have been the case. General Nuri al-Sa'id, who served longer than any other Iraqi under the monarchy as prime minister, and was the strong man behind the throne between 1941 and 1958, adopted very conservative and restrained military policies. He was careful never to test his army in a major confrontation against any of Iraq's neighbors. He had great respect for the Iranian and the Turkish armies, and refrained from any adventures in Kuwait because he had great respect for the British armed forces and, in any case, was keen on keeping on good terms with Great Britain.

General 'Abd al-Karim Qasim, who had won the respect of his peers when he commanded an Iraqi force in the Palestine War of 1948, was very careful, too, not to engage in battle against Iran, despite growing tension over the Shatt al-Arab. In June 1961 he announced the annexation of Kuwait, but when he realized that the British navy was on its way to protect Kuwait he decided to stay put, even though he had prepared forces to march on his tiny neighbor. It is quite possible that his annexation announcement was simply a test balloon to see how the British would react, and to act accordingly.

Generals 'Abd al-Salam and 'Abd al-Rahman 'Arif were just as careful not to get involved in war against any of their neighbors. The force that the latter 'Arif sent to fight in the 1967 Arab–Israeli war was half that sent in 1948 by the monarchy to 'liberate Palestine'. General Ahmad Hasan al-Bakr for his part, with Saddam as his deputy, managed his conflict with Iran (1969–75) with extreme caution. He allowed for small border skirmishes, especially around the Shatt al-Arab, but essentially limited himself to political struggle in the Arab world and the UN and to a fierce media campaign. Even when the Shah occupied the three strate-gic islands at the mouth of the Gulf, Bakr kept to the diplomatic sphere. It was then that Saddam, with or without his approval, embarked on military nuclear and biological programs, but this was a very long-term project. It is true that the Iranian provocation since 1979, inciting the Iraqi Shi'a to topple the 'atheist' Ba'th regime, and the potential for a revolt in the Shi'a south, went beyond anything that preceded the rise of the Ayatollah Khomeini to power in Iran. Still, Iraq was in no immediate danger from Iran, and the domestic unrest clearly subsided towards the middle of 1980. When Saddam attacked, the Shi'a population was already cowed most effectively.

It has to be pointed out, though, that any dictatorship headed by an army general and supported by the largely Sunni Arab officer corps, runs a real risk of clashing with the majority of the Shi'a population who live in Saddam City and in the south. This is a matter of socioeconomic priorities and of a clash of identities. If the new leader would be unable to give the majority of the Shi'a a sense of true equality plus some religious, cultural and educa-tional autonomy for the more traditional circles, he is sure to run up against growing opposition. This could lead both to repres-sion and foreign adventure. Without doubt, a democratic regime, enjoying full legitimacy in that it is representative, holds the best promise for an Iraq that will not seek to change the regional territorial status quo by force.

Could the army be expected to play any role in a regime change? A military coup staged by army officers (as opposed to RG, SRG or SSO officers) is difficult to imagine. The army suffers from low morale, massive desertion, shortage of spare parts and too little training. All army units are stationed at a considerable distance from the capital city. Between them and the capital, Saddam has stationed the RG units, which serve as an outer shield for the regime. Inside of the city, security is in most part in the hands of the SRG, a 20,000-strong commando unit with around 100 tanks. Their duty is to block city streets, seal off city quarters and clear the road for the regime luminaries heading to the airport. Most of them hail from Saddam's tribe and some other tribes that have been working closely with the regime for a long time (Harb, al-Jawa'ina, al-Shaya'isha, albu Bazun, albu Yasin, al-'Azza and others). Thus, the chances of an army unit penetrating through these protective shields are negligible.

The army, though, can be very instrumental in a situation in which the survival of the regime comes into question as a result of an American aerial bombardment, a mass Shi'a revolt, or a split at the heart of the regime – Saddam's family. In such a case, whole army units under their commanding officers may cross over or simply cease to take orders from Baghdad. The traditional disdain of the army officer corps towards Saddam and his family may become under such circumstances a crucial factor. All that will be needed is to create a situation in which fear of Saddam's reprisal would diminish. In such a case, despite all of Saddam's efforts to rub in the notion of the sacred nature of the *Bay'ah* (swearing of allegiance), he can expect little loyalty from his officers. However, to create such a situation is not an easy task.

The regular army could be of great help, however, in a post-revolutionary era. Following a regime change there would be a need to dismiss every single soldier and officer in the SSO and SRG. The RG would have to be integrated into the larger army. The new regime would have to ensure that the army's, rather than the SRG's, values would triumph. And the army would have the long-term role of defending Iraq against neighbors. Indeed, the army is still generally popular and would have to be a pillar for any new regime. As a young Shi'a revolutionary, whose position in Hilla was stormed by an army unit in March 1991, put it, 'No matter what it did, the Army is still the property of the people', meaning, apparently, 'the pride of the people'. One legacy, though, from Saddam's era will have to be upheld: the separation between the army and politics.

NOTES

1. The first time Salah al-Din appeared prominently in connection with Saddam's leadership was, apparently, in the new Iraqi national anthem, written by the politician-poet Shafiq Abd al-Jabbar al-Kamali under Saddam's instructions soon after the latter became president. It appeared in *al-Thawra*, 12 July 1981, and then in all school books.
2. Amir Iskandar, *Saddam Husayn: Munadilan, wa Mufakkiran wa Insanan* (As a Struggler, Thinker and Man) (Paris: Hachette, 1980), pp. 23–4.

3. Based on an interview with a Western intelligence officer who received reports of the purge in 1969 from sources within the Iraqi armed forces.
4. See Amatzia Baram, 'The Ruling Political Elite in Ba'thi Iraq 1968–1986', *International Journal of Middle East Studies*, Vol. 21 (1989), pp. 451–2.
5. Based on interviews conducted in London in the late 1990s by academic colleagues with Salah 'Umar al-'Ali, himself an RCC member in the first three years of Ba'th rule. Al-'Ali left his position as Iraq's chief envoy to the UN in August 1982 in protest against Saddam's policies and remained abroad ever since.
6. See Baram, 'The Ruling Political Elite', p. 451.
7. *Al-Thawra*, 6, 9 January 1976.
8. *Al-Muthaqqaf al-'Arabi* (Baghdad), March 1974, p. 183.
9. See, for example, his anti-Communist speech, *One Trench or Two Opposite Ones?* (Baghdad: Mizan, 1977).
10. *Babil*, 19 February 1994.
11. Tariq 'Aziz, an interview on Iraqi TV upon Kamil's defection, 11 August 1995.
12. Saddam in *al-Thawra*, 23 April 1988.
13. *Al-Tayyar al-Jadid* (London), 9 March 1989; *al-Iraq*, 24 April 1990.
14. *Baghdad INA in Arabic*, 11 April 1991, *FBIS-NES-DR*, 11 April 1991, p. 13; *Alif Ba*, 10 April 1991.
15. *Alif Ba*, 7 August 1991.
16. *Babil*, 29 December 1992.
17. *Al-Jumhuriyya*, 16 September 1993. He may have been made minister a few months earlier.
18. *Al-Thawra*, 17 August 1994; *Republic of Iraq Radio Network in Arabic*, 17 April 1995, *FBIS-NES-DR*, 21 April 1995, pp. 30–2.
19. General Khazraji interviewed by *al-Hayat* (London), 16 April 1996, *FBIS-NES-DR*, 18 April 1996, pp. 21–6.
20. Based on an interview with an Israeli intelligence officer who was then in charge of the Iraqi desk.
21. An interview between al-'Ali and a colleague, 1999.
22. See Anthony H. Cordesman and Abraham R. Wagner, *The Lessons of Modern War* (Boulder, CO: Westview Press, 1990), p. 142. This information has been corroborated by interviews with ex-soldiers.
23. An interview with an Iraqi expatriate now in the US, who served in the army during most of the war and who had access to his contemporaries, children of senior regime personalities.
24. *Al-Jumhuriyya*, 18 July 1988.
25. *Al-Thawra*, 1 May 1988.
26. *Al-Jumhuriyya*, 28 January 1988.
27. For details see Stephen C. Pelletiere, *The Iraq–Iran War: Chaos in a Vacuum* (New York, Westport: Praeger, 1992), pp. 105–9.
28. See his speech in *Baghdad Domestic Service* in Arabic, as in *FBIS-NES-DR*, 12 January 1989, p. 21.
29. *Al-Muharrir* (Paris), 8 May 1990.
30. Sa'd Bazzaz, in his two-day lecture in the US following his defection to the West, on 16–17 August 1995; see also Bazzaz, *Harb Talidu Ukhra: al-Ta'rikh al-Sirri li Harb al-Khalij* (Amman: al-Ahliyya lil-nahsr wal-Twzi', 1992–93), p. 50; Tariq 'Aziz in an interview to Milton Viorst, *New Yorker*, 24 June 1991, pp. 64–7; 'Aziz to *Milliyet* (Ankara), 30 May 1991. And an interview with the Iraqi brigadier general through an academic colleague, Summer 1999.
31. General Khazraji interviewed by *al-Hayat* (London), 16 April 1996, *FBIS-NES-DR*, 18 April 1996, pp. 21–6.
32. See, for examples, his meeting with brigade commanders, *al-Thawra*, 3 October 1988.
33. See description of Operation The Blessed Ramadan, *al-Thawra*, 19 April 1988. See

also description of Saddam as 'personally commanding' Operation In God We Trust (Tawakkalna 'Ala Allah), No. 3, deep inside Iran east of Baghdad, *al-Jumhuriyya*, 14 July 1988. Also *al-Thawra*, 20 April 1988.

34. *Al-Thawra*, 26 September 1988. Also a meeting between Saddam and senior officers, *Iraq TV Network* in Arabic, 14 November 1999, *FBIS-NES-DR JN1411195399*, 14 November 1999.

35. For Mahir's unwise interview, see *al-Thawra*, 20 April 1988.

36. See, for example, some graphic expressions of Saddam's intimacy with these and other historical heroic-military personalities in Amatzia Baram, *Culture, History and Ideology in the Formation of Ba'thist Iraq 1968–1989* (London, Oxford: Macmillan and St Antony's College, 1991), in the plates section.

37. *Al-Jumhuriyya*, 17 February 1986, front page.

38. An interview with a member of the Mukhlis family in the West, 1999.

39. Interview with a Western intelligence officer, Washington, DC, 1998.

40. *Arab Times* (Kuwait), 15 February 1989, p. 5.

41. *Al-'Iraq*, 15 December 1991.

42. *Al-Thawra*, 13 October 1991.

43. *INA*, 2 March 1992.

44. *INA*, 6 January 1992.

45. *Al-Thawra*, 26 March 1992.

46. *Al-Thawra*, 22 November 1992.

47. For more details, see Baram, *Building Toward Crisis: Saddam Husayn's Strategy for Survival* (Washington, DC: Washington Institute for Near East Policy, 1998), pp. 48–51.

48. Interviews with three senior UNSCOM officials in New York and Washington, DC, in October 1995 and again in 1998.

The Armed Forces of the Islamic Republic of Iran: An Assessment

MICHAEL EISENSTADT

In 1989, following a costly eight-year-long war with Iraq, Iran initiated an ambitious military build-up to rebuild, expand and modernize its war-ravaged armed forces and transform itself into a regional military power. As part of this effort, it has tried to acquire the air and naval forces needed to dominate the Persian Gulf, to develop missiles and non-conventional (chemical, biological and nuclear) weapons to enable it to intimidate neighbors, bolster deterrence and counter US influence in the Gulf, and to create – in conjunction with the Lebanese Hizballah – an infrastructure capable of supporting terrorist operations in the Middle East, Europe and South America.

Iran's economy, however, has been its Achilles' heel. Its economic woes – the legacy of war, ruinous policies, fluctuations in international oil prices, and US sanctions – forced Iran to reduce defense spending following the Iran–Iraq War, cut procurement of key items since 1989 by half, and prioritize the allocation of scarce financial resources among the various services.[1] During the 1990s, Iran lacked the funds for a sustained, across-the-board military build-up. Instead, it had to content itself with selectively enhancing its military capabilities, focusing on naval forces, missiles and non-conventional weapons. This happened in a decade when several of Iran's Arab neighbors purchased large quantities of advanced Western arms, and the United States dramatically increased its forward military presence in the region.

However, thanks to a disciplined effort to repay its short-term debt obligations during the second half of the 1990s, and the turnaround of world oil prices in the year 2000, Iran's short-term economic circumstances have improved substantially. As a result, Iran is now spending significantly more on defense than in previous years. Its defense budget for 2000–01 was 50 per cent higher than in the previous Iranian fiscal year, though it is not clear whether the additional funds went to arms imports, purchases from domestic arms suppliers, investments in the country's military infrastructure, or various classified programs (such as non-conventional weapons).[2] The Russian decision in November 2000 to continue arms transfers to Iran (in contravention of a 1995 commitment to the United States that it would fulfill only existing contracts by the end of 1999 and not sign any new ones) may indicate that major future deals are in the works.[3]

Iran's defense policies have shown remarkable constancy in the decade following the end of the Iran–Iraq War, and even after the 1997 election of reformist President Muhammad Khatami. Iran has continued its plodding efforts to expand and modernize its conventional military forces – increasingly through domestic procurement – though the main emphasis has been on the development of missiles and non-conventional weapons. Work on these latter systems has continued unabated, with Iran enjoying a number of breakthroughs in its missile program, due largely to Russian assistance. Experience has shown that the one thing Iran's liberal reformers and their hardline conservative rivals agree on is the need for a strong military, to enable Iran to play a dominant role in the Gulf and an influential role in the greater Middle East region.

IRANIAN DEFENSE PLANNING: THE STRATEGIC CONTEXT

Defense planning in the Islamic Republic has been driven by three major factors: first, a desire to achieve self-reliance in all areas of national life, as a fundamental goal of the Islamic revolution. Second, a determination to transform Iran into a regional power capable of projecting influence throughout the Middle East and beyond. Third, the need – in the wake of its war with Iraq, which was seen as the result of a tragic failure of deterrence – to strengthen its ability to deter and deal with various perceived threats in order to avoid a repetition of that experience.

Self-Reliance
Revolutionary Iran has placed a strong emphasis on military self-reliance. Under the Shah, Iran depended on the United States and Britain for nearly all its arms. Following the 1979 revolution, Tehran was isolated internationally and faced Baghdad virtually alone during the Iran–Iraq War. Tehran's sense of isolation and abandonment was heightened by the apathetic international response to Iraq's use of chemical weapons in that war – an experience that has left deep wounds in the Iranian national psyche to this day. In addition, a US-led arms embargo during the war greatly complicated Iran's efforts to replace its losses and sustain its war effort.

The bitter legacy of the war has bred a determination in Iran that these experiences should not be repeated. Iran has thus sought to develop its own military industries in order to reduce its dependence on foreign arms suppliers, minimize the impact of future embargoes, and create the foundation for a modern military capable of dealing with a range of potential missions.[4] It has also sought non-conventional weapons (particularly nuclear weapons) as a means of realizing self-reliance in the military field and enhancing its ability independently to secure its vital interests.

Status and Influence
Since 1979, Iran's foreign and defense policies have reflected the tension between two competing (though not necessarily contradictory) orientations: Islamic universalism and Persian nationalism.[5] These have, at different times and in different places, exerted varying degrees of influence over Iranian policy. The Islamic tendency generally dominated in the 1980s, while Persian nationalism prevailed in the 1990s, though geopolitics, economics and ethnicity have played an increasingly important role in shaping Iran's foreign and defense policies in recent years.[6]

Iran's clerical leaders believe that the Islamic Republic plays a key role in world affairs as standard-bearer of revolutionary Islam and guardian of oppressed Muslims everywhere. Accordingly, they believe that the fate of the worldwide Islamic community depends on Iran's ability to transform itself into a military power which can defend and advance the interests of that community. This perception also leads Tehran to support radical Islamic movements in the Middle East and elsewhere, in order to undermine US influence, to make the regional and international environment more amenable to Iranian interests, and to burnish the regime's Islamic credentials at home and abroad.

Most Iranians believe that their country is a regional power by dint of geography, demography, and natural resource endowments (gas and oil). In their view, destiny and geopolitics dictate that Iran be the dominant power in the Persian Gulf. It is the largest Gulf state, it has the longest coastline, and it has vital oil and gas interests there. This translates to a desire to dominate developments in the region, and to defend Iran's vital interests there against the United States, Iraq and Saudi Arabia.

Because of Iran's economic problems, and its corollary desire to attract foreign investment in its oil and gas sector, Iran has worked to improve relations with the West (particularly Europe), and it has made tentative gestures toward the United States in the hope that this might lead to renewed economic ties (which are much more important to Tehran than the resumption of political ties with Washington). Many among the clerical leadership realize that Iran's weak economy is a threat to stability, and a major obstacle to realizing their goal of transforming Iran into a regional power, and that the country's economic problems can no longer be ignored.

There is a large gap, however, between the self-image and the aspirations of the regime and the reality of Iran's military weakness. Tehran's efforts to expand and modernize its armed forces and enhance its military capabilities are intended to bridge this gap. Iran's financial problems, however, have prevented it from achieving its goal of building a large, capable military. Consequently, it has devoted much of its available resources to missiles and non-conventional weapons, which potentially provide the biggest 'bang' for Iran's limited defense 'bucks'. And given its financial problems, nuclear weapons may be the only way for Iran to become a military power without destroying its economy. While a nuclear weapons' program could cost billions of dollars, rebuilding its conventional military would cost tens of billions of dollars.[7]

Deterrence and Defense

Iranian defense planning is also motivated by a desire to enhance its deterrent capability. At various times, the Islamic Republic has perceived or faced threats from Iraq, the Soviet Union, the United States, Israel and, more recently, Turkey, Afghanistan and Azerbaijan. During the 15 years of the Islamic Republic, the main threats were seen as coming from the west (Iraq and Israel), and then the south (US naval forces in the Persian Gulf). The subsequent emergence of new threats to the north and east (Turkey, Azerbaijan, Afghanistan and – by extension – Pakistan) have greatly complicated Iranian defense planning.

The defeat of Iraq in the 1991 Gulf War temporarily removed Iraq from the roster of states threatening Iran. However, Iraq still possesses the largest armed forces in the Gulf region (though greatly weakened by war and sanctions) and retains a chemical and biological warfare (CBW) and missile capability. Accordingly, Iran sees a revitalized Iraq as the greatest long-term threat to its interests.

The demise of the Soviet Union was a mixed blessing. While it eliminated the only real threat to Iranian independence, the creation of new independent republics along Iran's northern border brought new fears that instability in the Caucasus and central Asia would spill over into Iran. Because of these fears, Tehran has successfully worked with Moscow to maintain stability in these regions.

Since the 1991 Gulf War, the United States has greatly increased its forward military presence in the Gulf region. Iran sees this as a threat, and it would therefore like to see an end to the US presence there. This would also enhance Iran's political and military freedom of action in the region. Iranian officials believe (not without reason) that the United States is attempting to create an anti-Iranian bloc to their north and north-east, while it is encouraging the building of regional oil and gas pipelines that bypass Iran. Thus, Tehran fears what it perceives to be American efforts at encirclement intended to harm its economy, reduce its diplomatic margin of maneuver and complicate its security situation.

Whereas Iraq and the Persian Gulf were the main focus for Iran's foreign and defense policies in the decade following the Iran–Iraq War, developments in Afghanistan have increasingly held the attention of Iran's leaders. Iran fears that the Pakistani-supported Taleban government could stir unrest among the two million Afghans in Iran and exacerbate Sunni–Shi'a tensions in eastern Iran, where the Sunni minority constitutes one-third of the population. In addition, some Iranians suspect that a series of assassinations and terrorist attacks by the opposition Mojahedin-e Khalq in 1998–99 originated from Afghanistan. Finally, Islamabad's support for the Taleban has been a source of tension between Iran and Pakistan. Tensions with Afghanistan (and by extension Pakistan) are likely to be a feature of Iran's threat environment for years to come.

Relations with Azerbaijan have also become strained. Iran tacitly supported Armenia in its war with Azerbaijan (which ended with a shaky ceasefire in 1994). Furthermore, Tehran is concerned that Azerbaijan might become a magnet for Iran's Azeris, who constitute about one-third of its population. Senior Iranian officials also fear that Azerbaijan is increasingly aligning itself with American and Israeli interests.

Finally, with Iran implacably opposed to the existence of Israel, the Jewish state has looked askance upon the Islamic Republic's efforts to develop non-conventional weapons and missiles capable of reaching Israel. Iranian decision makers have been alarmed at past threats by senior Israeli politicians and military officials directed at Iran's missile and nuclear infrastructure – undoubtedly with Israel's June 1981 air strike on Iraq's Osiraq nuclear reactor in mind. Moreover, as a result of growing military cooperation with Turkey, Israel now effectively has a presence on the Turkish border with Iran; it reportedly operates intelligence-collection facilities there, and Israeli reconnaissance or strike aircraft could overfly Turkey en route to Iran.

Iranian force deployments reflect these threat perceptions. Most of Iran's ground forces are deployed near the border with Iraq, while most of its air force is deployed toward Iraq and the Persian Gulf region. Its navy is almost exclusively deployed in the Gulf.[8] Moreover, since the end of the Iran–Iraq War, Iran has devoted the lion's share of its limited defense dollars to enhancing missile and non-conventional capabilities and expanding and modernizing its navy, with the ground and then air forces receiving the lowest funding priority. These deployment patterns and spending priorities reflect Tehran's preoccupation during the last decade with perceived threats from Iraq, the United States and Israel, and the fact that Iran's most important economic asset – its oil and gas industry – is concentrated largely in the vicinity of the Persian Gulf.

To bolster defense, Iran has sought to create its own deterrent triad, consisting of:

1. the ability to disrupt oil exports from the Persian Gulf should it desire to do so;
2. the ability to launch terror attacks on several continents in conjunction with the Lebanese Hizballah;
3. the development of non-conventional weapons and the means to deliver them throughout the Middle East, if not beyond, by missiles and various non-traditional means such as saboteurs, unmanned aerial vehicles and boats.

Iran has sought to bolster its deterrent capability by cultivating the image of Iran as an undeterrable state, whose soldiers seek martyrdom, and whose society is willing and able to absorb heavy punishment. While this image may have borne some relationship to reality during the heady days of the revolution in the early 1980s, it is certainly no longer the case. Years of revolutionary turmoil and a bloody eight-year war with Iraq have made Iranians weary of war and political violence, and transformed the Islamic Republic into a more 'normal' state – at least in terms of its ability to absorb casualties.[9]

THE STRUCTURE OF THE ARMED FORCES AND CIVIL–MILITARY RELATIONS

According to the Constitution of the Islamic Republic, the Supreme Leader, Ayatollah 'Ali Khamene'i, is Commander-in-Chief of the armed forces, which today consist of three main components:

- the regular military;
- the Islamic Revolutionary Guard Forces (IRGC), with its paramilitary Basij militia;
- the Law Enforcement Forces (LEF).[10]

The regular military and IRGC are subordinate to the ministry of defense and Armed Forces Logistics (MODAFL), which is headed by Admiral 'Ali Shamkhani (an IRGC officer who is considered sympathetic to the country's conservative hardliners). These organizations are responsible for defending Iran's borders and providing internal security. The LEF are formally subordinate to the ministry of interior, and play a key internal and frontier security role. While Interior Minister 'Abdolvahed Musavi-Lari is an ally of reformist President Mohammad Khatami, the senior leadership of the LEF consists of IRGC officers who remain loyal to the supreme leader and his hardline conservative supporters. As a result, Interior Minister Musavi-Lari has complained that he in fact does not control the LEF.[11]

Parallel Structures, Military Professionalism and the Problem of Unity of Command
The division of Iran's combat forces between the regular military and IRGC dates to the 1979 Islamic revolution, when the IRGC was formed in order to maintain internal security, safeguard the ideological purity of the revolution, and counterbalance the regular military.[12] The new clerical regime distrusted the regular army because of its association with the deposed Shah, and saw it as a potential counter-revolutionary force.[13] For this reason, relations between the regular military and the IRGC have been characterized by ambivalence, mistrust and, at times, outright

hostility. This distrust was also a major factor behind large-scale purges of the military after the revolution and the formation of a political-ideological directorate, which ensures clerical oversight of the military by placing personal representatives of the supreme leader in all major commands. These activities and organizations are all part and parcel of the regime's efforts – dating to the early days of the revolution – to 'Islamicize' the armed forces.

Such parallel structures are characteristic of the Islamic Republic, where throughout the government the authority of conventional political and military institutions is checked by that of revolutionary Islamic institutions. Thus, the powers of the president are circumscribed by those of the supreme leader; those of the parliament (Majlis) by the Council of Guardians; and those of the regular military by the IRGC. Paradoxically, this arrangement has been a source of both stability and tension within the Islamic Republic,[14] though the existence of parallel military structures has sometimes undermined unity of command and posed major obstacles to creating a modern effective military.

The dichotomy between the regular military and IRGC initially reflected divergent approaches to modern warfare. The regular military embraced a traditional approach to war, with a balanced emphasis on hardware, technology and the human element. Its force structure – which resembled those of most Western armies – reflected this fact. By contrast, the IRGC elevated the human factor above all others in the belief that faith, ideological commitment and morale would be sufficient to bring victory.[15] Accordingly, the IRGC originally consisted of poorly trained, irregular, mass infantry forces that specialized in human wave attacks. The IRGC's approach came to dominate Iranian thinking during the Iran–Iraq War, even though the IRGC eventually established quasi-conventional infantry, armor and artillery formations, as well as naval and air arms during the war.[16] The IRGC was also put in charge of Iran's missile forces and non-conventional weapons programs (which it still controls today).

In the light of lessons learned from the Iran–Iraq and Gulf Wars, the armed forces developed a greater appreciation of the relative importance of modern arms, technology and the human factor in modern warfare. Its exercises have moved away from the static attrition warfare practiced in the war with Iraq, to combined arms operations and maneuver warfare.[17] As part of this trend toward greater professionalism, the IRGC adopted new uniforms and rank structures, similar to those used by the regular military.

The regime has tried to resolve some of the unity-of-command problems created by this dual military structure. In June 1988, following several major battlefield reversals during the latter stages of the Iran–Iraq War, it created a joint Armed Forces General Staff that brought together the upper echelons of the regular military and the IRGC to ensure greater unity of command. Shortly after the war, however, Supreme Guide Khamene'i approved the re-establishment of a separate IRGC headquarters, in an apparent bid to curry favor with the Guard.[18] Under this arrangement, the supreme commander of the IRGC reported directly to Khamene'i, whereas the commanders of the various branches of the regular military (ground, air and naval forces), reported to the Chief of Staff of the Armed Forces, General Hasan Firuzabadi (a physician with no professional military credentials, who is close to Khamene'i).

In October 1998, however, at the height of the crisis with Afghanistan, Khamene'i created a new position, that of supreme commander of the regular military. This step put the regular military on a par with the IRGC for the first time (the latter has had a supreme commander since 1981), and represented an upgrading of the importance of the regular military. It derived from a recognition of the fact that, in the event of a war with Afghanistan, the regime could not rely on the IRGC alone but would have to depend on the regular military to bear the brunt of the fighting. The interests of the state thus made such a step imperative.[19] The dual structure of the armed forces, however, remains intact, and is likely to do so as long as the current regime survives – it reflects a fundamental organizational principle of the Islamic Republic, rooted in the political logic of the regime.

The Military, IRGC, and LEF: A Changing Division of Labor
According to the constitution of the Islamic Republic, the regular military is responsible for defending Iran's borders and maintaining

internal order, while the IRGC is responsible for protecting the regime (to this end, IRGC garrisons are located near all major cities). In practice, however, matters are not so clear-cut. During the Iran–Iraq War, military exigency required that the IRGC (and the Basij) be committed to the front, where they fought side-by-side with regular military units. Since the war, this ambiguity has been preserved: while the regular military and IRGC routinely hold joint military exercises, the regular military, IRGC and Basij have together participated in exercises that hone their ability to deal with domestic unrest. Thus, while the regular military retains a minor internal security role, the IRGC continues to have a conventional military role. The LEF, which was created in 1991 by uniting the urban police, rural gendarmerie and revolutionary committees (komitehs), initially assisted the IRGC and Basij in maintaining domestic order.

The unrest that has racked Iran since 1991, however, has exposed latent tensions between the country's political and military leadership, as well as political differences between the senior echelons of the armed forces and the rank-and-file, and it has called into question the prevailing organizational division of labor. The first sign of trouble was the refusal of regular army and IRGC units garrisoned near Qazvin (a major town north-west of Tehran) to obey orders to quash riots there in August 1994. The commanders of these units apparently refused to turn their weapons on the Iranian people. The regime was forced to airlift in special IRGC and Basij anti-riot units from elsewhere to put down the violence.

The May 1997 election of reformist candidate Mohammad Khatami to the presidency put further stress on civil–military relations. Though senior IRGC officers had endorsed his conservative opponent (Majlis Speaker 'Ali Akbar Nateq Nuri), credible post-election press reports indicate that IRGC personnel voted for Khatami in even greater proportions than did the general population (73 per cent versus 69 per cent).[20] This indicates that the IRGC – a military organization long thought to have been a bastion of support for conservative hardliners – is in fact riven by the same divisions as Iranian society, and divided into highly antagonistic reformist and conservative camps. This raises questions about the political reliability of these units, should they be needed to quell popular violence between supporters of the reformist and conservative hardline factions.

The student riots of July 1999 provided the backdrop for the next crisis in civil–military relations. These riots were put down by the LEF (often aided by the thugs of the Ansar-e Hezbollah, a shady vigilante group sponsored by senior hardline clerics), which was relieved by the Basij once the situation had stabilized. These events highlighted the fact that, by July 1999, a new division of labor had emerged: the LEF had become the regime's first line of defense against domestic unrest, with the Basij providing backup. When necessary, they might be reinforced by the IRGC's 'Special Units', followed by the IRGC's ground forces. The regular military's ground forces would be deployed only as a last resort.

At the height of the July 1999 unrest, 24 senior IRGC commanders sent President Khatami a letter that, in effect, threatened a coup should he not restore order quickly.[21] Such a threat was unprecedented in the history of the Islamic Republic, but, given the political divisions in the armed forces, it is unclear whether a coup would have succeeded. The result could well have been bloody street violence, perhaps even civil war. In the end, Iran's clerical leadership was able to restore calm, thereby pre-empting a coup, though the threat of overt military intervention was an unsettling new development.

In fact, however, hardline elements in the security services and armed forces had already covertly intervened in the political arena, participating in the murder of dissident and reformist intellectuals from the autumn of 1998 (and continuing into the spring of 2000).[22] Through these actions, the senior leaderships of the security services and armed forces have, in effect, thrown their weight behind the conservative rivals of President Khatami. This development not only raises doubts about the prospects of the reform movement, but also about the impact of the growing politicization of the armed forces on discipline and effectiveness.

IRAN'S MILITARY CAPABILITIES: AN ASSESSMENT

Conventional Forces

While the regular military and IRGC each have ground, air and naval components, the regular military is, by all measures, a much larger and better equipped organization than the IRGC. The regular military has about 400,000 men on active duty, the IRGC about 120,000. IRGC ground formations are much smaller and more lightly armed than corresponding regular army formations, and the best equipment is generally fielded by the regular army. As for the IRGC air force, it consists of no more than a few dozen trainer aircraft; most of Iran's 200 or so operational 'high performance' combat aircraft are owned by the regular air force. Likewise, the IRGC navy consists mainly of ten Chinese Houdong-class missile boats and more than 100 small boats, shore-based anti-ship missile batteries and a large combat swimmer (naval special warfare) force. Iran's dozen major surface combatant ships and three submarines are controlled by the regular navy.[23] Despite its relatively small size, the IRGC is a key institution in Iran today, due to its role as guardian of the revolution and the fact that many senior Revolutionary Guard officers have close personal and family ties to key members of Iran's clerical establishment. In addition, the IRGC plays a crucial role in the selection, ideological indoctrination, professional development and advancement of future senior officers.[24]

Iran's conventional military capabilities are relatively limited. Nearly a decade of war and revolution and two decades of financial hardship have taken their toll. Iran's operational equipment inventories are relatively small, given the size of the country and the magnitude of its security problems. It would take tens of billion of dollars – which Iran simply does not have – to make it a major conventional military power.

Major transfers between 1989 and 2000 include at least 104 T-72 tanks from Poland, 422 T-72s from Russia, 413 BMP-2 IFVs from Russia, self-propelled artillery from Russia and 106 artillery pieces from China; small numbers of SA-2 SAMs from China and SA-5 and SA-6 SAMs from Russia; five Mi-17 helicopters, 12 Su-24 strike aircraft and 24 MiG-29 fighters from Russia, and 20 older F-7 fighters from China; ten Houdong-class fast attack craft and C-802 anti-ship cruise missiles from China, three Kilo-class submarines from Russia, and large numbers of wake-homing torpedoes from Russia and advanced naval mines from Russia and China.[25] While these numbers may seem impressive, they constituted only a fraction of the weapons on Iran's military wish-list (see Appendix A), and pale in comparison with transfers over the same time-frame to many of its Arab Gulf neighbors. Nonetheless, despite these constraints, Iran has invested wisely, building on its strengths, attempting to redress its most critical weaknesses, and procuring weapons that could have the greatest impact on its own capabilities and those of potential adversaries.

Iran's offensive options are limited. It does not pose a ground threat to any of its neighbors, because of the small size and poor condition of its ground forces, although it can launch limited air strikes into neighboring countries (and has done so several times in recent years in Iraq). The main conventional threat from Iran is in the naval arena; specifically, the threat it poses to the flow of oil from the region, the security and stability of the southern Gulf states, and the ability of the United States to project force in the region. Iran could disrupt maritime traffic in the Persian Gulf using its submarines, coastal missiles and mines, and it could temporarily close the Strait of Hormuz, were it willing to use chemical or biological weapons against shipping. It cannot, however, block the strait (as it claims it can), which is too wide and too deep to be obstructed. Moreover, although the Gulf itself is a significant barrier to major acts of aggression against the southern Gulf states, Iran could conduct limited amphibious operations to seize and hold lightly defended islands or offshore oil platforms in the Gulf. Finally, its naval special forces could sabotage harbor facilities, offshore oil platforms and terminals, and attack ships which are in ports throughout the lower Gulf, disrupting oil production and maritime traffic there.

It is unclear, however, what policy objective could be served by an Iranian attempt to block the Strait of Hormuz. Even if Iran could do so, this action would harm Iran as much as any other state, since it has no other way to bring its oil to market. This is an option of last resort, to be played only in extremis, if Iran's vital interests were threatened or if it was denied use of the Gulf. In the near term, Iran is more likely to use the implied threat of disrupting shipping or closing the strait, to intimidate its neighbors or deter its adversaries. Nonetheless, the United States must plan to deal with Iran's growing ability to disrupt the flow of oil from the Gulf, even if it seems unlikely that Iran will use this capability in the foreseeable future.

Iran's defensive capabilities are also limited, although the military weakness of its neighbors, its strategic depth and its non-conventional retaliatory capability offset – to some degree – its conventional weakness. In the event of a conflict with the United States, Iran's air and air defense forces could do little to oppose US airpower, which would roam Iran's skies at will, while its navy (which has been routed by the US navy in the past) would be rapidly defeated. However, it might succeed in inflicting some losses on US forces and disrupting shipping in the Gulf. Perhaps the most effective weapon in Iran's hands, in such a scenario, would be its ability to strike directly at the United States and its interests in the region through subversion and terror.

Non-Conventional Forces

Iran's non-conventional weapons programs are among the regime's top priorities, and Tehran continues to devote significant resources to acquiring such capabilities, despite severe economic constraints and efforts to reduce tensions with its neighbors and the West. Its current efforts focus on the stockpiling of chemical and biological weapons, acquiring the means to produce nuclear weapons, and the acquisition and production of missiles (and perhaps other means) to deliver these. Because of the politically sensitive nature of these programs and capabilities, they come under the purview and control of the IRGC.

Iran is pursuing the acquisition of nuclear weapons, despite being a signatory of the nuclear Non-Proliferation Treaty (NPT). Iran's civilian nuclear infrastructure is, at present, still rather rudimentary. However, it is believed to be trying to acquire fissile material by various means – including diversion from facilities in the former Soviet Union – and its procurement activities in the past decade indicate an interest in acquiring both overt and clandestine capabilities to indigenously produce plutonium or highly enriched uranium.[26]

Of greatest concern have been Iran's attempts, during the past decade or so, to acquire:

- enriched uranium from a poorly guarded facility in Khazakhstan;

- fuel fabrication and reprocessing capabilities from Argentina;

- research reactors from Argentina, India, China and Russia;

- nuclear power plants from Russia and China;

- gas centrifuge enrichment technology from Switzerland and Germany;

- a gas centrifuge enrichment plant from Russia;

- a uranium conversion plant from China or Russia;

- a laser enrichment plant from Russia.[27]

Nearly all these known attempts have been thwarted by US diplomatic efforts and political pressure. Of abiding concern, however, are possible procurement activities that may not have come to the attention of Western intelligence agencies. Moreover, in addition to trying to acquire fissile materials and nuclear fuel cycle-related technologies, Iran may be trying to acquire the components needed for weapons to work. In 1999, an Iranian student in Sweden was caught trying to smuggle thyratrons to Iran. Though a dual-use item, these may be used in the explosive package of a nuclear weapon, and may indicate that Iran is conducting work in the area of weaponization as well.[28]

Were Iran to acquire diverted fissile material today, it might be able to produce a nuclear weapon within a year or two. Should such diversion efforts fail, it could take years to acquire the means to produce fissile material at home. Progress will depend greatly on the amount of foreign assistance obtained. Thus, there is a broad margin of uncertainty regarding the potential timeline for Iran's acquisition of nuclear weapons. There is no question, however, that the acquisition of civilian research reactors, nuclear power plants and nuclear technology from Russia will ultimately aid this effort. Without significant outside help, Iran would face considerable obstacles to realizing its nuclear ambitions.

How Iran would employ a nuclear capability, should it acquire one in the coming decade, is unclear. Iran faces a dilemma: to acquire the perceived benefits of nuclear weapons, it needs to declare its capabilities. However, doing so while remaining a member of the NPT might subject it to painful economic sanctions. Thus, Tehran has several options that could influence the political utility of an Iranian bomb:

1. remain silent about its nuclear capabilities until it becomes absolutely necessary to unveil them, meanwhile using its missile force as a symbolic surrogate for the range of non-conventional capabilities that Iran possesses but cannot brandish, because of its various arms control commitments;
2. withdraw from the NPT and then declare itself a nuclear weapon possessor state;
3. pursue a policy of opacity by leaking hints to the foreign press that raise questions about Iran's true nuclear status.

In the event of a military crisis, however, all bets are off. Because Iraq's CBW capabilities did not deter the United States during the Gulf War, Tehran may believe that, in the event of a military confrontation with Washington, only a nuclear capability could enable it to avert defeat. In such circumstances, it would likely reveal its capabilities, if it had not already done so.[29]

Iran has a significant chemical warfare capability. It is believed to have stockpiled several hundred tons of chemical agents in bulk and weaponized form, including nerve, blister, choking and blood agents. It produces bombs and artillery rounds filled with these agents, and probably has deployed chemical missile warheads.[30] While Iran has signed and ratified the Chemical Weapons Convention – obligating it to destroy its stocks of chemical weapons within ten years of accession – it is hard to believe that Iran would give up the pillar of its strategic deterrent when Baghdad may still retain CBW capabilities. Thus, it might be pursuing several options:

1. clandestinely retaining stocks of CW (chemical weapons) while ostensibly complying with its treaty obligations;

2. considering its options during the ten years it is allowed to retain CW, while perhaps seeking an extension at the end of the ten-year period (it would probably not be alone were it to do so);

3. destroying its CW capabilities while retaining a rapid breakout capability.

Iran is also developing biological weapons.[31] It probably is researching such standard agents as anthrax and botulin toxin, and it has shown interest in acquiring materials that could be used to produce various toxins. At this time, Iran has probably deployed biological weapons, which it could deliver via terrorist saboteurs, spray tanks mounted on aircraft or ships, or via missiles. It is unclear, however, whether Iran has overcome the various technical problems related to the efficient dissemination of BW agents.

Biological weapons can be produced quickly and cheaply, and are capable of killing thousands in a single attack. Moreover, no early warning capability for biological weapons exists, and vaccines are not stocked by the US in sufficient numbers or variety to be of use in an emergency. Thus, Tehran's biological warfare program provides Iran with a true mass destruction capability for which the US currently lacks an effective counter – beyond deterrence. In light of the uncertainties confronting its nuclear effort, Iran's biological warfare program assumes special importance, since it could provide Tehran with a strategic weapon whose theoretical destructive potential approaches that of a low-yield nuclear weapon.

The backbone of Iran's strategic missile force consists of 300 North-Korean produced Shahab-1 and 100 North Korean-produced Shahab-2 missiles (with ranges of 320 km and 500 km respectively), a handful of locally assembled or produced Shahab-3 missiles (with a range of 1,300 km), and some 200 Chinese CSS-8 missiles (with a 150 km range), armed with conventional, and perhaps chemical, warheads.[32] Iran is also reportedly working on a Shahab-4 missile (reportedly based on the Soviet SS-4, it is said to have a range of 2,000 km) and a Shahab-5 (reportedly a paper design with an estimated range of 5,000–10,000 km).[33] Iran's missiles could reach major population centers in Israel, Turkey, Iraq, Saudi Arabia and the smaller Arab Gulf states. Many of the technical and financial problems that have long plagued the program seem to have been overcome, at least in part due to significant Russian assistance since about 1994. However, Iran still seems to be dependent on foreign technology inputs from Russia, North Korea and China; for instance, it is not clear whether Iran can locally produce the rocket motor for the Shahab-3, and it may still depend on North Korea for this component.[34]

From Iran's perspective, the Shahab-3 (and subsequently the Shahab-4) will provide a variety of new capabilities. The Shahab-3 will enable Iran to target Israel, Turkey and Egypt, and in the now unlikely event of an Iranian–American confrontation, the knowledge that they are within range of Iranian missiles could influence decision makers in Cairo and Ankara during a crisis. Moreover, American missile defenses could have problems intercepting a Shahab-3 flying a depressed (low-level) or lofted (high-altitude) trajectory against targets in the Gulf region. Likewise, the Shahab-4, if and when it becomes operational, will be capable of flying depressed or lofted trajectories against Israel, Turkey and Egypt, complicating the defense of these countries, and it will be able to reach southern Europe by following a maximum-range medium-level trajectory.

For now, however, the main value of these missiles is political. They serve as a symbolic surrogate for Iran's non-conventional capabilities, while the fact that Iran possesses missiles capable of hitting targets throughout the region will alter the risk calculus of potential adversaries. And while these missiles are of uncertain reliability and accuracy, prudent policy-makers will have to assume that the Iranian missiles will perform in wartime as intended, and act accordingly.

Terror and Subversion

Terrorism has been a key instrument of Tehran's foreign policy since the Islamic revolution in 1979. Because of its military weakness, the Islamic Republic has favored ambiguity, indirection and covert action through surrogates, over direct confrontation, as the means of dealing with its enemies. Moreover, Iran's use of terrorism as an instrument of foreign policy appears to be a corollary to the use of shadowy violent pressure groups in the Islamic Republic's domestic politics, and may therefore represent a manifestation of the political culture of the Islamic Republic.[35]

Iran's involvement in terrorism was most intense in the decade following the 1979 revolution. During this time, Tehran's preferred methods included kidnapping, assassination and bombing. Its arena of operations spanned the Middle East, western Europe and Asia. After peaking in the mid-1980s, the number of Iranian-sponsored terrorist incidents declined, in response to changes in Iran's regional and international environment.

However, Iran continues its efforts to hunt down dissidents abroad, to support groups that use terrorist violence to undermine the Arab–Israeli peace process, and to use terrorist groups as a lever against some of its neighbors (such as supporting the Kurdish Workers' Party, the PKK, against Turkey). In recent years, Iran has generally restricted attacks on oppositionists to those based in northern and central Iraq. This marks a continued evolution in Iranian policy since the early to mid-1990s away from high-profile terrorist actions in the heart of Europe (which harmed Tehran's ties with countries such as France and Germany) toward less conspicuous acts in less politically sensitive locations. Iran also supports various groups violently opposed to the Arab–Israeli peace process – like Hamas, the Palestinian Islamic Jihad (PIJ), as well as its longstanding ally, the Lebanese Hizballah – which it continues to arm, train and finance. In 2000, Tehran redoubled its efforts to encourage these groups to work together and coordinate their activities in order to undermine Israeli– Palestinian peace talks.[36]

Several organs of the Iranian state – the intelligence services, the IRGC, the foreign ministry and the Islamic culture and guidance ministry – play important roles in Tehran's sponsorship of terrorism. The ministry of intelligence and security (MOIS) plays the lead role in organizing and conducting terrorist operations abroad, and it runs operations out of Iranian embassies, consulates and Islamic cultural centers overseas. It is sometimes helped in these efforts by IRGC intelligence personnel based in Iranian embassies, overseas branches of Iranian-owned businesses and charitable foundations. The IRGC Qods (Jerusalem) Force is responsible for training foreign personnel in Iran and abroad (in the past, in Lebanon or the Sudan) to organize and participate in terrorism and subversion, and the export of the revolution. The ministry of foreign affairs plays an important supporting role by providing logistical assistance to Iran's agents overseas through Iranian embassies and consulates. MOIS and IRGC personnel often travel and serve overseas under diplomatic cover, and weapons and explosives are sometimes transported to them by diplomatic pouch, via regularly scheduled Iran Air flights. Finally, Iranian bonyads (quasi-official charitable foundations) play an indirect role in the sponsorship of terrorism by funneling money to radical Islamic groups and organizations overseas.

In terms of advancing its national interests, Iran's involvement in terrorism has yielded mixed results. On the one hand, Iranian terrorist successes in the early 1980s burnished the regime's popular image in the first years of the revolution and helped it to consolidate its domestic power base. Moreover, Hizballah hostage-taking also facilitated secret deals between Iran and the United States, France and others, that enabled Tehran to recover financial assets impounded abroad and to trade hostages for arms from the United States.

On the other hand, Iran's involvement in terrorism has sullied Tehran's image and contributed to the country's isolation, straining its relations with key Western countries and leading many of these to adopt a pro-Iraqi tilt during the Iran–Iraq War. Moreover, Iran's attempts in the 1980s to use terrorism to subvert the Arab Gulf states have prompted these states to rely more heavily on the United States for their security, thereby complicating Iranian efforts to achieve a key goal – ending the US military presence in the Gulf.

The Lebanese Hizballah is Tehran's biggest success story. But even here, Iran's success is mixed. While Hizballah succeeded in evicting Israel from south Lebanon, it has so far failed in its efforts to establish an Islamic Republic in Lebanon. On the other hand, Hamas and PIJ terror (supported by Iran) helped complicate implementation of the Israel–PLO Declaration of Principles of September 1993, thus contributing to the eventual breakdown of Israeli–Palestinian negotiations and the subsequent outbreak of the 'Al-Aqsa Intifada' in September 2000. While Iran certainly is

251

not the primary moving force behind these organizations, Tehran can claim indirect credit for their successes.

Finally, Iran has succeeded in killing a number of key expatriate opponents of the regime. While these acts have hurt the opposition and may have bolstered the self-confidence of the clerics, most of the individuals killed by Tehran never were a serious threat to the rule of the mullahs. In the long run, as a result of the regime's corruption, inefficiency and repressive policies, growing popular disenchantment and widespread unrest will pose a greater threat to clerical rule than exiled opposition members.

Iran's capacity for terror and subversion remains one of Tehran's few levers in the event of a confrontation with the United States, since – barring the use of non-conventional weapons – it otherwise lacks the ability to challenge the US on anything near equal terms. In the event of such a confrontation, Iran might sponsor terrorism in Kuwait, Bahrain, Qatar, the UAE and Oman – all of which host important US military facilities – in order to intimidate them and thereby undercut US power projection capabilities in the region. Further, through its ties to the Lebanese Hizballah, Iran has the means to launch a destructive terrorist campaign spanning several continents that would be very difficult for the United States to counter. Although neither Iran nor Hizballah are known to have targeted American personnel or interests since 1991, Iran is keeping its options open: Iranian agents have continued to covertly observe US missions and personnel from time to time, and Iran could resume attacks on US interests in the Middle East, Europe, South America and elsewhere should it decide to do so. And while funding for Iran's intelligence services has been cut in recent years due to the country's financial woes, their ability to carry out terrorist spectaculars has probably not been hampered, since these operations cost relatively little to carry out.

CONCLUSIONS

Iran's military capabilities are most robust on the two extremes of the conflict spectrum: Tehran's capacity for terror and subversion on the one hand, and its non-conventional capabilities on the other. Iran has in the past shown it is able to use terrorist surrogates to strike painful blows against the interests of the United States and its allies, while obscuring its involvement in order to escape retribution. Moreover, an Iran armed with non-conventional (particularly nuclear) weapons could, at the very least, raise the potential risks and stakes of US military intervention in the Gulf, and reduce the freedom of action of the United States and its allies in the region.

The United States faces a secondary threat to its interests in the form of Iran's naval build-up in the Persian Gulf. While the United States and its allies in the region are reasonably prepared to deal with this threat, Iran could nonetheless disrupt the flow of oil from the Gulf and inflict losses on US naval forces there, if it desired to do so. And, if it were willing to use chemical or biological weapons against US forces, American casualties could potentially be heavy (particularly should biological weapons be used).

However, the costs of a major confrontation with the United States could be devastating for Iran, resulting in the destruction of much of its military and civilian infrastructure, and leaving it without the ability to defend itself by conventional means. Moreover, hard experience over the past decade has shown Iran that it has neither the funds needed to replace significant combat losses, nor a reliable supplier capable of doing so. And an open provocation by Iran could generate international support for economic sanctions against Tehran. Having seen what happened to Iraq after it invaded Kuwait in August 1990, the mullahs are unlikely to make the same mistake Saddam Husayn did. Consequently, Iran will continue trying to avoid a major confrontation with the United States that could lead to losses it cannot afford to replace, while it will continue its efforts to expand and modernize its armed forces, reduce US influence in the Middle East through anti-peace process terrorism, and woo the Gulf Arabs from the American embrace through a diplomatic charm offensive.

The greatest threat posed by Iran in the coming years is that of a nuclear breakout, which – if Iran were to succeed in diverting fissile material from the former Soviet Union – could happen without warning, at any time. Accordingly, even as Washington continues its efforts to forestall such an eventuality, the United

States and its allies have to consider how they will respond, if and when this happens.

APPENDIX A:
IRAN: MAJOR WEAPONS DESIRED AND ACQUIRED, 1989–2000

	Quantity Desired	Quantity Acquired
Tank	1,000–1,500	526
IFVs	1,000–1,500	413
Artillery	200–300	108+
Combat Aircraft	100–200	72
Warships	10–15	13

Sources: Estimates are based on: United Nations, *Register of Conventional Arms, 1992–1999*; S. Brom and Y. Shapir (eds), *The Middle East Military Balance, 1999–2000* (Cambridge, MA: MIT Press, 2000), pp. 182–3; International Institute for Strategic Studies, *The Military Balance: 1999–2000* (London, IISS, annually), p. 125; and other sources.

APPENDIX B:
THE PERSIAN GULF MILITARY BALANCE, 2000

	Personnel	Tanks	APCs	Artillery	Aircraft	Warships
Iran	500,000	1,500	1,500	2,000	220	25
Iraq	400,000	2,000	2,000	1,950	200	2
S. Arabia	165,000	1,000	3,000	300	250	17
UAE	46,500	335	800	425	55	12
Oman	34,000	150	150	130	30	6
Kuwait	20,000	400	650	100	60	6
Qatar	12,000	44	200	50	14	7
Bahrain	7,400	180	250	50	24	7

Sources: Figures have been rounded off, and are derived from Brom and Shapir, *The Middle East Military Balance, 1999–2000*; International Institute for Strategic Studies, *The Military Balance: 1999–2000*; and other sources.

NOTES

1. Following the Iran–Iraq War, Iran's Majlis (parliament) announced plans to spend $2 billion a year over five years for weapons purchases. Actual spending during most of the 1990s, however, fell far short of this target. According to Iran Central Bank figures, actual spending on arms imports reached $1.625 billion in 1989–90; $1.6 billion in 1990–91; $1.678 billion in 1991–92; $808 million in 1992–93; and $850 million in 1993–94 – the last year Tehran published such figures (International Monetary Fund, *Islamic Republic of Iran: Recent Economic Developments*, 19 September 1995, p. 74, and 5 October 1993, p. 38). These figures are roughly consistent with US government estimates that Iranian foreign-exchange expenditures on arms dropped from a high of $2 billion in 1991 to less than $1 billion in 1997. Bruce Riedel, 'US Policy in the Gulf:

Five Years of Dual Containment', Washington Institute for Near East Policy, Policy Watch No. 315 (8 May 1998), p. 2.

2. According to statistics compiled by the International Monetary Fund, Iranian expenditures on defense have increased dramatically in the last year or two. Tehran spent about 10,440 billion rials on defense in 1998–99, and budgeted 11,240 billion rials for defense in 1999–2000, and 16,939 billion rials for 2000–01. (These figures do not include capital expenditures in the defense field, which are incomplete for the 2000–01 fiscal year.) International Monetary Fund, *Islamic Republic of Iran: Recent Economic Developments*, 12 July 2000, pp. 112–13.

3. For details about the original Russian commitment and the recent decision to renege on it, see John M. Broder, 'Despite Secret '95 Pact by Gore, Russian Arms Sales to Iran Go On', *New York Times*, 13 October 2000, p. A1; Jim Hoagland, 'From Russia, With Chutzpah', *Washington Post*, 22 November 2000, p. A27.

4. Shahram Chubin, *Iran's National Security Policy: Capabilities, Intentions, and Impact* (Washington, DC: Carnegie Endowment for International Peace, 1994), pp. 17–28.

5. David Menashri, *Revolution at a Crossroads: Iran's Domestic Politics and Regional Ambitions* (Washington, DC: Washington Institute for Near East Policy, 1997), pp. 69–82.

6. Daniel Byman, Shahram Chubin, Anoushiravan Ehteshami and Jerrold Green, *Iran's Security Policy in the Post-Revolutionary Era* (Santa Monica, CA: RAND, 2001). For a more detailed treatment of these issues, see Michael Eisenstadt, *Iranian Military Power: Capabilities and Intentions* (Washington, DC: Washington Institute for Near East Policy, 1996), pp. 2–7, and 'Living with a Nuclear Iran?', *Survival*, Vol. 41, No. 3 (Autumn 1999), pp. 125–9.

7. Conventional arms are extraordinarily expensive: a tank may cost $1–$3 million, a combat aircraft $25–$50 million, while a warship may cost anywhere from $50 million for a fast-attack craft to $500 million for a modern frigate. These sums do not include associated weapons, training and maintenance costs. Thus, creating a large modern military could cost tens of billions of dollars. By contrast, a well-planned, well-managed nuclear program might require an initial investment of a few billion dollars.

8. Anoushiravan Ehteshami, 'The Armed Forces of the Islamic Republic of Iran', *Jane's Intelligence Review*, February (1993), pp. 76–80.

9. For a more detailed elaboration of this argument, see Eisenstadt, 'Living with a Nuclear Iran?', pp. 134–7.

10. The responsibilities of the supreme leader are set forth in Article 110 of the Constitution of the Islamic Republic of Iran. See Hamid Algar, *Constitution of the Islamic Republic of Iran* (Berkeley, CA: Mizan Press, 1980), pp. 67–8. For subsequent amendments to the 1979 constitution made in 1989, see *Tehran Times International*, 3 August 1989, pp. 4–11, in Foreign Broadcast Information Service Daily Report, *FBIS-NES-89-181*, 20 September 1989, pp. 63–4.

11. Wilfried Buchta, *Who Rules Iran?* (Washington, DC: Washington Institute for Near East Policy, 2000), p 143.

12. The missions of Iran's armed forces are formally defined in Articles 143 and 150 of the Constitution of the Islamic Republic of Iran. Whereas the role of the army is defined as 'guarding the independence and territorial integrity of the country, as well as the order of the Islamic Republic', the role of the IRGC is defined as 'guarding the Revolution and its achievements'. Algar, *Constitution of the Islamic Republic of Iran*, pp. 79, 81.

13. For more on civil–military relations in Iran, see Nader Entessar, 'The Military and Politics in the Islamic Republic of Iran', in Hooshang Amirahmadi and Manoucher Parvin (eds), *Post-Revolutionary Iran* (Boulder, CO: Westview Press, 1988), pp. 56–74; Sepehr Zabih, *The Iranian Military in Revolution and War* (London: Routledge, 1988); Kenneth Katzman, *The Warriors of Islam: Iran's Revolutionary Guard* (Boulder, CO: Westview Press, 1993); Ahmed Hashim, *Civil–Military Relations in Iran: A Case Study*,

study prepared for the Central Intelligence Agency Office of Near Eastern, South Asian and African Analysis, January 1999; Byman *et al.*, *Iran's Security Policy*.

14. Buchta, *Who Rules Iran?*, p. 3.
15. Chubin, *Iran's National Security Policy*, pp. 17–18, 20.
16. Katzman, *Warriors of Islam*, pp. 86–91.
17. Ahmed Hashim, 'Iranian National Security Policies Under the Islamic Republic: New Defense Thinking and Growing Military Capabilities' (Washington, DC: Henry L. Stimson Center, July 1994), p. 9; Glen E. Howard, 'Zohd-1: An Iranian Combined Arms Exercise', Analytical Note A92-007/UL, Foreign Systems Research Center of Sciences Applications International Corporation (FSRC) (Greenwood Village, CO), 9 March 1992.
18. Katzman, *Warriors of Islam*, p. 105.
19. Buchta, *Who Rules Iran?*, p. 147.
20. Ibid., p. 125. The IRGC has traditionally recruited from the same social base as the universities: poor families with solid revolutionary credentials (i.e., participation in the revolution, Iran–Iraq War service, and the like). In light of the fact that the universities are a hotbed of support for reformist President Khatami, it should come as no surprise that most members of the IRGC would share the politics of the students. This trend may have been reinforced by the fact that in recent years the IRGC has increasingly come to rely on conscripts to meet its manpower needs, due to a drastic decline in volunteers.
21. For more on this episode, see Buchta, *Who Rules Iran?*, pp. 187–92.
22. For more on these events, see ibid., pp. 156–70.
23. Figures are from Shlomo Brom and Yiftah Shapir (eds), *The Middle East Military Balance: 1999–2000* (Cambridge, MA: MIT Press, 2000), pp. 181–98.
24. Byman *et al.*, *Iran's Security Policy*.
25. These figures are drawn mainly from the *UN Register of Conventional Arms*, 1992 and *passim*, and have been cross-checked with the International Institute for Strategic Studies' *Military Balance*, and the Jaffee Center for Strategic Studies, *Middle East Military Balance*, for various years. In addition, some figures are from Igor Korotenko, 'Russia and Iran Renew Collaboration: Tehran May Take Third Place in Volume of Russian Arms Purchases', *Nezavisimoye Voyennoye Obozreniye*, 12 January 2001. They are at best rough approximations, however, as not all countries contributed entries to the *UN Register of Conventional Arms* for every year in which the register has been in existence since 1992, and some surmise is necessary in order to identify the model of weapon referred to in the Register.
26. Testimony of A. Norman Schindler, Deputy Director, DCI Nonproliferation Center, before the International Security, Proliferation and Federal Services Subcommittee of the Senate Governmental Affairs Committee, 21 September 2000; Testimony of Robert J. Einhorn, Assistant Secretary of State for Nonproliferation, before the Senate Foreign Relations Committee, 5 October 2000.
27. For more details on Iran's nuclear procurement activities, see Eisenstadt, *Iranian Military Power*, pp. 9–25, 108–9.
28. For more on this episode, see Susanna Loof, 'Swedish Student Suspected of Smuggling Nuclear Weapon Technology to Iran', *AP Worldstream*, 11 October 1999.
29. For more on the various considerations that will influence Iranian nuclear decision making, see Eisenstadt, 'Living with a Nuclear Iran?' pp. 132–7.
30. Schindler, *Testimony*; Einhorn, *Testimony*.
31. Ibid.
32. Brom and Shapir (eds), *The Middle East Military Balance: 1999–2000*, p. 186. The Shahab-1 is reportedly the North Korean Scud-B, the Shahab-2 is the North Korean Scud-C, and the Shahab-3 is a locally produced version of the North Korean Nodong-1, presumably with some Russian content. For more on North Korea's missiles, see Joseph S. Bermudez Jr, *A History of Ballistic Missile Development in the DPRK*, Monterey

Institute of International Studies, Center of Nonproliferation Studies, Occasional Paper No. 2 (November 1999).

33. Clifford Beal, 'Iran's Shehab 4 is Soviet SS-4, Says US Intelligence', *Jane's Defence Weekly*, 17 February 1999, p. 5; and Donald H. Rumsfeld, *Report of the Commission to Assess the Ballistic Missile Threat to the United States: Executive Summary* (Washington, DC: Government Printing Office, 1998), pp. 12–13.

34. Bill Gertz, 'North Korea Sells Iran Missile Engines', *Washington Times*, 9 February 2000, p. A1; Andrew Koch and Steve Rodan, 'Concern as Test Boosts Iranian Missile Development', *Jane's Defence Weekly*, 26 July 2000, p. 3; Testimony of Robert D. Walpole, National Intelligence Officer for Strategic and Nuclear Programs, before the International Security, Proliferation and Federal Services Subcommittee of the Senate Governmental Affairs Committee, 21 September 2000.

35. Violent pressure groups have played a key role in Iranian politics since the Constitutional Revolution of 1906, and have been a feature of modern Iranian politics under both the monarchy and the Islamic Republic. Michael Rubin, *Into the Shadows: Radical Vigilantes in Khatami's Iran* (Washington, DC: Washington Institute for Near East Policy, 2001). The use of terrorist 'pressure groups' as an instrument of Iranian foreign policy is, however, unique to the Islamic Republic, and may derive from the rejection of 'foreign' norms and standards of interstate behavior as a fundamental element of the regime's revolutionary legitimacy.

36. John Lancaster, 'Iran Gives Terrorists More Aid, US Says', *Washington Post*, 4 December 1999, pp. A1, A16.

Index